W9-BUP-802

AUGUSTUS

Introduction to the Life of an Emperor

Augustus, Rome's first emperor, is one of the great figures of world history and one of the most fascinating. In this lively and concise biography, Karl Galinsky examines Augustus' life from childhood to deification. He chronicles the mosaic of vicissitudes, challenges, setbacks, and successes that shaped Augustus' life, both public and private. How did he use his power? How did he manage to keep reinventing himself? What kind of man was he? A transformative leader, Augustus engineered profound change in Rome and throughout the Mediterranean world. No one would have expected such vast achievements from the frail and little-known eighteen-year-old who became Caesar's heir amid turmoil and crisis. A mere thirteen years later, after defeating Antony and Cleopatra, he had, in his words, "power over all things."

Karl Galinsky is the Cailloux Centennial Professor of Classics at the University of Texas at Austin. The author and editor of several books, including *Augustan Culture* and *The Cambridge Companion to the Age of Augustus*, he has received awards for his teaching and research, including fellowships from the National Endowment for the Humanities, the Guggenheim Foundation, and the Max-Planck Society.

filiis meis

AUGUSTUS

INTRODUCTION TO THE LIFE OF AN EMPEROR

Karl Galinsky
University of Texas, Austin

CAMBRIDGE
UNIVERSITY PRESS

CAMBRIDGE UNIVERSITY PRESS
Cambridge, New York, Melbourne, Madrid, Cape Town,
Singapore, São Paulo, Delhi, Mexico City

Cambridge University Press
32 Avenue of the Americas, New York, NY 10013-2473, USA

www.cambridge.org
Information on this title: www.cambridge.org/9780521744423

© Cambridge University Press 2012

This publication is in copyright. Subject to statutory exception
and to the provisions of relevant collective licensing agreements,
no reproduction of any part may take place without the written
permission of Cambridge University Press.

First published 2012

Printed in the United States of America

A catalog record for this publication is available from the British Library.

Library of Congress Cataloging in Publication data
Galinsky, Karl, 1942–
  Augustus : introduction to the life of an emperor / Karl Galinsky.
    p. cm.
  Includes bibliographical references and index.
  ISBN 978-0-521-76797-2 (hardback) – ISBN 978-0-521-74442-3 (pbk.)
    1. Augustus, Emperor of Rome, 63 B.C.–14 A.D.   2. Emperors – Rome – Biography.
  3. Rome – History – Augustus, 30 B.C.–14 A.D.   4. Rome – Political and
  government – 30 B.C.–68 A.D.   I. Title.
  DG279.G175   2012
  937'.07092-dc23[B]   2011049017

ISBN 978-0-521-76797-2 Hardback
ISBN 978-0-521-74442-3 Paperback

Cambridge University Press has no responsibility for the persistence or accuracy of URLs
for external or third-party Internet Web sites referred to in this publication and does not
guarantee that any content on such Web sites is, or will remain, accurate or appropriate.

CONTENTS

LIST OF MAPS, GENEALOGICAL CHART, AND ILLUSTRATIONS

Map 1. The Augustan empire and its provinces.

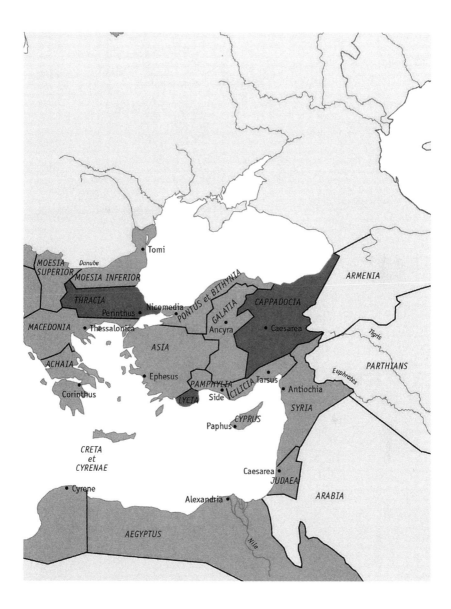

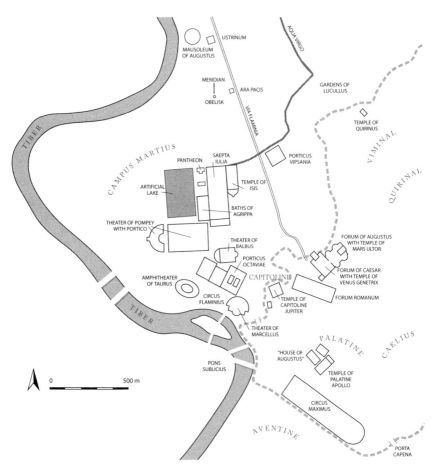

USTRINUM

MAUSOLEUM
OF AUGUSTUS

AQUA VIRGO

MERIDIAN

ARA PACIS

GARDENS OF
LUCULLUS

OBELISK

VIA FLAMINIA

TEMPLE OF
QUIRINUS

TIBER

CAMPUS MARTIUS

VIMINAL

PANTHEON

SAEPTA
IULIA

PORTICUS
VIPSANIA

QUIRINAL

ARTIFICIAL
LAKE

TEMPLE OF
ISIS

BATHS OF
AGRIPPA

THEATER OF POMPEY
WITH PORTICO

THEATER OF
BALBUS

FORUM OF AUGUSTUS
WITH TEMPLE OF
MARS ULTOR

PORTICUS
OCTAVIAE

FORUM OF CAESAR
WITH TEMPLE OF
VENUS GENETRIX

AMPHITHEATER
OF TAURUS

CAPITOLINE

CIRCUS
FLAMINIUS

TEMPLE OF
CAPITOLINE
JUPITER

FORUM ROMANUM

TIBER

THEATER OF
MARCELLUS

PALATINE

CAELIUS

"HOUSE OF
AUGUSTUS"

PONS
SUBLICIUS

TEMPLE OF
PALATINE
APOLLO

0   500 m

CIRCUS
MAXIMUS

AVENTINE

PORTA
CAPENA

Map 2. The City of Rome AD 14.

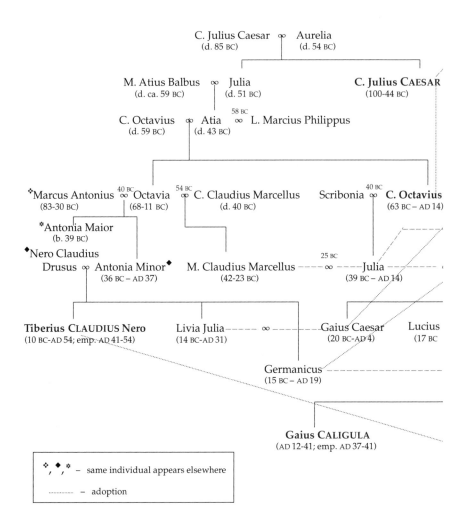

Genealogical chart of the family of Augustus.

The Julio-Claudian Family

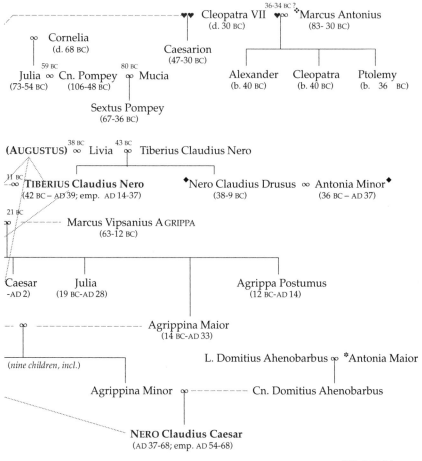

TIMELINE

39	late Dec.	Birth of Julia
38	Jan. 17	Marriage to Livia
37	autumn	Renewal of Triumvirate (Treaty of Tarentum); Antony permanently returns to Cleopatra
36	Sept. 3	Battle of Naulochus. Defeat of Sextus Pompey
35–34		Octavian campaigns in Illyria
34	late	Beginning of propaganda war between Octavian and Antony
32		Consuls and c. 300 senators flee to Antony. Antony divorces Octavia
31	Sept. 2	Battle of Actium
30	Aug. 1	Fall of Alexandria. Suicide of Antony and Cleopatra
29	Aug. 13–15	Octavian celebrates triple triumph
27	Jan. 13–16	Senate meetings confirming return to constitutional government; Octavian named "Augustus"
27–24		Augustus in Spain and Gaul
23		Augustus almost dies. Reorganization of his powers: he receives tribunician power and overriding *imperium*. Death of Marcellus
22–19		Augustus in Sicily and the east
21		Agrippa marries Julia
20		Parthian "victory": Parthians return Roman military standards captured in 53 BC. Birth of Gaius Caesar
19	Sept. 21	Death of Vergil. Posthumous publication of *Aeneid*
18		"Moral" legislation: Julian Laws about marriage and adultery
17		Birth of Lucius Caesar. Augustus adopts both grandsons. Secular Games
16–13		Augustus in Gaul
15	May 24	Birth of Germanicus
12		Augustus becomes *pontifex maximus*. Death of Agrippa. Birth of Agrippa Postumus

11		Marriage of Tiberius and Julia
11–10		Augustus in Gaul
9	Jan. 30	Dedication of Ara Pacis
8		The month of *Sextilis* is renamed *Augustus*. Reorganization of the city of Rome into XIV Regions. Augustus again in Gaul
6		Tiberius withdraws to Rhodes
2		Augustus named *pater patriae*. Dedication of Forum of Augustus
AD 2		Tiberius returns from Rhodes. Death of Lucius Caesar. Banishment of Julia
4		Death of Gaius Caesar. Augustus adopts Tiberius following Tiberius' adoption of Germanicus
6		Banishment of Agrippa Postumus
6–9		Rebellion in Pannonia
9		Defeat of Varus in Germany; loss of three legions. Revision of marriage laws
10–12		Military campaigns of Tiberius in Germany
13		Augustus writes his final will. Germanicus campaigns in Germany
14	Aug. 19	Death of Augustus in Nola
14	Sept. 17	*Divus Augustus* by decree of the senate. Tiberius named Augustus' successor with title *Augustus*
29		Death of Livia

NOTE ON MAJOR ANCIENT SOURCES

GREEK AND ROMAN HISTORIANS AND BIOGRAPHERS

Only three of these are contemporary with Augustus; there were others whose works have not survived. For **Nicolaus of Damascus**, see Chapter 1. **Velleius Paterculus** (c. 19 BC–after AD 30) participated as a high-ranking military officer in the campaigns of Tiberius and Augustus' grandson Gaius Caesar and became a senator in AD 7. A major part of his two books of *Roman Histories* deals with the period of Augustus and Tiberius. Even though he is an unabashed fan of these two (cf. Boxes 3.3 and 5.6), he provides a valuable "boots on the ground" perspective that is missing from later writers. **Strabo** (c. 64 BC–AD 24), an educated and well-traveled Greek who spent much of his time in Rome, wrote a seventeen-book description of the world known to Romans at the time of Augustus and Tiberius. Its title is *Geography*. It is highly informative, even if not accurate in all details (cf. Box 7.2).

Of the later writers, the following stand out:

Suetonius (c. AD 70–c. 130). One part celebrity journalist, one part gossip wag, Suetonius served in the Communications Office under the emperors Trajan and Hadrian, where he oversaw the imperial correspondence. He had access to the imperial records and used them, especially the letters of Augustus, for his *Lives of the Caesars* that are rich in anecdotal details. Suetonius is a great read even today but needs to be enjoyed with a lump, rather than a grain, of salt.

Tacitus (c. AD 56–117). Cut from the cloth of the Roman elite, Tacitus was a senator, consul, and provincial governor. In his *Annales*, which covers the period from Tiberius' ascension to power in AD 14 to the death of Nero in 68, and his *Dialogue on Orators*, he is the voice of that elite, lamenting the demise of the Republic while being realistic about the impossibility, and even undesirability, of its revival; mordant wit and innuendo provide an outlet. Tacitus did not follow through on his plan to write a separate work on the reign of Augustus, but the memory of Augustus, which was still in its communicative stage at his time, is woven throughout his jaundiced account of the successors.

Plutarch (c. AD 45–after 120). Plutarch, a resident of the Greek east, is best known for his *Parallel Lives*, which were famously used by Shakespeare and others. His stand-alone *Life of Augustus* is among his lost works. Still, he provides much information through his biographical sketches of Caesar and Antony. The multitude of his other works includes a collection of quotations from Augustus.

Appian (c. end of the first century AD–c. 160). Born in Alexandria, later a resident of Rome, Appian treats a wide array of topics in his multivolume *Roman History*, which ranges from the beginnings of Rome to his own times. Particularly relevant to Augustus are the three books on the civil wars of the triumviral period. Appian's strengths include his interest in social issues, knowledge of finance, and relative objectivity. Probably because he was a native of Egypt, he gives the events there special attention and thus is a major source for information on Cleopatra.

Cassius Dio (c. AD 164–after 229). He was the scion of a prominent Greek family in Bithynia (Northwest Turkey; see Map 1) and had a distinguished public career as Roman senator, consul (twice), and provincial governor. Like Appian's, his eighty-book *Roman History* began with the origins of Rome and proceeded to his own day. Unreliable as he is in many ways, Dio is the major continuous narrative source we have for Augustus from his beginnings to 10 BC. The subsequent books, 55–60, dealing with the period from 9 BC to AD 46, exist mostly in abridged form, with a major lacuna for the years 5 BC–3 BC. Like other ancient historians, Dio creatively composed speeches for his protagonists in order to illustrate key issues; see Box 3.2.

Others: Given Augustus' abiding place in Roman memory, it is not surprising that scattered bits and pieces about him are found in the writings of several other Roman authors, including Pliny the Elder's (AD 23/4–79) *Natural History* (see Box 4.1). Another source is the collections of diverse topics by literati such as Aulus Gellius' (c. AD 130–c. 180) *Attic Nights* (see Box 5.9) and Macrobius' (early fifth century) *Saturnalia* (see Boxes 5.3, 5.10, and 5.11).

Inscriptions (Epigraphy)

Under Augustus, inscriptions became a mass medium of both written and visual communication; on major buildings in Rome, for instance, the inlaid letters were large and made of gilded bronze. The number of known "monumental" inscriptions (i.e., all durable inscriptions on stone and bronze plaques posted on stone, but not writing tablets or other equivalents for domestic use) increased exponentially, from 3,000 during the five centuries of the Republic to some 300,000 in the empire; their actual total has been estimated as high as 20 million to 40 million. The main reason was not the increase in territory, but the discovery of the power of inscriptions, analogous to the power of images. Augustus literally inscribed himself, and was inscribed, on the Roman empire (cf. Boxes 7.3 and 7.4). It is obvious that this is a rich source of information; good examples include the largest of them all, Augustus' *Res Gestae* of which copies were set up in several of the cities of the empire, but also private funerary inscriptions (cf. Box 2.5).

Papyri

Papyrus, made from the plant in Egypt, was a very common writing material in Greco-Roman antiquity. Unfortunately, it is also more perishable than stone. Most of the surviving papyrus documents, therefore, come from the sands of Egypt and their dry climate. For Augustus' time, they comprise mostly administrative documents, at various levels, for that region. An exception of more general relevance is a snippet from Augustus' funeral oration on Agrippa; see Box 5.2.

Coins (Numismatics)

Because they are hardware that has survived, coins figure prominently in many discussions of Roman civilization. They can be quite informational (cf. Fig. 7), but often that information is only supplementary. Their "propaganda" value, in particular, has been overrated; one of the reasons is that major coin catalogues, such as those of the British Museum, were published at a time when the propaganda of authoritarian rulers in Europe loomed large and when Augustus was cast as their godfather. It is important to realize that the gold and silver coinage (*aurei* and *denarii*) with the most striking designs did not wind up in the hands of most of the populace. The designs on the lower-denomination Roman base-metal coins were rather humdrum and would hardly sway hearts and minds. The basic unit was a *sestertius* (HS); four *sestertii* were one *denarius*, and 100 *sestertii* were an *aureus*. The annual salary of a Roman legionnaire was 900 HS, which explains, among other things, why Roman soldiers relied on booty in addition to their base pay. For further comparison, the price for an unskilled slave was some 200–1,000 HS, and the value of the free annual allocation of grain to heads of household in the city of Rome was worth between 300 and 360 HS.

PREFACE

The story of Augustus' life is as stunning as his achievements. Frail and only eighteen years old, he stepped on the stage of history when Caesar, slain on the Ides of March of 44 BC, named him, his grandnephew then known as Octavius, as his heir and posthumously adopted him. If the young man had followed the counsel of his mother and stepfather and refused to accept the will, history would have taken a different course and this book (and many others) would not have been written. He had no résumé to speak of at the time, yet some thirteen years later he defeated Antony and Cleopatra and, in his own words, had "power over all things." He became the sole ruler of Rome's Mediterranean empire and profoundly reshaped it and its culture. In the process he reinvented himself from a murderous warlord who took no prisoners to the model of an effective leader who gave Rome stability for almost two centuries. No question, then, that he is a key figure not only of classical antiquity but also of world history.

Given his tumultuous ascent to power, the range of his actions and policies, his immense impact, and the many sides of his personality, unanimity of opinion is the last thing we should expect, let alone wish, from biographers and historians, whether on the myriad of individual issues or on his overall attainments. Not waiting for others, he presented the latter, with his own perspectives, in the most monumental inscription from Roman times, the *Res Gestae*. It is not an autobiography – the one that he wrote has not survived – and the focus is not on personal details; his wife Livia, for instance, is not mentioned, although she was a great influence on his life.

That brings me to the genesis of this book. Over the years, I had dealt with many aspects of the Augustan age. It is a fascinating period to study because of its creativity, dynamics, and many dimensions in all its areas of cultural, political, and social activity. When my friend Beatrice Rehl of Cambridge University Press approached me about the new series of key figures in classical antiquity it gave me an opportunity to concentrate on Augustus' life and impact. That is, therefore, what this book is mostly about. As always, there was a challenge: as every scholar knows, it is often easier to write longer than shorter books. On just about every point in this book there has been extensive scholarly debate and discussion, starting with the nature and reliability of our sources. For each sentence I wrote, there could have been three or four more with additional elaboration in scholarly footnotes. The series chose not to adopt such a format and I therefore have followed the advice given to me long ago by a prolific scholar I have always admired, Erika Simon: *souverän auswählen*, which is, roughly, "select with authority" (and don't look back). The book's purpose is to provide a concise and informative introduction, to set some accents, and to stimulate the reader to explore any of its topics further. Another welcome emphasis in this series is to illustrate how we know what we know; hence the incorporation of a good number of "boxes."

A few months after I signed the contract I received a generous award from the Max-Planck Society for a multidisciplinary research project on the role of memory in ancient Rome. Building up and administering the project, which now involves some thirty grantees, with the apparatuses of two state universities in different countries has been another challenge. I am most grateful to this sponsor, however, for funding the necessary release time from which the writing of this book has benefited. I also want to thank the following for various kinds of assistance: Beatrice Rehl and Amanda Smith for their guidance; the clearance reviewer of the Press for his/her constructive suggestions; Peter Wiseman for advice on some very controversial points; and Darius Arya, Robert Daniel, Erica Firpo, Andrea Morgan, Stefan von der Lahr, and Henner van Hesberg for help with some of the illustrations. My greatest thanks go to Dr. Douglas Boin, whose keen reading improved the manuscript in many ways and whose efficient help with some research issues and the coordination of the photo permits was invaluable.

Sis felicior Augusto, melior Traiano ("may you be [yet] more fortunate than Augustus and better than Trajan") – that was the formal wish of the senate at the accession of every new emperor after Trajan. One area where Augustus would not count himself fortunate was his children. He had only one daughter, who caused him as many problems as he did her, and he had no sons; hence he doted on his two grandsons, both of whom died early. So I have been *felicior Augusto* and happily dedicate this book to my two wonderful sons and friends, Robert and John.

Karl Galinsky

1

FROM VELITRAE TO CAESAR'S HEIR

Childhood and adolescence, synonymous in our times with "formative years," did not arouse nearly the same interest in Roman biographers as in their modern counterparts. Concern with developmental psychology was slim at best; just as most characters in ancient literature are presented as fully formed while their different facets are being illuminated, so Roman art generally depicts children as little adults. Reliable information about Augustus' early life, therefore, is scant and centers on some basic data, such as his birth, and on noteworthy events like the funeral oration he gave in Rome, at an early age, in honor of his grandmother Julia. In addition, and as could be expected in light of his later prominence, there is a goodly number of accretions, most dealing with miracles and portents – there was a public for those – that were clearly later inventions.

Augustus Gets a "Life"

As always, there is the proverbial exception. That in this case is the biography by Augustus' contemporary, Nicolaus of Damascus, written perhaps around 20 BC. Nicolaus, a highly educated Greek, was not only an extremely versatile author but also a close adviser to Herod the Great and involved in several diplomatic missions, and it is likely that he met Augustus on one of these. The full title of his work is significant: *On the Life of Caesar Augustus and His Agōgē*; *agōgē* connotes upbringing, education, and direction. Given the stature and impact of Augustus, we might expect such a work to be a bestseller, but such was not the case. In fact, it is not cited by any ancient author and owes its survival, which is only partial, to a Byzantine ruler of the tenth century AD. He had it excerpted and then excerpted again: the various passages, sometimes shortened, were assigned to fifty-three subject categories, such as "Virtue and Vice" and "Conspiracies against Kings." The *Life*, such as we have it in its reassembled state, breaks off amidst the events a few months after Julius Caesar's death. Even so, the main significance of Nicolaus' work is that it was based, to a great extent, on the autobiography that Augustus, always the innovator, wrote not late in his life, but in his mid-thirties. Entitled *De vita sua*, it is another work from antiquity that has not survived. Suetonius, for one, used it but does not cite from it directly anywhere in his *Life of Augustus*.

Nicolaus' *Life*, then, is by far the most complete account of Augustus' early years, but how trustworthy is it? "Leave no superlative behind" seems to have been one of Nicolaus' unspoken maxims as his treatment of the young Augustus is panegyrical and then some. Discernibly, it reflects the tenor of Augustus' own *Vita*: a recurring theme is the emphasis on the justness of his actions that needed to be demonstrated after a gruesome thirteen years of civil war, if only to instill confidence in his abilities now that he was sole ruler. But especially when it comes to Augustus the child and adolescent, it is impossible to tell where Augustus' *Vita* leaves off and Nicolaus' begins. Nicolaus may have decided to lay things on yet more thickly. The result is that the youngster emerges as a paragon whose probity was never impeded, even by a cherry tree.

Still, we can use Nicolaus' work judiciously because some topics, such as the influence of Augustus' mother, the young man's respect for his teachers, and his sickliness, sound authentic. There is ample middle ground for us between a lapidary summary of the unchallenged data and a fulsome recital of Nicolaus/Augustus. The result may not be enough for psychohistory, which is not necessarily a drawback, but the future emperor's background readily contributed to shaping his mentality and some of his attitudes and actions.

Augustus was born on September 23 – some scholars have recently argued for September 22 (see Box 1.1 with Fig. 1) – not as Augustus, a name with which he was honored by the Senate in 27 BC, but as Octavius. This followed Roman custom: the family he was born into was that of the Octavii and, as was often the case, the first (and as it turned out, only) son also was given the father's first name, Gaius (abbreviated C.). The family was not from Rome but from Velitrae (modern Velletri), a small town in Latium about 25 miles southeast of the capital. It may well be that Octavius was actually born there, although other sources place his birth at Rome, not far from the Palatine where he came to live as emperor; that version may reflect the attempt to associate him with Rome from the cradle. Similarly, Rome won the battle of one-upmanship for the physical presence of the birthplace: in the capital, the house that was shown as his birthplace was made into a shrine whereas all that tourists in Velitrae got to see was a pantry-sized room in the family's suburban villa. There can be little doubt, however, that some of Octavius' upbringing did take place in small-town Velitrae.

BOX 1.1. AUGUSTUS' BIRTH SIGN: WHY CAPRICORN?

Figure 1. *Denarius* minted in Spain, ca. 17–15 BC. Hirmer Fotoarchiv 2001.613R, Hirmer Verlag, Munich.

Augustus was born on September 22 or 23. His sun sign, therefore, was Libra. Why, then, does Capricorn appear as his birth sign on coins, gems (such as the Gemma Augustea; cf. Box 5.8), glass pastes, and architectural decorations? That was, to be sure, his moon sign, but there is hardly any evidence from antiquity that people, let alone rulers, adopted that norm. And yet all of our ancient sources, including Augustus, hold to the September date, even Suetonius (*Aug.* 94.12), who states that Capricorn was his birth sign. One explanation for this seeming inconsistency is that after the calendar reform of Julius Caesar, Augustus' birth retroactively would have fallen around the winter solstice and, therefore, in the sign of Capricorn.

(continued)

3

Another solution is that Capricorn denotes the time of Augustus' conception, reckoned by one ancient authority as taking place 273 days before the birth date. That might work, even if we allow for the fact, obvious to any parent, that hardly any child arrives on the predicted day; but this kind of reckoning is also very rare, although it was used in connection with Romulus' birth and, for that matter, Augustus' association with Rome's founder. The basic answer, in Tamsyn Barton's apt formulation (1995, 44), is that "accurate dates of birth were not essential to the enterprise of the ancient astrologer.... [T]he astrologer was quite prepared to look for a horoscope *appropriate to the circumstances of the client.*" The popularity of Capricorn is a paradigm of the Augustan era because it was polyvalent – it could mean different things to different people just like "liberty" in politics, Vergil's poetry, or the Altar of Augustan Peace. Besides the possibilities above, Capricorn signified luck; in fact, in the September 22 horoscope Capricorn, though not the sun sign, controls the principal "point" or "lot," that of fortune. Further connotations include rule over the west and even revenge (via the murder of Osiris that was avenged by Horus) on the murderers of Julius Caesar.

In the end, the Augustan Capricorn is the equivalent to a logo in a modern advertising campaign. It is typical, too, that its representations are not heavy-handed and leave room for play and whimsy (cf. the chubby Cupid and the squashed snout of the dolphin by the feet of the hallowed Prima Porta Augustus statue; see Box 3.4). The coin above, minted in Spain between 17 and 15 BC, is a good example: the Capricorn holds a globe in his spindly front legs and a cornucopia pivots on his back.

Main sources

T. Barton, "Augustus and Capricorn: Astrological Polyvalency and Imperial Rhetoric," *Journal of Roman Studies* 85 (1995) 33–51.
A. Schmid, *Augustus und die Macht der Sterne* (Cologne 2005).

It is an experience he had in common with most inhabitants of Italy; as it turned out, he comprehended their sensibilities much better than did most city politicians and his ultimate victory, as Sir Ronald Syme rightly emphasized, was the victory of the nonpolitical classes of Italy, at least in great part. While there is no "typical" Italian town – Pompeii tends to be overrated in that respect – Velitrae's history was not isolated but shared in a spectrum of vicissitudes, characteristics, and peoples that were central to the making of Italy. To begin with, Italy did not consist of "Italians," let alone Romans. Instead, it was an aggregation of several peoples, tribes, and ethnicities, each with their own culture and language. The Volsci were one of these. They founded Velitrae even though the Latins later claimed to have done so. At any rate, soon after 500 BC it became part of the Latin League of some thirty cities of which Rome was one, only to see itself conquered by the Romans a few years later. Unrest, however, continued, until the Romans lowered the boom in 338 BC, razing Velitrae's fortifications and forcibly relocating the city fathers and their families "to the other side of the Tiber," certainly quite a distance in those days. Like many others, the city became a *municipium* under Roman control and its men could not vote. That changed after the Social War (90–88 BC) when all of Italy seceded over this very issue and it is only from that point on that Italy became more Roman.

It stands to reason that exposure to all this – life in a small town with its variegated cultural and political history, not to mention its pieties – contributed to Octavius' perspectives. So did his family, which did not belong to the Roman aristocracy on the basis of either money or descent. There were Octavii in Rome, but their relation to the Octavii of Velitrae is uncertain. Status and snobbery, however, were not prerequisites for comfortable circumstances and Octavius was born into such. His grandfather was a banker and member of Velitrae's municipal aristocracy and he had no further ambitions, living to a happy old age. His son, Octavius' father, aimed higher. With the family's wealth, he met the property qualifications for the senatorial class in Rome and, embarking on the time-honored *cursus honorum* (career path), advanced to the rank of praetor in 61 BC, an office which was just below that of the two highest executives, the consuls. He adhered to the traditional term limit of one year and then was awarded the governorship of Macedonia. On the way, he put down a slave insurrection in southern Italy and achieved even greater military successes in his province that qualified him for a future triumph in Rome. His civil administration also was exemplary; Cicero held him up as model to his somewhat less than exemplary brother Quintus, who was governor of the neighboring province of Asia (mostly today's Turkey) at the time.

Octavius the father, however, was not to consummate his triumph but suddenly died upon his return, at Nola near Naples in 59 BC. He was some 42 years old at the time. Given the prevailing conditions of health, hygiene, and medical knowledge – and that is one of the key differences between the Roman world and ours – the mundane reason was probably some kind of infection. In gross terms, average life expectancy in the Roman empire has been calculated at about 35 years and deaths of fathers and mothers while their children were still in infancy were anything but uncommon (see Box 1.2). Nor was it uncommon for the widowed parent to remarry quickly. Octavius had done so after the death of his first wife, Ancharia, with whom he had a daughter, Octavia the Elder. He then had married Atia and they had two children, Octavia the Younger, born in 69, and Octavius; the latter thus had two older sisters. In 58, Atia married Lucius Marcius Philippus, a member of the Roman nobility, who would be consul in 56.

BOX 1.2. LIFE EXPECTANCY IN ANCIENT ROME

One aspect that makes our world completely different from theirs is the much higher life expectancy we have in modern countries today. In the course of world history, this demographic transition is a relatively recent development that was not attainable until scientific breakthroughs such as those of Louis Pasteur and Alexander Fleming.

While much work has been done of late on life expectancy and mortality in the Roman empire, any precise figures that would apply to that diverse population, which counted in the millions, are beyond the meager evidence that is available. Tomb inscriptions and skeletal analysis will go only so far. By analogy with other premodern populations, life expectancy at birth probably ranged between twenty and forty years, with a major concentration in the lower half of this range. The figures are heavily impacted by the high infant mortality rate in Rome, which has been calculated as 300 out of 1,000.

An additional calculator is provided by the annuity table of the Roman jurist Ulpian (writing in the early third century AD) that can be used as a "life table." It assumes an average life expectancy at birth of approximately twenty-one years; once you turned ten, you could expect to live another thirty-five years or so. But again, these are not figures applicable to everyone in the empire. Of course, there are examples of considerable longevity, too, such as Augustus and his grandfather.

The situation hits home, however, when one realizes – and again this is a rough estimate – that at the age of twenty, only one-fifth of Roman women would have a father who was still alive. As one scholar reminds us, "average life expectancy is today usually regarded as one basic measure of quality of life" (Frier 1999, 89). We should not lose sight of these conditions amid the "Golden Age" of Augustus. At the same time, since life was precarious under the best of circumstances, we can understand the relief of the empire's populace that the additional ravages of decades of civil war were finally over.

Main sources

B. Frier, "Roman Demography," in D. Potter, ed., *Life, Death and Entertainment in the Roman Empire* (Ann Arbor 1999) 85–109.
T. G. Parkin, *Demography and Roman Society* (Baltimore 1992).

FAMILY CONNECTIONS

It is useful to pause here and look at the network in which young Octavius was embedded at this point. He may have been *ignobilis loco* ("not noble by origin"), as his later rival Mark Antony would point out with a sneer, but that did not mean he was unconnected. Octavius' marriage to Atia brought together not only the two leading families of Velitrae and the neighboring town of Aricia but established connections with two of Rome's most powerful figures: Atia's mother, Julia, was a sister of Julius Caesar while the mother of her husband Atius was the aunt of Pompey the Great. The Julian clan had been of long standing in Rome; it traced its descent back to Julus, the son of Rome's mythical ancestor from Troy, Aeneas, whose mother was the goddess Venus. Like other Roman *gentes*, or families, the Julians had had their ups and downs and were somewhat in eclipse by the end of the second century. They regained considerable profile shortly thereafter, only to lose some key members in the civil wars between Marius, with whom they were allied, and Sulla. The family's most prominent surviving scion, Julius Caesar (born 100 BC), had to go underground during one of Sulla's persecutions, but the very year of young Octavius' birth, 63 BC, marked Caesar's undoubted reassertion on the Roman political scene: he was elected *pontifex maximus* and thereby in charge of the far-reaching apparatus of Roman religion, which was an integral part of the

Roman state and its politics. At the same time, Pompey, after a series of stunning military victories, was practically Rome's viceroy in the eastern Mediterranean and the Near East. He and Caesar joined forces a short four years later along with Crassus, Rome's biggest financier. The so-called First Triumvirate did not suspend Rome's constitution, but it was a power junta that ran the table. The alliance fractured over the next decade amid a great deal of turmoil in Rome and Italy. Returning from Gaul, Caesar crossed the Rubicon in early 49, marched on Rome, and defeated Pompey at Pharsalus in northern Greece in August of 48.

The father figure with whom young Octavius grew up during those tumultuous times, his stepfather Lucius Marcius Philippus, again was anything but *ignobilis*. The *gens Marcia* was one of the most illustrious and well connected in Rome. In the third century, one of its male members had opted for the surname (*cognomen*) Philippus rather than the previous Tremulus, probably in admiration of Alexander the Great, the son of Philip. Lucius Marcius was neither tremulous nor audacious like Alexander but, as a leading member of the Roman senate during perilous partisan struggles, excelled at staying out of harm's way by cautious maneuvering and the wide range of his network. Through Atia, he was connected with Julius Caesar while simultaneously being the father-in-law of the younger Cato, one of Caesar's most relentless opponents. What was self-preservation for him sometimes looked like double-dealing to others, but he was universally recognized for being a careful operator who avoided missteps and prevailed at the end of the day. Not the least of his achievements was that he kept his considerable personal wealth and did not fall victim to the preferred means of political fundraising in Rome during civil wars, the proscription list (cf. Shakespeare, *Julius Caesar*, Act 4, Scene 1).

If, without stretching the point, we want to gauge these various influences on the formation of the future emperor, we can reasonably arrive at the following composite (and we will turn to his mother and teachers shortly). He was at home both in small-town Italy whose mindset he understood full well and in Rome where he could observe politics and the shaky state of the republic first hand. His grandfather's example may have impressed on him the importance of solid finances and their administration while his stepfather showed him how to navigate a minefield and err on the side of caution. The Octavii did not belong to the old nobility and Octavius' father, like Cicero, was one of the many "new men" (*novi homines*) who made their way into the highest echelons of government by virtue of their own efforts. Through Marcius Philippus, however, the young Octavius also had a foot inside the traditional establishment. This diverse background, and the concomitant experiences, were going to serve him well.

THE INFLUENCE OF HIS MOTHER

He was also served well by his mother. While the legal rights of Roman women seem pale by modern standards – though they were able to make wills, be in charge of businesses, and sponsor building activities – their real power, which was considerable, came by way of what the Romans called *auctoritas*, that is "clout" or "influence" rather than simple "authority." Unlike statutory power, *potestas*, which it complemented, it did not rest on a body of law or permanent enactments but was far more wide-reaching and dynamic, expressing a material, intellectual, and moral dimension of initiative and superiority. This quality was a traditional attribute of a Roman *mater familias*, and while it was "a cultural thing," to use a current phrase, it was not a given but had to be constantly validated – thus living up to its derivation from *augēre*, which means to increase or augment, or simply, to keep working at it. The distinction between *potestas* and *auctoritas* was operative in public life, too – the Roman senate, for instance, in contrast to its modern counterparts, was not an upper house with legislative powers but exerted its will through its *auctoritas* – and we will see that *auctoritas* became a pivotal part of Augustus' rule.

In that light, the frequent mention of his mother in the narrative of his youth and upbringing is not surprising. Atia was an *auctoritas* figure. She involved herself closely in young Octavius' education, conferring with his teachers, and forcefully stepped in as an adviser even after his assumption of the *toga virilis* in 48 BC – a step that marked the formal beginning of his adult life. When he wanted to join Caesar's campaign in Africa in late 47, Atia expressed her reservations and Octavius acquiesced. And when, in early 45, he departed for Spain to meet up with Caesar, Atia wanted to accompany him, though he was able to dissuade her. This was not mere possessiveness on her part: her son's health and constitution were brittle and, as we shall see, he sometimes ignored this weakness at his own peril.

Similarly, Atia immediately contacted Octavius after Caesar's assassination when it was announced that he was Caesar's heir. She was concerned about attempts on his life and asked him to seek sanctuary with her and "her entire house," which can mean various domiciles. Her husband, Philippus, even advised Octavius strongly not to accept Caesar's will and opt for a quiet life instead. But it is telling that Augustus in this instance of self-stylization, filtered as it may be through Nicolaus' biography, gives pride of place to his mother. Her *auctoritas* prevails: she sees both the potential for his greatness and glory and the huge risks and dangers that lie ahead. Hence she counsels neither acceptance nor rejection but leaves the choice to her son, being the first, however, to approve that he should take Caesar's name. And she remains a presence up to the point where Nicolaus' account breaks off. The final, decisive juncture comes with Octavius' decision to go to Campania to recruit his private army from among Caesar's veterans. He does not want to initiate her into this plan because, as reported by Nicolaus, he reasons that "her motherly and womanly affections would be an obstacle to his great designs." Instead, he pretends to her that he is merely trying to sell some of his father's properties in the region. He was, however, "not able to convince her entirely."

What matters in all this is not absolute historical accuracy but the portrait Augustus develops of his mother and of their relationship. That alone tells us something about her influence on him. She was a great presence in his life – even Tacitus, who was no fan of Augustus, would praise her for that (*Dialogue of the Orators*, 28.6) – and someone whose advice he took seriously. The same was going be true, in all respects, of his future wife Livia, Rome's first empress. Nor should we be surprised, therefore, that Augustus was the first Roman statesman to put mothers, and their children, on a public monument, the Altar of Augustan Peace (Ara Pacis; cf. Fig. 20).

EDUCATION

Growing up in an aristocratic household Octavius received a first-rate education. The unusual detail with which we are informed about his teachers again reflects his respect for those who participated in his upbringing. His elementary education in Philippus' household was entrusted to a Greek slave named Sphaerus in close collaboration with the parents – a recipe for success that is anything but a modern discovery. As *grammaticus*, Sphaerus taught the child reading, writing, and arithmetic, along with Greek because aristocratic Romans were cosmopolitan and Greek culture had been adapted and revitalized in Rome for more than two centuries, a synthesis that would reach new heights in Augustan poetry, art, architecture, and religion. Like other aristocrats, Octavius/Augustus never became fluent as a Greek speaker, but he habitually interspersed Greek with Latin in his correspondence and even tried his hand at composing poems in Greek. As for Sphaerus, Octavius freed him and took time out in 40 BC to grant him a state funeral even while being embroiled in an arduous civil war.

In his teens, Octavius' education continued with an emphasis on Greek philosophy and rhetoric. Again, we know the names of the teachers – Alexander may have had Aristotle, but Octavius had a team. His two philosophical teachers, Areios of Alexandria and Athenodorus of Tarsus (the birthplace of the Apostle Paul), prominently represented the leading school of the day, Stoicism, which emphasized, among other tenets, ethical responsibility and a divinely ordered universe. Typically, these philosophers were not unworldly; Augustus maintained connections with both and entrusted them with diplomatic and administrative tasks in Sicily and the east. Yet another example of continuing closeness came with Athenodorus' addressing a treatise to Octavia the Younger, whose son Marcellus died when he was only nineteen. Another telling episode is that, coming from a part of the world that had been ruled by Hellenistic monarchs, Athenodorus was concerned about Augustus' being overly accessible. Hence, to demonstrate the lack of security surrounding the emperor, he once disguised himself as a woman and was brought into Augustus' room in a covered litter. He leapt from it, sword in hand, and cried to the emperor: "Aren't you afraid that someone may come like this and kill you?" Augustus' reaction, according to Dio (56.43.2), was that, "far from being angry, he thanked him for the suggestion" – not an uncommon way to handle an old teacher's well-meaning advice – and seems to have issued no call for special protection. Later, he did employ a bodyguard of several Germans whom he dismissed after the German uprising in AD 9.

Professional training in rhetoric was the *sine qua non* for any Roman in the public realm who aspired to higher office. Defining an issue, constructing a speech, familiarity with literary tropes, and various techniques of delivery – all these were components of the systematic knowledge and skills an effective speaker had to master. It readily followed that there were competing schools of thought and practice. While rhetoric at first had been the domain of Greek teachers, Latin rhetoricians had entered the market for several decades by Octavius' time, and he studied with both a Latin and Greek teacher. Both were leading figures: Marcus Epidius, who also taught Antony and perhaps Vergil, and, on the Greek side, the even more famous Apollodorus of Pergamon, whose textbook was duly translated into Latin and who advocated for a style that was clear, direct, and free of bombast and artifice. That Octavius was able to pay him handsomely is evident from Apollodorus' leaving his school in Rome and following Caesar's protegé in late 45 BC to Apollonia (in today's Albania). There, Octavius was to train with some of Caesar's troops prior to a planned expedition against Rome's main enemy in the east, the Parthians; it was there that Octavius got the news of Caesar's assassination.

The incident also illustrates that Octavius needed ongoing rhetorical supervision and practice. Command of rhetoric did not come easy to him because it tended to strain his voice. Typically, however, and setting a pattern for the rest of his life not only in regard to rhetoric, he never desisted but made up for this deficit of nature with tenacity; Nicolaus even records what may have been one of the more successful applications of abstinence

training as we know it, that is, Octavius' refraining from sex for a year
to strengthen his voice and constitution (cf. Box 1.3). Similarly, though
Suetonius and others attest that he was good at speaking extemporane-
ously and quite a few of his surviving dicta show his quick wit and gift
for repartee (see Box 5.10), he methodically wrote out every speech, in
striking contrast to established practice. Again, this would not be the only
instance of his ability to be contrarian.

Another aspect of his education was physical training. In the early stages,
this task was usually entrusted to Roman fathers or their surrogates; later,
professionals would take their place. Roman nobles were destined to be
officers in the army and had to be trained in hand-to-hand combat. The
training included swimming, riding, swordsmanship, and throwing a spear.
Here again nature did not cooperate. Octavius had among other debilities
a weak left leg that sometimes caused him to limp, and was prone to illness
and heat exhaustion. Yet again he kept at it, although there were instances
when he overdid it and was overcome by stress. A striking example occurred
when Caesar put his barely seventeen-year-old grandnephew (instead of
a magistrate) in charge of the organization of the Greek games in Rome
in connection with his triumphal celebrations. Overworked, Octavius col-
lapsed, probably from heat stroke, and was bedridden for some time. He
learned from it: there were exponentially greater instances of stress later in
his life and he lived on to an old age for a Roman at the time, seventy-six
years. What made it possible was undoubtedly a great deal of self-discipline.
And in his youth, as later in his life, his frailty was no impediment to relations with the other sex; Nicolaus again dutifully reports that Octavius'
mother was very protective of him in this regard, too, because the young
man was very handsome and much sought after (Box 1.3).

Box 1.3. Nicolaus on the Young Octavian

"He went to the temples on the regular days, but (only) after dark on
account of his youthful charm, seeing that he attracted many women
by his handsome looks and high lineage; though often tempted by
them, he seems never to have been enticed. Not only did the watchful
care of his mother, who guarded him and forbade his wandering, pro-
tect him, but he too was prudent now that he was advancing in age.
During the Latin Festival when the consuls had to go to the Alban
Mount to perform the customary sacrifices and the priests took over

the jurisdiction of the consuls, Octavius sat on the Tribunal in the center of the Forum. And there came many people on legal business and many on no business at all except for a wanting to see the youngster; for he was well worth beholding, especially when he assumed the dignity and honorable aspect of office."

FGrH (= *Fragments of the Greek Historians*, ed. F. Jacoby) 90 F127.5

"Octavius lived soberly and in moderation; his friends know of something else about him that was remarkable. For an entire year at the very age at which youths, particularly those with wealth, are most wanton, he abstained from sexual gratification out of regard for both his voice and his strength."

FGrH 90 F129

"After this Caesar celebrated his triumphs for the Libyan War and the others which he had fought; and he ordered the young Caesar, whom he had now adopted, and who was in a way a son even by nature, on account of the closeness of their relationship, to follow his chariot, having bestowed upon him military decorations, as if he had been his tent companion in the war. Likewise, at the sacrifices and when entering the temples he stationed him at his side and he ordered the others to yield precedence to him. Caesar already held the rank of Dictator, which was the highest according to the Roman usage, and he was highly esteemed in the state. The young man was his companion both at the theater and at the banquets, and he saw that Caesar conversed kindly with him, as if he were his own son. He gained some more self-confidence as many of his friends and citizens asked him to intercede for them with Caesar, in matters in which they were in need of aid. Looking out for the opportune moment, he respectfully asked and was successful; and he became of great value to many of his kinsfolk, for he took care never to ask a favor at an inopportune time, nor when it was annoying to Caesar. And he displayed not a few sparks of kindness and natural intelligence."

FGrH 90 F127.8

Like many other outstanding ruler figures, Augustus was not a natural. His intellectual gifts were considerable, though they were hagiographically exaggerated by ancient writers. Nicolaus, for one, offers an exact counterpart in the boy wonder, Octavius, to Luke's presentation of the young

Jesus in the Temple (2.46–7): in one scene the seventeen-year-old expertly answers technical legal questions when he is city prefect for a day while the consuls are out of town (Box 1.3). He was not a gifted orator and his physical constitution was far from ideal. What made him successful is that he learned to work with these deficiencies and compensated for them with ongoing effort and determination. That was the grandnephew whom Julius Caesar began to notice and whom he would make his heir.

OCTAVIUS AND CAESAR

Our sources do not report one particular meeting or incident that would constitute an epiphany, neither do modern scholars emphasize nearly enough that Caesar was away from Rome for most of those years. Between his crossing of the Rubicon on the night of January 11, 49 BC, and his return from Spain, where he defeated the last army of his opponents, in early October of 45, he was in the city very intermittently: for two months in late 47 and some four months in 46. Octavius joined Caesar in Spain in June of 45 and then set out in the fall for Apollonia where he remained until Caesar's death. Probably because he is aware of these lacunae, Nicolaus makes up for them with much gushing detail that is meant to document Octavius' closeness to Caesar, but it is best not to follow him here too much. Further, some of Octavius' profiled appearances, such as the funeral oration on his grandmother Julia in a public assembly when he was barely twelve years old (Nicolaus, typically, makes him nine) – Caesar was in Gaul at the time – and his serving as city prefect for a day when he was seventeen, were not unusual honors that need to be ascribed to Caesar's doing. Others, however, were. They included his adlection into the most prestigious of all Roman priesthoods, the college of *pontifices*, who had broad supervisory powers over Roman religion, which, as we saw earlier, was closely intertwined with the life of the state. It was an appointment for life, and Octavian was only sixteen at the time. Then there was his assumption, at the age of seventeen, into the ranks of the patricians, the highest echelon of Roman senatorial society. Further, as we have seen, Caesar charged Octavian with the organization of important games that were normally under the purview of a magistrate, and upon his return from Spain, he rode with Brutus in the back of Caesar's carriage; Antony was in front with Caesar.

The final and most striking instance of Octavius' increasing visibility and prominence was Caesar's selection of him as *magister equitum*. Literally, it meant "Master of the Cavalry," and Octavius was duly sent to Apollonia to practice with Caesar's legions. The office, however, had traditionally been political rather than military. The *magister equitum* was the deputy of the dictator, which was a legal office in the Roman constitution, albeit limited to emergencies and a tenure of no more than six months. Like other constitutional provisions, such as one-year terms for the consuls, this one had fallen by the wayside amid the disorders of the first century; Caesar, at the time of Octavius' appointment, was in his fifth year as dictator and, on the Ides of February of 44 BC, was declared dictator for life, a life that lasted exactly one more month. At any rate, there could be little doubt about the role Caesar contemplated for Octavius. Yet when Caesar wrote his will in late 45, he did not tell Octavius about it. It provided that Octavius should be heir to three quarters of Caesar's estate (the remainder was divided between two nephews) and take on his name. These provisions, however, were contingent on Caesar's not having a son (his son by Cleopatra, Caesarion, had no legal claim) and, in case Octavius deceased or did not accept the will, Mark Antony was named a contingent heir. Octavius learned of all this soon after the Ides of March by letter from his parents and was given yet more details after he landed in southern Italy.

Caesar's Heir

The choice Octavius had to make was indeed monumental. Being Caesar's heir – what exactly did that mean? It must have been clear to most of his contemporaries that this was not simply a matter of a private inheritance, limited to taking possession of Caesar's material estate. An immediate official and very consequential public dimension was, in fact, built in: the heir was charged with distributing 300 sesterces to 250,000 heads of household of the plebs in Rome. That was a huge amount, equivalent to paying almost 85,000 legionnaires for an entire year – a truly unprecedented stimulus program. And there were other obligations that would propel the heir onto the center of the public stage. While Brutus and Cassius might crow about liberation, the fact was that Caesar had been murdered and his heir had the manifest duty to avenge him and bring them to justice. Roman customs in this regard and others were different from ours – some modern interpretations of Rome's Augustan epic the *Aeneid*, for instance, have been bedeviled by an unwillingness to make such distinctions – and the issue figures prominently in our sources about Octavius' decision. They are careful to present him as taking his time for careful deliberation and listening to various advisers. The final decision lay between two extremes: rejection, as urged by his stepfather, and immediate recruitment of a private army of Caesar's veterans to march on Rome and hunt down the assassins. Octavius, then, accepted the will and had it duly probated in early May by the legal magistrate in charge, one of the praetors, who also happened to be a brother of Mark Antony.

Of course the dimensions of the will did not end here. It was not just a will, but also a testament: there was the whole aspect of being heir to Caesar's political fortunes and legacy. Caesar, by the time of his death, was indeed the Colossus who bestrode the world. No Roman had ever been able to concentrate so much power in his hands; similarly, his military achievements had finally begun to surpass those of Pompey and, among many other attainments, even Cicero ranked him among the best orators of the age. If that was the legacy, how could an eighteen-year-old – a "boy" as Antony and Cicero immediately labeled him – without any military and political résumé, and plagued by a weak constitution and less than compelling rhetorical gifts, be expected to step into those boots and assume that mantle? And how would he avoid the many liabilities the dictator had accumulated along with his achievements? There was no way for anyone to predict the outcome we know. This is, of course, precisely what makes history so compelling, and what followed turned out to be one of the most fascinating chapters in world history. Moreover, to look at it from Octavius' perspective: even when, in a public speech later that year, he made the pronouncement, which left many in the audience aghast, that he "aspired to the honors of my father," he, too, must have realized that he was not going to be a copy of Julius Caesar. Instead, he would have to, and want to, chart his own path. The dynamic between continuing Caesar's legacy and establishing his own identity was, in fact, a major characteristic of his early career and reign.

No doubt, given the lack of any notable achievements by the youngster prior to the Ides of March of 44, there was much truth in Antony's derisive comment: "Boy, you owe everything to Caesar's name" (see Box 1.4). As we have seen, Caesar had stipulated in his will that his heir take his name and Octavius did so, calling him himself forthwith Gaius Julius Caesar. In order to avoid confusion with, well, Gaius Julius Caesar – there was no way to designate a son as Jr. – Cicero and other contemporaries started referring to him, besides informally calling him "the young Caesar," as Gaius Caesar Octavianus because of his actual descent. It needs to be stressed that Octavius never used that name himself. Neither did Brutus, who kept referring to him as Octavius and thereby implicitly denied Caesar's testamentary powers and, even more so, his reincarnation. "Octavian" has become conventional, however, and therefore he would be "Octavian" from the death of Caesar until January 27 BC when the senate officially conferred on him the name Augustus.

Figure 2. Marble head of Octavian. Copy from the 30s BC of an original dating to his political beginnings. The veil he wears marks him as belonging to a priesthood. Private collection in La Alcudia, Mallorca. Photo DAI Madrid R 1–71–11.

Box 1.4. Cicero Attacks Antony for Calling Octavian "Boy"

"But you, who cannot deny that you also were made illustrious by Caesar, what would you have been if he had not showered so many kindnesses on you? Where would your own good qualities have taken you? Where would your birth have conducted you? You would have spent the whole period of your manhood in brothels and eateries and in gambling and drinking, as you used to do when you were always burying your brains and your chin in the laps of mime actresses.

"'And you too, o boy – '"

"He calls him a boy whom he has experienced and shall again experience to be not only a man, but one of the bravest of men. It is

(continued)

indeed the name appropriate to his age; but you are the last man in the world who ought to use it, when it is your own madness that has opened to this boy the path to glory.

"'You who owe every thing to his [Caesar's] name – '"

"He does indeed owe everything, and nobly is he paying it.

"For if he [Caesar] was the father of his country, as you call him – I will make clear later what my opinion of that matter is – why is not this youth still more truly our father, to whom we certainly now owe our lives, snatched from your most criminal hands?"

Philippics 13.11, 24–5

There was another sequel. Adoption in Rome worked in different ways than today. At its center were not young children who needed a home but grown males in mostly upper-class families who, with the consent of their parents, were adopted into another such family that was lacking an heir. Commonly this was done by the adoptive parent when he was still alive. Testamentary adoption was somewhat unusual, though not unprecedented, and there is no indication whatever from friends or foes, let alone Caesar's veterans and the general populace, that Octavian's adoption was considered invalid. Still, Octavian sought formal ratification from Rome's most ancient, if not antique, assembly, the Comitia Curiata. It traced its beginnings back to the time of Romulus and most of its original powers, such as the election of magistrates, had been steadily taken over by other assemblies.

What message did Octavian intend to send here? It was typically dual: he forcefully pursued the aura of being Caesar's heir, but he also differed from Caesar by evincing respect for some of the old ways. Caesar would only have scoffed at the procedure. His contempt for Republican traditions was obvious in word and deed and his alleged pronouncement that "the Republic was nothing – a mere name without form and substance" (Suetonius, *Caesar* 77.1) was yet another stepping-stone to his assassination. In contrast, Octavian, even though he did not have to, chose not to bypass a formality steeped in tradition. It is an attitude that was going to be characteristic of the way he governed and his program in general. Further, the Curiate Assembly, being organized on the basis of thirty wards (*curiae*), retained a more democratic character than Rome's main electoral assembly, the Centuriate Assembly, which was egregiously plutocratic. We will see, too, that, perhaps paradoxically, Augustus' shift to an imperial and more autocratic government was accompanied by an authentic involvement of much wider strata of the population in civic affairs. This is not to say that Octavian already had it all planned out – such an assumption would be preposterous – and historical hindsight is an all too convenient commodity. Still, it is interesting to see the young Octavian's actions here prefigure what he would do as Augustus on a much larger scale.

2

POWER STRUGGLES AND CIVIL WAR

Caesar's Heir Asserts Himself

Caesar once, after a blitzkrieg campaign, famously claimed that "I came, I saw, I conquered" (*veni, vidi, vici*). Octavian's lightning debut on the Roman scene, when one looks at it in retrospect, may seem marked by similar success: entering Rome in May of 44 BC, he became the youngest consul in Roman history a mere sixteen months later, in August of 43. These months, however, are instructive not for their outcome, which was only the beginning of even greater challenges, but for amply illustrating that this outcome was anything but preordained. It could easily have been different because the amount of variables involved was immense. They were a mosaic of calculations and miscalculations, steps and missteps, sudden vicissitudes that required instinctive response, and both human actors and turns of events that were not susceptible – there and then – to the kind of careful analysis that is afforded to historians later. Certainly, a major reason Octavian prevailed was his determination. At the same time, he was at the mercy of circumstances that were not easily controlled.

After the Ides

What was the situation like after Caesar's death? Who were the major players who could influence events? We can begin with Brutus and Cassius. As Shakespeare's Antony said, they were honorable men – denizens of Cyprus, whom Brutus charged 48 percent interest on loans, might have had a different perspective – but their action exemplified the shortsighted mindset typical of their class: they had no constructive program whatsoever. Happy days would simply return after Caesar was out of the way. In essence, we are looking at a major reason both for the failure of the Republic and the failure of their coup. Caesar was dead, but the problems that had beset the Roman Republic for several decades did not die with him. In Rome, the urban plebs, numbering in the hundreds of thousands, continued to be a volatile mass, even though or precisely because they were on the dole. The army of some 500,000 had gotten used to fighting civil wars as much as foreign opponents, and most of the soldiers had greater allegiance to their commanders, who could deliver the goods, than to the *res publica*, the commonwealth. Further, Rome had long ceased to be a small city-state on the Tiber and could not be governed as if it still were. Its empire stretched all around the Mediterranean; besides increased economic opportunity, this expansion had led to striking social change throughout the area and the provinces could not be expected simply to persist as tax-paying appendages to the capital and Italy. On top of it all were an economy and infrastructure ruined by internecine warfare and other dislocations.

These problems demanded solutions. Caesar had aggressively initiated some, like drastically reducing the number of recipients of the dole and shifting welfare to workfare, during the few short months he was in Rome prior to the Ides of March. The senatorial oligarchy, however, kept to its insulated ways: its members enjoyed their privileges and that lessened their sense of urgency. In other words, vision was not their forte. For the huge populace outside of that class, in both Rome and the provinces, things looked and were different. Hence the assassination, besides its temporary *éclat*, was basically a fiasco. Absent any program by the liberators for addressing underlying social, economic, and other problems, there were sympathizers, but no popular groundswell of support materialized. Brutus and Cassius soon found themselves rattling around outside of Rome, first in Campania and then in Greece. Both were praetors that year; a stunned senate along with Antony, who was consul, on March 17 had quickly agreed to an amnesty to prevent further bloodshed. But they departed soon enough and, despite some allies, were not a factor in the capital itself.

Mark Antony

Others were, Antony foremost. It is well known that history is written by victors and we can therefore discard caricatures of Antony like the libertine, hyped in Cicero's *Philippic Orations*, who drunkenly staggers about the Roman scene (cf. Box 1.4), and his equally lurid portrayal as the reincarnation of the Greek wine god Dionysus and Cleopatra's besotted love slave. Julius Caesar was not in the habit of picking incompetents and Antony was his right-hand man both in the field and in affairs of state. He had the résumé, several times over, that Octavian lacked and he was consul in 44 BC. As such, he was at the levers of power: he could convene the senate, he commanded several legions, and he had the backing of Caesar's veterans, who expected vengeance. Of all the protagonists, he was in the strongest position to set the agenda. His failure was that he did so very indecisively. Again, a systemic rather than personal reason may be cited. Honorable as one-year term limits were in the early republic, they precluded continuing leadership in a larger and more complex environment – another reason why so many problems were left simmering – and since a consul, after his one-year tenure, automatically spent his remaining years in the senate, his understandable inclination would be not to rattle the cage but to go along in order to get along; innovation and truly decisive action often had to come about in other ways. Antony, then, was a creature of the old order by not being farsighted, or at least farsighted enough. Politics triumphed over policy, an affliction that was shared by others, including Cicero.

Antony's objectives, then, made sense for the immediate term. Chief among them was to put down the young heir of Caesar and show him up as an inexperienced Caesar wannabe and pretender. Antony, therefore, made it a point to obstruct Octavian's every move. They had an early meeting where the consul and true political heir of Caesar treated the youngster with deliberate condescension, for all to see. He blocked the Comitia Curiata from acting on Octavian's formal adoption by Caesar. The contestation then moved on to Rome's most public venues, the games. When Caesar was still alive, the senate had awarded him a golden throne to sit on during his public appearances. Octavian wanted to have it set up in full view at the games in April, ritually enshrining his adoptive father's lasting presence. The city official in charge, however, turned him down. Antony backed that decision.

A few weeks later, at the end of July, Octavian tried again on occasion of yet more prestigious games that he himself organized and financed with the help of influential backers, the games for Caesar's Victory. Their divine patron was the goddess Venus, the ancestress of the Julian family. Again Antony denied him, though the games went on. Absence, however, can be just as effective as presence in provoking memory. In light of the immense publicity, therefore, about the whole controversy, the empty spot where the throne would have been placed must have stood out just the same. And Octavian did more to fill in the blank. He distributed thousands of glass tokens to the rapt masses; they featured his head and Caesar's throne (Fig. 3, see Box 2.1). Celestial media stunningly complemented their terrestrial counterparts: during the games, a comet appeared (Box 2.2) and the word was given out that this was the soul of Julius Caesar streaking into heaven. Caesar now was *divus*, divine. That made Octavian the son of the divine – an incomparable asset in politics to our day – and he wasted no time to affix the star to Caesar's images and style himself as *divi filius*. He insisted that Caesar be officially deified in the Roman state religion; again, Antony obstructed and the final ratification, like the adoption, did not occur until later. The media advantage, however, clearly belonged to Octavian, who repeatedly upstaged Antony. So far from being able to ignore Octavian, Antony now had to deal with his rapidly increasing presence and his just as rapidly increasing acceptance as Caesar's real heir.

Box 2.1. A Mass Medium: Glass Pastes

Figure 3. Glass paste, Berlin. From A. Furtwängler, *Beschreibung der geschnittenen Steine im Antiquarium*, Berlin 1896, no. 5172.

Far more so than even the cheapest coin, which had to be produced by one of the official mints, glass tokens were inexpensive to manufacture and could be produced quickly by the thousands. They were more perishable, too, a circumstance that has contributed to the over-emphasis, by modern scholars, on coins as means of "propaganda."

(continued)

Glass tokens conveyed such messages much more effectively to a targeted audience; besides, they were distributed for free. In this example Octavian combined three visuals that were easy to understand: his head, Caesar's throne (which he was not allowed to display during the games), and two horns of plenty (cornucopiae) that symbolized prosperity and referred to the payout Octavian had made from Caesar's estate to the urban populace. Medium and message were direct, clear, and effective.

Box 2.2. Caesar's Star

No fewer than thirteen literary sources attest the appearance of a comet in late July 44 BC. Extremely luminous, it was visible in Rome for seven days that happened to coincide with the duration of the impressive games staged by Octavian. Octavian had made two significant changes: (1) he moved them to July from September, the month in which Caesar had inaugurated them in 46 BC along with the Temple of Venus Genetrix, ancestress of the Julians; and (2) they took on a strong commemorative aspect for Caesar. Another objective was to trump the games sponsored by Brutus earlier that month in honor of Apollo.

Was Octavian prescient? The same comet – it was not Halley's – was sighted in China in June; about its reality there is no doubt. It seemed to be a godsend. Besides its effect on the populace – yet another departure from tradition was the skillful interpretation of the phenomenon as beneficent rather than as a baleful harbinger of disaster – it also had a deep effect on Octavian himself: "He took pleasure in the view that it [the comet] had come into being for him and that he was coming into being in it" (Pliny, *Nat. Hist.* 2.94). How so? One reason may be that Capricorn, his birth sign (see Box 1.1) was in the ascendant when the comet appeared. It was not difficult to interpret this as a sign of his own "(re)birth" as a Julian and of the destiny, as "son of the divine," of his own future divinity. In a world where astrology ruled, Octavian was forever hitched to Caesar's star.

Main source

J. T. Ramsay and L. Licht, *The Comet of 44 B.C. and Caesar's Funeral Games* (Atlanta 1997).

Building a Base

More substantive issues converged on the same result. There was the matter of distributing the immense largess Caesar had willed to the Roman populace. A major source for it was the many properties Caesar had confiscated from enemies after crossing the Rubicon in 49. Octavian put them up for sale. A sale this massive, of course, was going to depress property values in Italy, but that was not the reason Antony tried to slow down the process by insisting that the courts should allow the original owners to present their claims in each and every case. The motive was obvious: not to let Octavian gain any popularity and clout. It soon proved to be a miscalculation. Caesar's followers and the intended plebeian recipients resented having to wait for their payments while seeing Antony invoke lofty legal principles. Octavian moved quickly. He rallied financial support, including from the two other heirs, sold many properties of the family of Octavius, dipped extensively into his private inheritance from Caesar, and diverted some of the Caesar's public funds, including his war chest for the planned campaign against Rome's eastern enemies, the Parthians – after all, his grandfather had shown him how to handle money. The bottom line was that the Roman populace received the first half of the payments without delay – and exactly during the Caesarian Victory Games, which thus turned out to be the perfect storm or trifecta: the publicity over Caesar's throne on the ground, the appearance of the comet overhead, and the money in the pockets of the people squarely put Octavian at the center of the action.

Once more Antony could only react and at one point had Octavian dragged from one of the property trials by the lictors. Octavian acted with savvy and used the opportunity to present himself as the injured party. He sought refuge in his house while claiming that his life was endangered from Antony's threats when he, Caesar's heir, was only trying to make sure that the monies willed by Caesar – "when that the poor have cried, Caesar hath wept" – reached the masses. The fracas reached a point that had many of Caesar's followers concerned and, significantly, it was Antony's bodyguard of some 6,000 veterans who insisted that Antony publicly reconcile with Octavian. That was done amid great ceremony and pomp in Rome's holiest shrine, the Temple of Jupiter Optimus Maximus on the Capitol (see Map 2). The clear beneficiary was Octavian because it established him as Antony's equal yet more visibly.

Not in all ways, of course. Octavian had ample resources, but Antony commanded an army. Antony held a constitutional office whereas Octavian, for all Caesar's aura, was only a private citizen. For the next few months, therefore, Octavian's agenda was to close that gap and do so in a hurry. Of course he could not do it all by himself and we therefore need to look at his support, and supporters, and at the actions, or lack thereof, of institutions like the senate.

His support came from many quarters. His supporters were a loose but cohesive aggregation; they were not a party or faction. As Caesar's heir, he would have the loyalty of many of Caesar's veterans. The financial crowd also had been largely in Caesar's camp in addition to many well-to-do freedmen who had no civic, but considerable economic, status. Then there were Caesar's trusted operatives, Gaius Oppius and Cornelius Balbus, who had minded his affairs in Rome during his frequent absences. Forerunners of the executive staff of the "imperial presidency," they were not elected officials nor approved by the senate but handpicked by Caesar on the basis of expertise and ability; Balbus, in fact, was from a wealthy family in Spain, had acquired Roman citizenship, and was to be Rome's first foreign-born consul (in 40 BC). Further, Octavian could count on influential senators, including his stepfather Philippus, who acquiesced in Octavian's decision to accept Caesar's testament and then supported him staunchly. Caesar had packed the senate in ways Franklin Roosevelt could only have envied when he tried to do the same with the Supreme Court. The senate had swollen to 900 members, and while the Caesarian majority showed little initiative, it provided a fairly reliable block against efforts hostile to Octavian. At the same time, the Caesarians were not a monolithic group. Antony had his share of supporters among them. That made it imperative for Octavian to win more over to his side.

Cicero and the Senate

What about the senate, then, that repository of *auctoritas*? It is easy to be misled here by a less than careful use of one of our main sources for the period, Cicero. His letters during these months and the much read invectives that he gave or published later in the year against Antony, the famous fourteen speeches called *Philippics* (the model was the Greek orator Demosthenes who had excoriated Alexander the Great's father, Philip), may conjure up the image of beehive-like activity and Rome's elder statesman being constantly engaged in stirring up senatorial energies. The telling fact is that Cicero, while busily writing letters, did not attend any senate meetings between March 17 and September 2 and he probably was not alone. The pace would quicken considerably later that year, but the protracted initial inertia again worked in Octavian's favor. He made nice with

Cicero, paying a courtesy visit to one of Cicero's estates in Campania in the spring before he moved on to Rome. That was only the beginning of a long effort of cultivation, which fully exploited the great man's equally great susceptibility to flattery. That is clear even though we have only Cicero's letters; Octavian may have taken care not to have his published, being prescient enough, perhaps, that he was going to make his mark on history in other ways. And what could he possibly have said about vain boasts by Cicero – to Brutus, of all people – such as "this young Caesar... derived from the headspring of my mentorship" (Cicero, *ad Brut.* 24.6)? Cicero wrote this in late July of the following year, 43 BC, five months before his death by proscription (cf. Box 2.4) on which Octavian signed off, and his delusion of "mentorship" shows how effectively Octavian had courted him.

There were further factors in the unfolding scenario. One was the acute shortage of real leaders due to the carnage of the civil wars. It is not that distinguished ancestry with its aura of *dignitas* automatically produced individuals with true leadership qualities, but the aristocratic families provided a pool of potential movers and shakers. That pool was severely diminished: in the senate of some 900, there were but seventeen *consulares*, individuals with consular experience. That is a very small number when one realizes that often more than two men held the consulship in a given year, due to the death, natural or other, of one of their colleagues. Of course, the longer a political career, the greater the baggage. It was an issue that worked against Antony; boast about his superior experience as he might, there were some very ugly things on his record that did not make him the favorite of the urban populace nor of quite a few of the Caesarians. In contrast, Octavian was unencumbered. Here was a new face from outside Rome that was not part of the usual crowd, and to many he may well have represented hope, especially hope for a better future. It is hard to gauge such things because our written sources are elitist and do not come from the common people. It is clear, however, that his arrival resonated widely – we have accounts of enthusiastic crowds greeting him in Campania – and he could tap into much favorable sentiment.

The Rogue Operator

All these pluses, however, added up to only so much. Octavian realized soon enough that his real need was military muscle. There was no constitutional way for him to get it since he held no office. He therefore recruited, in October of 44 BC, a small army of some 3,000 of Caesar's veterans. He marched into Rome with them in early November and gave a speech that showed his political immaturity. As "a servant of the state who harkened to its needs" (Appian, *Civil Wars* 3.41), he offered the use of his troops against the machinations of Antony with the result that many of his veterans quit while keeping their generous pay – they had expected to be enlisted, at last, for revenge against Brutus and Cassius rather than a fellow Caesarian. And it was the occasion for the dramatic gesture of stretching out his hand towards Caesar's statue and swearing that he aspired to honors of his father. It prompted Cicero (*Letters to Atticus* 16.15.3) to call him "that boy" (*iste puer*); something he gave up on quickly, only to attack Antony for it all the more vigorously (cf. Box 1.4).

The reason was that the boy quickly learned from his mistakes. He had to vacate the city for the arriving Antony but through emissaries immediately capitalized on the disaffection of the troops whom Antony had left behind south of Rome so as to show his good will in negotiating with the senate. Traditionally, Rome was off limits to the legions, but this prohibition had been breeched frequently by that time and Antony's soldiers were in a rebellious mood for precisely the same reason Octavian's hired troops had walked off a little earlier: they had expected to march on Rome and against the senate in order to avenge the death of their slain leader. Had Antony done so, our story might well have come to an end right here. Antony could have taken over the city and imposed his regime, and Octavian would have been in no position to stop him.

Instead, Octavian's agents went to work and won over two of Antony's veteran legions with appeals of "coming to the help of his father," and, even more decisively, with generous donatives. Antony had to make a choice: either lead his remaining four legions against these two and have Caesar's veterans fight each other or move on to secure northern Italy where an army loyal to the Republic was entrenched. That situation seemed more threatening – Cisalpine Gaul, as it was called, controlled access to the heartland of Italy – and Antony chose to deal with it first. Again Octavian got a reprieve.

By that time, the senate showed signs of life. This is the place not to detail the various maneuvers and tergiversations of that body, but to focus on how the situation presented itself to Octavian. Antony's consulate was going to expire at the end of the year, and he would then be proconsul of a province allocated by the senate, which meant command over several legions. That province was to be Macedonia, but Antony had effected a plebiscite to give him Cisalpine Gaul instead. The current commander there, chosen by Caesar in early 44 BC, was Decimus Brutus, who then went over to the conspirators. He made it clear that he would not hand over his own legions, who remained loyal to him, to Antony, whose own support in the senate was beginning to show signs of erosion. Antony simply was looking too high and mighty even to a senate whose majority was comprised of Caesarian sympathizers.

Octavian saw an opening. Negotiating with Cicero, he offered the use of his private army against Antony to the senate in return for some benefits to be voted on: preferred membership, equal to that of a *consularis*, in the senate and legitimation of his position by being given a command equal to that of constitutional praetor. An additional bonus was the reduction of his waiting period for a consulate by ten years. The constitutional age requirement was forty years and that still put Octavian at twelve years' remove; subsequent events quickly made that provision obsolete. The deal having been worked out, Cicero mightily launched his remaining thirteen *Philippics*.

It is worthwhile to pause here for a moment and briefly survey what it all meant. Cicero's actions were typical of his career: he had always excelled at great rhetoric and scintillating invective, but they did not make up for the deficit of substantive programs directed at the real social and economic issues. Hence, as Syme, who was no fan of Octavian's, trenchantly noted, Cicero's fanatic intensity now was his final, desperate attempt to redeem himself and assert leadership: "He knew how little he had achieved for the Republic despite his talent and his professions, how shamefully he had deserted his post after March 17 when concord and ordered government might still have been achieved" (1939, 144). It is a sad irony that the program of this talented man now amounted to an exact perversion of anything republican. He saw to it that the senate legitimatized the rogue army of a warlord against the rightful consul of the Republic. He broke with all precedent by having the senate itself co-opt a new member. And he did that by officially exempting Octavian from the republican age requirement for holding Rome's highest office. The goal was to come to the aid of Decimus Brutus, defender of the Republic, but the means triumphed over the end and, once more, so did politics over policy.

What did this convey to Octavian? It definitely was a formative experience for him. He could see first hand that the constitutional apparatus of the Republic was broken, if not bankrupt. When, therefore, he rebuilt the *res publica* as Augustus later, his emphasis was not on restoring every technicality but to focus on substance. Growing up in a family from Velitrae, he had respect for the traditional values of Italy, which he would try to re-instill in its people. On the other hand, coming to power quite unconventionally by bypassing the usual *cursus honorum* and its attendant rigmarole, he was not a product of the old political system and therefore saw free to update and outflank it. The combination of these two aspects – traditionalism in some areas, new departures and innovation in others – was going to be a hallmark of his reign.

More immediately, he was aware his troops would never allow him to fight on behalf of a murderer of Caesar against Caesar's closest friend. Cicero divined that much. He was satisfied with the evolving stalemate in northern Italy, Decimus' success at breaking out of the besieged city of Mutina in April of 43, and Antony's defeat that forced him to withdraw his troops further north. He also stayed in contact with Brutus and Cassius. The Republic wasn't dead yet, and its icon let on that Octavian might not be needed and be better off somewhere else. And where might that be? Cicero expressed it with a coy ambiguity: "The young man should be praised, adorned, and uplifted" (*ad fam.* 11.20.1), which could mean either to the next level on earth or to the great beyond. The young man's response was that he was in no hurry getting to the latter place. While he aspired "to his father's honors," and especially divinity, he was equally determined to choose a different route – and he soon helped Cicero beat him to that destination handily.

Octavian's Coup

In the meantime, the nineteen-year-old displayed a knack for making the right calculations and using events which could easily have harmed him to his advantage. The two consuls of the year, Hirtius and Pansa, headed up the anti-Antonian Caesarians in the senate and commanded the legions that were sent against Antony in relief of Decimus Brutus. They won the engagement, but both died in a battle in which Octavian was decorated for bravery. Cicero tried to fill the void by entreating Brutus and Cassius to return to Italy with their troops and the senate began to treat Octavian dismissively. Octavian realized the danger and was well equipped to deal with it. He was the only commander in Italy who had a viable army in place – eight legions – and he further realized that only force was going to carry the day. Still, he first proposed to Cicero, and then to the senate, that he and Cicero should be the new consuls, an offer that both the senate and Cicero saw fit to refuse. And so, at the end of July of 43 BC, Octavian marched on Rome again without letting the senate slow him with increasing last-minute concessions. The populace in Rome received him enthusiastically and his centurions obtained senatorial cooperation at sword point. Brushing the usual and complex preliminaries aside, he was legally elected consul on August 19 by the proper electoral assembly and, not entirely by coincidence, the Curiate Assembly finally ratified his adoption by Julius Caesar on the same day. In retrospect, especially looking at the welter of events in those preceding months, we can see quite clearly that Octavian's success was far from guaranteed and that his fate hung in the balance time and again.

Pivotal as his coup and his assumption of the consulship were, they were only the beginning of years of grave challenges and difficulties. The contours of these years are clearer – only to blur again when we come to the transition between republic and monarchy – and we can proceed with them more rapidly, though we will never approach the succinctness of Augustus' own summary. This is how he began the *Res Gestae* (1.1–4):

> 1. At the age of nineteen, on my private initiative and at my private expense, I raised an army with which I redeemed into liberty the *res publica* when it was oppressed by the tyranny of a faction. 2. On that account, in the consulship of Gaius Pansa and Aulus Hirtius, the senate passed decrees in my honor, enrolling me in its order, assigning me the right to give my opinion among the former consuls and giving me power of command (*imperium*). 3. It ordered me as a propraetor along with with the consuls to see to it that the republic should suffer no harm. 4. In this same year, when both consuls had fallen in battle, the people appointed (*creavit*) me consul and triumvir for setting the republic in order.

It is a brilliant passage – short on details, especially unpleasant ones, and long on evocations. Nineteen: that puts him in the company of Alexander the Great. The private citizen coming to help the state: here is the real heir to Brutus, who overthrew Rome's last Etruscan king and founded the *libera res publica*, and to statesmen like Pompey, that virtuous paragon of the Republic. Liberating the commonwealth from factional oppression: again, that phrase, with its good ring, had been used by others before; here it presents the young Octavian, and not Brutus and Cassius, as the true liberator. No mention of the messy maneuvers and the military coup – it was the people who "created" the young consul and triumvir; the triumvirate, with Octavian very much the junior partner, was the junta established by him, Antony, and Lepidus in November of 43. Intentionally, then, the passage is notable as much for what is left out as for what is set in bronze and stone.

The Bloody Years

That applies even more to the events from late 43 until 30 BC, when he was the only leader left standing. Antony and Cleopatra had been defeated at Actium on September 2, 31 BC, and Octavian had conquered Alexandria after the couple's suicide in August of the following year. Augustus chose, in the *Res Gestae*, not to give a chronological account, however brief, of the period but incorporated only occasional references to it throughout the work. One of his successors, the scholarly emperor Claudius, who was Livia's grandson, commenced his history "with the murder of Julius Caesar, then skipped a few years and started again at the close of the Civil Wars; because he realized, from his mother's and grandmother's lectures, that he would not be allowed to publish a free and unvarnished report on the intervening period" (Suet., *Claud.* 41; trans. R. Graves) – the subject was too close for kinship comfort. The reason for both silences is that Octavian's behavior in those years was quite different from that of his later incarnation as Augustus. Many of his contemporaries never came to trust that transformation and kept fearing the old Octavian lurking behind the placid, supremely composed, and paradoxically youthful features of Augustus' ubiquitous portraits. It was a period of extreme violence and excess – "without law and custom," as Tacitus put it – and it is precisely because Octavian was at its center and under unbelievable duress that we see more of his raw emotions and passions in those years than later, when he had time to stylize his persona carefully. This is not to say that here, for once, we see the "real" Augustus or "the man behind the mask." He did evolve, but his actions and behavior during this period of extreme stress left an indelible impression. They cover a large and fascinating spectrum and we will, therefore, engage with some of these moments first and then fill in the historical narrative.

Octavian Up Close: Negatives

As we saw earlier, Octavian's constitution from childhood was not the best. Illness, therefore, continued to be his abiding companion at crucial times. At Philippi, he did not battle Brutus and Cassius as much as he did a kind of dropsy. His charge was to defend the camp, but on the day before the battle he removed himself from that task both on his doctor's advice – he had been ill for some time – and because of a dream. He then hid in the surrounding swamps for three days, only to emerge with "his belly and sides having puffed up and swelled with a waterish humor that had spread between the flesh and the skin" (Pliny, *Nat. Hist.* 7.148, on the authority of Agrippa and Maecenas, no less; cf. Box 4.1). The actual battle was won due to the generalship of Antony. Unsavorily, Octavian made up for his embarrassment by raging against the corpse of Brutus like a Homeric warrior, defiling it by having the head cut off and ordering that it be shipped to Rome for display in the Forum (it never arrived there because the ship lost its cargo in a storm). Here Shakespeare got it right: Antony was the more magnanimous of the two and the peroration on "the noblest Roman of them all" is appropriately spoken by him, and not by Octavian. The subsequent arrangements between the victors stuck Octavian with the explosive task of having to expropriate the landowners of eighteen Italian cities for the resettlement of some 50,000–60,000 soldiers; this stress factor may well have contributed to his falling ill upon his arrival in Italy. As always, however, he recovered and did not falter even when all hell broke loose because the assigned lands were not enough and additional properties had to be confiscated.

Perhaps the most famous instance of his being ill while a crucial battle was being fought came at Actium. The image of the seasick Octavian bobbing up and down in the sickbay of the command ship has had a good run, especially in the literary and cinematic tradition. Alas, it is far from proven. The battle itself, as historians now agree, was a rather lame affair, and its outcome was foreseeable well in advance. Since it marked a turning point, however, layer upon layer of descriptive efflorescence accrued; "the true story," as Syme (1939, 296) tersely noted, "is gone beyond recall." The vignette of the out-of-combat Octavian does not occur in the texts of the major historians but may reflect the effort of Antonian sympathizers to debase his stature and reduce him to a coward whose timely illnesses always left the fighting to others. Vergil may also have responded to it when, in one of the most glorifying passages in the *Aeneid*, he presents Augustus emphatically as "standing tall on the stern of his ship" (*Aen.* 8.680) – a phrase the poet had used earlier for his ancestor Aeneas – and, with the help of Apollo and Caesar's star overhead, "leading the Italians into battle" against the mongrel hordes (and gods) of the east. Augustus let the more experienced Agrippa be in command of the battle while he directed operations from a smaller brigantine, and the hostile tradition may be a spin on those actualities. If anyone was sick, it was many of Antony's troops who were suffering from famine and a variety of diseases. In Dio's lurid tableau, a large number were roasted on their ships when Octavian ordered an assault with fiery missiles. Others jumped in the water only to drown or be "torn apart by wild sea beasts." Evidently, the inventiveness of our historical sources was not limited to stories about the sick Octavian (see Box 2.3).

BOX 2.3. SCENES FROM THE BATTLE OF ACTIUM

"Vivid in the center [of the shield] were two fleets of bronze, engaged in the battle of Actium; all about Cape Leucas you saw
brisk movement of naval formations; the sea was a blaze of gold.

(continued)

On one side Augustus Caesar, high up on the stern, is leading
the Italians into battle, the Senate and People with him,
with his home-gods and the great gods: two flames shoot up from
   his helmet
in jubilant light, and his father's star dawns over its crest.
Flanking him is Agrippa, favored by winds and gods,
towering, leading his column; the naval crown adorned with beaks
of ships shines forth from his head, a proud decoration of war.
On the other side, with barbaric wealth and motley equipment,
is Antony, fresh from his victories in the east and by the Red Sea;
Egypt, the powers of the Orient and outermost Bactra
sail with him; also – a shameful thing – his Egyptian consort …

"In the midst, Cleopatra rallies her troops with the rattle of Isis,
for she cannot yet see the two serpents of death behind her.
The barker Anubis, a whole progeny of grotesque
deities are embattled against Neptune and Minerva
and Venus. Mars is raging in the thick of the fight…."

Vergil, *Aeneid* 8.675–88, 696–700
(C. Day Lewis trans., with modifications)

This is one of only three places in Vergil's epic where Augustus is mentioned by name. The occasion is the shield the god Vulcan, husband of Aeneas' mother Venus, makes for Aeneas, the ancestor of Augustus and Rome. With its depiction of scenes from Roman history, the shield is the updated counterpart of that of Achilles in Homer's *Iliad*. Vergil deftly concludes the episode by writing that although Aeneas (who was a contemporary of Achilles, whom he had fought at Troy) did not understand the meaning of the shield's representations, he rejoiced at their sight and "shouldered his people's glorious future."

While Dio's account is in prose (50.35.1–4), he also knew how to be highly dramatic:

"When the fire spread to the encircling walls of the ships and descended into the hold, the most horrible of fates came upon the men. Some, and particularly the sailors, perished by the smoke before the flame so much as approached them, while others were roasted in the middle of it as though in ovens. Others were consumed in their armor when it became heated. There were still others, who, before they should suffer such a death, or when they were half-burned, threw

off their armor and were wounded by the shots that came from a distance, or again leaped into the sea and were drowned, or were struck
by their opponents and sank, and were mangled by sea-monsters.
Considering the sufferings which prevailed, the only ones who found
a tolerable death were those who were killed by their comrades in
return for the same service, or killed themselves before any such fate
could befall them; for they not only had no tortures to endure, but
these dead had the burning ships for their funeral pyres."

Loeb trans. E. Cary, with modifications

A far more reliable example, related by Pliny (*Nat. Hist.* 7.148) as part
of his catalogue of Augustus' vicissitudes (Box 4.1), is the incident when,
for once, he really reached the breaking point and became suicidal. The
pressures on him had been relentless. There was ongoing unrest because
of the land confiscations, the war in Italy against Antony's brother Lucius,
and the ever-present threat of a naval blockade of Italy and its food supply
by Pompey's son Sextus, who had amassed a large fleet and held Sicily. To
characterize all this (and more, as we shall see) as a life and death struggle is no exaggeration. In the effort to subdue Sextus, which succeeded
at sea off the coast of the Sicilian city of Naulochus a few weeks later (in
September of 36 BC), Octavian was able to land three of his legions in
Sicily, but he then suffered a crushing defeat against Sextus' fleet that cost
him more than half of his ships. He was cut off from his troops and the
Italian mainland and, in utter despair, asked his friend Proculeius to kill
him. Proculeius refused and, sure enough, Octavian soon reached Italy and
was welcomed by a friendly contingent of soldiers.

There were other ways, however, in which he went over the edge. The literature about his conspicuous cruelty during that time is ample and would
not have taken off, even to the point of extensive exaggeration, if there
had not been some truth at its core. The mutilation of Brutus' corpse is
one example; another, in an equally Homeric vein, was his response to the
request, prior to their execution, by some of Brutus' prominent comrades
for a decent burial: "Let the carrion-birds take care of that" (Suet., *Aug.* 13).
It certainly was an exception to the general civil convention that Augustus
himself affirmed in his autobiography, according to the third-century jurist
Ulpian. On the same occasion, Suetonius proceeds to another incident: a
father and son were pleading for their lives. Octavian told them he would
spare one of them and told them to settle the issue by playing the Roman

equivalent of rock, paper, scissors. Instead, the father decided to sacrifice himself whereupon the son committed suicide as Octavian watched the entire proceedings. His most spectacular display of cruelty occurred after the surrender of the city of Perusia (today's Perugia) where Octavian had besieged and starved out Lucius Antonius and his supporters: he is said to have sacrificed some 300 members of the local upper classes at the altar of the Divine Julius on the Ides of March of 40 BC. While the figure may be high, our sources, which include Dio and Appian, are not untrustworthy. To the numerous others who begged for their lives his repeated, routine reply was: "It's time to die." The impersonal character of the phrase (*moriendum est*) reflects an unemotional indifference and cold-bloodedness that Octavian displayed along with more passionate outbursts.

The general context was a landscape of unmitigated violence and, as was the custom of ancient historians, a protagonist like Octavian prominently served to personify that atmosphere. One of its major aspects was the horror of the proscriptions. Proscription, like gladiatorial combat, did not mean automatic death. Many who were on these hit lists escaped with their lives and even some property, but the tone was set by numerous executions and the horror stories about them, which were an ever-increasing and titillating narrative genre. The scenarios ranged from Cicero's death (Box 2.4) to tabloid tales like the one about the wife who arranged for her husband to be put on the list and celebrated his execution that night by having sex with her lover. But even if we allow for some attendant sensationalism, the widespread trauma caused by the proscriptions is undeniable and the same applies to the numerous other dislocations at the time.

Box 2.4. The Death of Cicero

"In the meantime [Cicero's] assassins came to the villa. They were Herennius, a centurion, and Popillius, a tribune, who had once been prosecuted for parricide and defended by Cicero, and they had helpers. After they had broken in the door, which they found closed, Cicero was not to be seen, and the people in the house said they did not know where he was. Then, we are told, a youth who had been educated by Cicero, and who was a freedman of Cicero's brother Quintus, Philologus by name, told the tribune that the litter was being carried through the wooded and shady walks towards the sea. The tribune, accordingly, took a few helpers with him and ran around towards where Cicero had left, but Herennius hastened on the run through the walks, and Cicero, perceiving him, ordered the servants to set the litter down where they were. Then he himself, clasping his chin with his left hand, as was his custom, looked steadfastly at his murderers, his head all squalid and unkempt, and his face wasted with anxiety, so that most of those that stood by covered their faces while Herennius was hacking at him. For he stretched his neck forth from the litter and was slain, being then in his sixty-fourth year. Herennius cut off his head, by Antony's command, and his hands – the hands with which he wrote the *Philippics*. For Cicero himself entitled his speeches against Antony "Philippics," and to this day the documents are called *Philippics*.

"When Cicero's extremities were brought to Rome, it so happened that Antony was conducting an election, but when he heard of their arrival and saw them, he cried out, 'Now let our proscriptions have an end.' Then he ordered the head and hands to be placed over the ships' beaks on the rostra, a sight that made the Romans shudder; for they thought they saw there not the face of Cicero, but an image of the soul of Antony."

Plutarch, *Life of Cicero* 48–9 (trans. B. Perrin);
cf. Appian, *Civil Wars* 4.19–20

Dio (47.8.4) adds this detail:

"Fulvia took the head into her hands before it was removed, and after abusing it spitefully and spitting upon it, set it on her knees, opened the mouth, and pulled out the tongue. She pierced it with the pins that she used for her hair and uttered many brutal jests all the while."

Octavian Up Close: Positives

We need to take stock, however, and recognize that Octavian would never have won out in the long run if he had been simply a perpetually ill, absentee general; a violent poltroon; or the unrelenting epitome of cruelty. The reason I have paid some attention to these negatives is that the rawness of the times is matched by rawness in his behavior, which seems uncharacteristic from the perspective of the "Augustan" period, when he was not known to be prone to such excesses and their earlier occurrence was played down, if not silenced; Octavian conspicuously ordered many records from that time to be destroyed. That, however, is not the only reason to avoid a one-sided portrayal of him during the triumviral period. His more positive qualities were amply in evidence, too, including in the very areas of his shortcomings. During the protracted war in the mid-30s in Illyria (today's Serbia), for instance, he fought near the front and was wounded at least twice. He also was honored twice for his military successes with an *ovatio*, a victory celebration just a step below the triumph. It involved an acclamation of him as *imperator* and Octavian used the first such occasion, in 40 BC, to do Caesar one better: instead of taking the title in perpetuity, as Caesar had done, he took it as his first name. Henceforth his name was Imperator Caesar Divi Filius. "Gaius Octavius" was gone forever.

Physically, as we have seen, the former Gaius Octavius was not destined to be an outstanding combatant, nor was Imperator Caesar D. F. a brilliant general. Neither was necessary as others could compensate for it. It was far more important for Octavian to earn, and keep, the respect of his troops – money and land assignations amounted to much, but not everything – and he did that, as so much else, by virtue of his tenacity. A good example is in the immediate aftermath of the victory over Sextus Pompey in Sicily in 36 BC. It was a joint operation with Lepidus, and Octavian thought the moment opportune to assert himself over the army – in this case, modeling his actions on Antony, who seven years earlier and with only a few bodyguards had walked into the camp of Lepidus in order to relieve him of his army. But whereas Antony had succeeded, Octavian's show of bravado, which was meant to impress the soldiers that day, failed miserably. Some mocked him and many were angered that he had not let them pillage the enticing city of Messina; besides their pay, Roman legionnaires counted on plunder for their income. Some of Octavian's own guards were actually killed and he himself barely escaped. The episode is a salutary reminder that history, while always instructive, rarely copies, let alone repeats, itself. In any event, afterwards came the show of force: Octavian cordoned off Lepidus' camp with his troops and before very long, Lepidus' soldiers, some 70,000 strong, started coming over – some as individuals, others in groups, and then in complete units. Lepidus, who was from a noble family and chosen by Caesar mostly for his diplomatic skills, was not known for personal courage in battle, closeness to his soldiers, or perseverance. He had lost his soldiers' support as much as Octavian had gained it. At the end of it all, it was now he who went into Octavian's camp as a suppliant in clothes of mourning.

Octavian's treatment of Lepidus that day, however, is complemented by acts of leniency and mercy. No *moriendum est* this time; instead, he packed Lepidus off into early retirement in the pleasant seaside town of Circeii. Likewise, when it came to pleas by those who had been proscribed or whose lands were about to be confiscated, Octavian could be a locus not necessarily of charity, but certainly of tangible reprieve. A moving example comes from a long inscription, the so-called *Praise of Turia* (*Laudatio Turiae*). It was composed by a man who was proscribed and whose wife (Turia) effected a pardon from Octavian, which Lepidus tried to ignore (Box 2.5). Another well-known literary testimony is the first poem of Vergil's *Eclogues*. It centers on a "divine young man" restoring to the farmer Tityrus, who made a special journey to Rome, his property that was about to be given to a veteran. Tityrus' praise is effusive, especially as his fate contrasts with that of the poem's other main character. But the young triumvir's motives were not those of Mother Teresa nor do they reflect a kinder, gentler Octavian. They came from the intelligent realization that favors win support, and he could never have enough support in those days.

Box 2.5. Octavian Helping Out

The following excerpts are from one of the lengthiest private Roman inscriptions in stone. A Roman noble, who had been proscribed, is eulogizing his wife upon her death (late first cent. BC). The woman's name is not found in the extant fragments of the inscription nor is her husband's; her name was imported from a similar story in our literary sources about a woman named Turia.

"Caesar [Octavian] was right when he said that it was you who made it possible for him to restore me to my native land because, if it had not been for the arrangements you made for him to save me, even his promises of help would have been in vain....

"But I must say that the bitterest thing that happened to me in my life befell me through what happened to you. When thanks to the kindness and judgment of Caesar, who was abroad, I had been restored to my country as a citizen, Marcus Lepidus, his colleague, who was in Rome, was confronted with your request concerning my recall, and you lay prostrate at his feet, and you were not only not raised up but were dragged away and carried off brutally like a slave. But although your body was full of bruises, your spirit was unbroken and you kept reminding him of Caesar's edict with its expression of pleasure at my reinstatement, and although you had to listen to insulting words and suffer cruel wounds, you pronounced the words of the edict in a loud voice, so that it should be known who was the cause of my deadly perils. This matter was soon to prove harmful for him.

(continued)

"What could have been more effective than the virtue you displayed? You managed to give Caesar an opportunity to display his clemency and not only to preserve my life but also to brand Lepidus' insolent cruelty by your admirable endurance ...

"When peace had been restored throughout the world and the lawful political order reestablished, we began to enjoy quiet and happy times."

> *ILS* (= *Inscriptiones Latinae Selectae*, ed. H. Dessau) 8393,
> supplemented with a fragment published in 1950. This collection
> of Latin inscriptions is available online at various websites.

Marriages

When Octavian was twenty-three, he was able to find some lasting support in his private life, albeit not without causing quite a stir, but then anything at the time was tumultuous. Marriages among the Roman upper classes were mostly political. When Octavian was feuding with Antony, therefore, in the months after Caesar's assassination, he became engaged to Servilia, the daughter of a prominent Caesar supporter who had been Caesar's colleague as consul in 48 BC, Publius Servilius Isauricus. The moment he joined forces with Antony in late 43 BC, his and Antony's soldiers, eager to see the two stay reconciled, insisted that Octavian marry Antony's step-daughter Clodia, although she was not yet "of nubile age." That union was dissolved before long when Fulvia, Antony's wife and now Octavian's mother-in-law, became the leader, along with Antony's brother Lucius, of the uprising against Octavian in Italy, which calamitously ended at Perusia; Octavian made it a point to stress that the marriage was never consummated. Next, in 40 BC, came the marriage to a considerably older woman, Scribonia, and the political reasons were transparent: coming from a well-connected noble family, she was the aunt of Sextus Pompey's wife, and Octavian was aiming to eliminate the dual threat of Antony and Sextus at the time by establishing family bonds with the latter. That did not work out, as we already have seen, because Sextus and his fleet continued their operations against him. It was probably the major reason the marriage was going to be short-lived, although our sources here engage in an orgy of sexism, portraying Scribonia as a "morose" harridan and "tiresome, disagreeable" shrew. Much of the reason behind this was the return to Rome of an "affable" (according to

Tacitus) and striking young woman, barely twenty years old, with whom Octavian fell totally in love. That was Livia Drusilla, married already and even several months pregnant at the time.

Our accounts are colored by some malice and spite on both sides of the issue. To Antony, who would later desert his wife Octavia, Octavian's sister, in order to carry on openly with Cleopatra, the affair between Livia and Octavian provided a more than welcome diversion from his own bad publicity. The attraction between the two lovers was high-powered in every sense of the word. It was physical; at the same time, Livia had more than the requisite status of nobility as a member of the Claudian family, one of Rome's oldest and most prestigious. The Claudii's ancestry stretched as far back in time as the Via Appia stretched in distance. Over the centuries, the Claudian clan had produced several outstanding leaders, as well as its share of madcap characters. Livia was married at the age of fifteen or sixteen to Tiberius Claudius Nero, her elder by some twenty years; she was no ingénue by the time she met Octavian. Her husband had backed Antony and then joined the uprising of Lucius Antonius and Fulvia. He, Livia, and their son, the future emperor Tiberius, escaped from Perusia and then again from Naples, where he had tried to instigate a slave uprising. Then it was off to Sicily, where Sextus Pompey gave him the cold shoulder, and after that on to Athens and Sparta. During that time, Livia's husband had been proscribed but was allowed to return to Rome after a rapprochement between Antony and Octavian that granted some amnesties in 39 BC. Livia had stood by her man then, but she was not the only one to see that he was basically an opportunist with a knack for winding up as a loser. Her father, a highly principled man, had committed suicide in the aftermath of Philippi.

The marriage of Octavian and Livia, therefore, was made not in heaven, but in the crucible of extraordinary hardships and the bracing realities of power struggles and civil wars. Perhaps that is why it lasted for fifty-two years, until Augustus' death parted the two. The wedding ceremony did not take place until after Livia's second child, Drusus, was born in January of 38 BC, but the engagement or, more formally, the betrothal, occurred three months earlier. It provided enough salacious fodder for wags – some referred to the "the three-month child" – though it did involve a class act: so far from stomping off angrily and swearing revenge, it was Tiberius Claudius Nero who graciously gave Livia away. A little earlier, Octavian himself had obtained a divorce from Scribonia, the moment after she gave birth to their daughter Julia. Thus the only child he ever had was born not under the luckiest star, and that destiny would remain with her (see Chapter 5).

THE BLOODY YEARS: HISTORY

Triumvirate

Back to the narrative of the events! The alliance that Octavian entered with Antony in October of 43 BC set an end to the anomalous situation of Caesar's heir and his army coming to the aid of Caesar's assassins such as Decimus Brutus. Placing his hired soldiers at the disposal of the senate, which had been quick to proclaim an amnesty for the conspirators, had been Octavian's temporary means to the end of gaining some legal standing. After that objective had been achieved it was time for the forces of nature to take their course. Given the history of discord between Antony and Octavian, Lepidus was called in as a sort of mediator and the three hammered out the shape of the new government: for the next five years they became – and the legislative assembly quickly ratified the arrangement – *tresviri rei publicae constituendae*, triumvirs in charge of, literally, "putting the state together" (hence our term "constitution"). In effect it was a triple dictatorship. Territorial and other spheres of influence were outlined and, as could be expected, Antony emerged as the heavyweight he was; among other things, Octavian had to give up his consulship and two of Antony's followers became consuls. The wave of proscriptions immediately followed and then came the campaign, long awaited by the soldiers who had served under Caesar, to avenge their slain leader's death. It was not easy; Brutus and Cassius had garnered considerable strength, even if by ruthless impositions on the provincials in the east, and their army was much better supplied for the oncoming winter. For the triumvirs, it was a do or die situation. The armies squared off against one another near Philippi in Thessaly first on October 23 of 42, when Octavian had to hide in the swamps – Cassius was in even worse shape and committed suicide – and then again in mid-November, when the left wing commanded by Octavian contributed decisively to the victory, though there was no doubt that Antony's military expertise and bravura were the key factor in both encounters. The combined losses numbered some 40,000 men and Brutus also ended his life, followed by Octavian's vengeful mutilation of his corpse.

Italy and Sextus Pompey

In early 41 Octavian returned to Italy and faced the horrendous task of having to settle some 60,000 veterans on lands that were legally owned by others. Collateral chaos ensued; many soldiers did not wait but took things into their own hands, and owners were evicted even from properties that were not located in, but simply adjacent to, the eighteen towns that had been selected. The dispossessed found their champion in Antony's brother Lucius, who was consul, and his ever-vocal wife, Fulvia. Several mediation attempts failed and, to make things worse, Sextus Pompey blockaded Italy, strangling its food supply. The civilian population increasingly supported Lucius, but Octavian had learned his lesson well from his early power struggles after Caesar's death: he needed the support of the soldiers and their needs had priority. In the end, Lucius and the core of his supporters were pushed into Perusia and had to surrender after a siege whose horrors lived on in memory.

They had their randy side, too. Lead missiles from Octavian's catapults bore messages like "Lucius and Fulvia, open your butts wide," and the poet Martial (11.20) cites some racy verses by Octavian as a remedy against sad-sack readers of Latin verse:

> Because Antony shagged Glaphyra, Fulvia determined that my punishment should be to hook up with her. Me do Fulvia? I don't think so, if I've got my wits. "Bang me," she says, "or there'll be war." Well, what if I care more for my life than for my tail? May the clarions sound!

That is a far cry from the Augustus whose criterion for literature was "moral salubriousness, both public and private" (Suetonius, *Aug.* 89.2). So was Octavian's participation in a themed costume party and dinner in those famine-plagued years, where he came dressed as Apollo and joined in a fraternity-type food fight. It may have been a moment of welcome relief from all the pressures, but popular reaction was decidedly hostile.

For good reason: conditions in Italy continued to be miserable. One did not have to be on a proscription list to be hit up for a large share of one's wealth or property. Since the state's deficit was enormous, the triumvirs wasted no time upon taking office to levy taxes that included 50 percent of the yearly income derived from property, a 2 percent tax on net worth for those who had accumulated wealth in excess of 100,000 denarii, a levy of twenty-five denarii for each slave, and a tax on the separate property of the 400 richest women. Enforced collections of this kind continued right down to 31 BC, the year of Actium. Early that year, freedmen who possessed property worth more than 200,000 sesterces were ordered to contribute 8 percent of it. The measure caused widespread rioting, murder, and arson, which Octavian had to quell by armed force. That done, freedmen who owned land had to pay one quarter of its worth to the tax collector. Thoroughly frightened, they complied.

Neither could the soldiers be relied on for unquestioning loyalty and professional behavior. Instead, a constant refrain throughout these years is the challenge their continuing demands and mutinies posed for Octavian. Even when he was on his way to Egypt after the battle of Actium, he had to hurry back to Italy in the middle of winter to end a serious uprising of veterans who had hoped for more bounty and lands. The young Caesar was no pushover in these situations. For obvious reasons, he usually tried to strike a balance, which had to be contingent, between concessions and standing tough. Unsurprisingly, therefore, one of his top priorities as Augustus was expeditiously to retire most of this civil war army of some 500,000 because they were an ethically challenged liability and replace them with a force of 300,000 professionals who would fight the real wars of consolidation and expansion.

There is no conclusive evidence to show that Antony was actively supporting his brother's war against Octavian. Following the demarcation of tasks among the triumvirs after Philippi, he had gone to the east to settle affairs there and, as it turned out, to begin a new and lasting one with Cleopatra. The division of territorial commands was spelled out even more clearly when Antony, after his brother's fiasco, returned to Italy and in 40 BC was a party to the treaty of Brundisium that put him in control of the eastern provinces; Octavian got the west and Lepidus, Africa. The rapprochement was further cemented by Antony's marriage to Octavian's sister Octavia; Fulvia had died a few months earlier and therefore could be conveniently blamed for the Perusine War instead of Lucius Antonius, whom Octavian had prudently chosen to treat with utter lenience. The joker in this game was Sextus Pompey, whom Octavian at first refused to recognize as an official player. He accepted reality, however, a year later when a supplementary treaty was made at Misenum that granted Sextus Sicily, Sardinia, Corsica, and the Peloponnese in return for vacating his bases in Italy and lifting his blockade. In fact, he now was officially charged with taking care of the grain supply of Italy.

It was clear that this was not going to last. Hostilities between Octavian and Sextus soon resumed, but Octavian had made massive preparations for countering Sextus' superiority at sea. It brings up an aspect that is typical of him during that time, too: the ability to delegate. As we have seen, he had not had enough time to gather extensive military and strategic experience and he therefore turned to a friend from his youth, who had been with him at Apollonia and became his right-hand man. That was Marcus Vipsanius Agrippa (more detail in Chapter 5). His family background is largely unknown, but it is safe to say that like the Octavii, they did not belong to the noble upper tier. Hence many members of that class disdained him although, or because, he became basically Augustus' viceroy – even after all those years, meritocracy was still a hard pill to swallow for those privileging their descent, and we will view their resistance in a wider context, which is both political and cultural, later. In this regard, too, Octavian was very much Julius Caesar's heir. Caesar had favored and rewarded many individuals and groups, such as one of his legions, especially with coveted grants of citizenship on the basis of ability and achievement. Agrippa, then, in 38/37 BC created an extensive naval base – a true engineering marvel involving the conversion of a lake – near Cumae for the building and training of a large fleet to match Sextus'. The final victory, soon after Augustus had despaired of his life, came off the Sicilian anchorage of Naulochus.

The arrangement for the encounter was unique and can be considered an early triumph of game theory, or at least an example of the intersection of war games and reality. Sextus and Octavian agreed that both sides would have the same number of ships, three hundred. At a given signal, they would attack each other like two gladiatorial teams while the two generals and their armies would watch from ashore. And that is exactly what happened. Agrippa's new and taller ships, equipped with efficient grappling hooks for boarding, and his thoroughly trained troops carried the day resoundingly. He lost only three ships compared to Sextus' twenty-eight in the initial onslaught; the rest of Sextus' fleet burned or sank while trying to escape, or surrendered. Agrippa was honored like a victor at the games with new sea-blue standard and a golden crown of ship beaks (cf. Vergil's reference in Box 2.3). Sextus managed to get away and ordered his eight legions in Sicily to march to Messina in order to regroup with him. Before they got there, however, he panicked and left Sicily for the east. Octavian's incubus was finally gone; there was no more blockade of Italy and the food supplies resumed, with the welcome result that the rioting in Rome died down. Just as important, and foreshadowing the outcome of his final clash with Antony, in this constant war of nerves and relentless emotional and mental stress on top of all the physical exertion and exhaustion it was Octavian's cool head and calculation, often combined with ruthlessness, which helped him prevail over his more emotion-driven opponents.

Antony in the East

This brings us back to Antony. He had been active in the east and very competently so; much of the reorganization he effected there, involving both the administration of the Roman provinces and the use of client kings, was largely left intact by Octavian after Antony's death. While he may have paraded in Athens as the New Dionysus – something that was of no consequence for his standing in Italy where local versions of that god were quite popular – he was far more than a drunken *bon vivant*. His real crux was the war against the Parthians. They were the heirs to the Persian empire after the demise of the largest of Alexander's successor states and were stirring just beyond Rome's frontiers and the buffers of the client kingdoms. Crassus had suffered a spectacular defeat against them in 53 BC, and the notion that Rome had lost some of its standards kept rankling even quite literally. Caesar had planned a revenge expedition, cut short by his assassination, and it fell to Antony to deal with that enemy. To that end, he and Octavian arranged for a swap in 37 BC after renewing their triumviral powers for another five years: Antony made some 120 warships available to Octavian in return for 20,000 legionaries, whom Octavian never sent. That contributed to the failure of Antony's campaign against the Parthians in 36 BC, which ended with a major defeat and a retreat that cost him at least another 8,000 men.

It also made him more dependent yet on Cleopatra. While still married to Octavia, Antony had fathered three children with Cleopatra, including the twins Alexander Helios (Sun) and Cleopatra Selene (Moon). In return for giving him more of the resources he needed, she exacted recompense. The goal of the queen of queens, a real survivor who had accompanied her father on diplomatic missions as a teenager and experienced the cost of his subservience to Rome, was to strengthen Egypt and keep it independent. Even before his Parthian campaign, Antony had conceded some territories to her, mostly at the expense of King Herod of Judaea, and the pace quickened after his defeat. With the new resources, he launched a campaign into Armenia, arrested its king during a diplomatic meeting, and returned to Alexandria in 34 BC to celebrate a great victory. In the following year, he campaigned again in Parthia with at least some partial success.

Then came the event, in 34 BC, that would be grist for Octavian's propaganda mills. In an elaborately staged ceremony in Alexandria's Gymnasium, Antony and Cleopatra were seated on two golden thrones while the children took seats on similar but smaller thrones. They included Caesarion, Julius Caesar's fourteen-year-old son with Cleopatra; she was proclaimed queen of Egypt, Cyprus, Cyrene, and parts of Syria, and with Caesarion as her co-regent. Alexander Helios and Ptolemy, six and three years old at the time, received other territories, including the yet to be conquered Parthia. The problem was that in his pursuit of a grand strategy for the future of the east, Antony reassigned some Roman provinces, such as Cyprus, to foreign ownership. It required approval by the senate and Octavian kept capitalizing on the propagandistic value of "the donations of Alexandria." With Italy under reasonable control after the departure of Sextus, who was executed in the east by one of Antony's governors, Octavian had started a war in Illyria, the area of today's Serbia and Croatia. Besides conquest and pacification, the objectives were to keep the greater part of his army busy so they were delayed in asking for lands and to have a seasoned fighting force for the confrontation with Antony. Typically, Octavian saw it coming far more clearly than his fellow triumvir; he planned it and he planned for it.

The Final Stage: Octavian vs. Antony

Soon after the events in Alexandria, therefore, the volleys started flying. They were purely verbal to begin with, but much was at stake and their intensity made it easy especially for twentieth-century scholars to see them as precursors of modern propaganda and defamation campaigns. And, no doubt, the aim was a massive mobilization of public opinion. Nothing was left untouched that could help discredit and demonize the rival. For Antony, that meant caricaturing Octavian as a lowborn coward, Caesar's boy toy, womanizer, and monster of cruelty. Octavian kept hammering away at Antony as being in the thrall of alcoholism and that foreign woman "who was plotting crazed ruin against the Capitol and the empire's burial with her band of men stained with foul perversion," as Horace would put it (*Odes* 1.37.6–10) before moving on to a far more ennobling perspective on the Egyptian queen. Antony even was forced to defend himself with a pamphlet "On His Drunkenness." Neither did it help that in early 32 BC he publicly broke off with Octavia, who had faithfully held out all these years, and asked her to move out of their house in Rome while he was not even living there.

In a move again akin to modern practice, Octavian accompanied this barrage with a concentrated campaign of visuals and images. They mattered in a world where literacy was not widespread, especially among the non-elites. Most of the surviving visual evidence we have today is coins, and scholars have sometimes been too zealous to play up their role in effecting propagandistic persuasion; out of necessity, the focus has been on these surviving witnesses and other hardware that is not perishable, although the organic context of the times was much more inclusive. A balancing consideration in this case is that Octavian's coinage often reflects monuments, such as statues, that have been lost to us, though we know of their existence from literary sources. Adding to the visual effectiveness was an imagery that, in contrast to many previous Republican issues, was clear and straightforward. Closeness of the *divi filius* to the gods, victory, and a return to order and stability were key themes (Fig. 4). As Paul Zanker has noted, "Never before had coins of such beauty been minted in Rome," and he continues with the observation that "it was a case of aesthetics in the service of political ends" (1988, 54). Again, we should not imagine every Roman, especially the poorer classes, as palming these coins assiduously in their hands and being swayed by their "messages." People in those times had access to a wider spectrum of visual communication, which has been preserved rather incompletely. But this latest round, even if far more intense, was not surprising: already in his early struggles with Antony Octavian had proved to be a master of the media, as we have seen, and one of the high points of the Augustan age proper would be its visual culture.

Barbs and insults were traded almost daily. They ranged from titillation about the protagonists' sex lives to demands that the other side obviously would not accept. Antony, for instance, asked for joint rule over Italy and Octavian promptly countered by asking for the same over Armenia. More explosive, and threatening to Octavian, was the expiration of the triumvirate at the end of 33 BC. Antony grandly offered that they should not continue as triumvirs. That was definitely to Octavian's disadvantage because the murky legalities, such as they were, would allow Antony to retain substantial powers in the east until he came to Rome – not a desirable prospect either – whereas Octavian, who already was on the scene, would be left in just about the same position as where he started in the months after the Ides of March: as a private citizen with an army. Of course his stature had risen incomparably, as had the size of his troops, but the prospect was troubling because there had to be some legal foundation for his continuing role as an officer of the state. The consulships for 32 BC had already been allocated, as part of the earlier agreement between the triumvirs, to two followers of Antony, and other options, such as the dictatorship or formal continuance as a triumvir, were politically unpalatable. And even the sort of supplementary mechanisms that had accrued to Octavian and enhanced his public stature, especially since Naulochus, did not amount to a secure legal standing. These honors included the sacrosanctity, that is, the basic personal inviolability, of a tribune of the people, and cities in Italy honored him by "setting him up with their gods," as reported by Appian (*Civil Wars*, 5.546). We can see now, too, that the massive effort to mobilize public opinion was needed to compensate for the looming deficit of Octavian's constitutional role.

His opponents wasted no time. On the very day Antony's consuls took office, January 1 of 32 BC, one of them, Gaius Sosius, while wisely refusing to move for a ratification of Antony's new dispensation of the east,

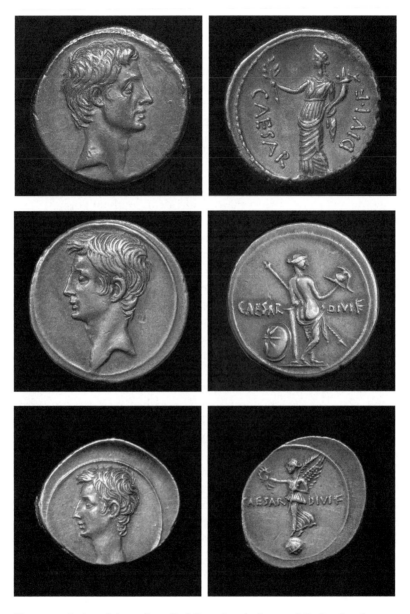

Figure 4. Series of three *denarii* of Octavian, before 31 BC. On the obverse,
Octavian. On the reverse, the goddesses Pax, Venus, and Victoria.
Bibliothèque Nationale de France. A testimony to the exceptional quality
of these images is a direct copy of the Octavian Venus on coins showing
the empress Sabina, Hadrian's (AD 117–138) wife.

49

sharply attacked the absent Octavian, who was huddling with his advisers, and made the formal motion that both triumvirs resign from that office forthwith. That motion, which apparently had a good chance of passing, was squelched by the veto of a tribune and the senate adjourned. When it met again, Octavian was there with a contingent of armed soldiers and friends who carried concealed daggers – visibly so, it seems – and he seated himself "on an official chair" between the two consuls. Dio continues his account (50.2) by saying that Octavian gave a long and moderate speech defending himself, accusing Antony and Sosius, and letting on that he was in possession of "certain documents" to prove Antony's misdeeds. There was no word of opposition. Intimidated, the two consuls fled to Antony, followed by one third of the senators. Octavian let them go.

What were these documents? The most important and spectacular one was not in Octavian's folder in January but came into his possession a few months later. It was clear by then that the mass arrival of his senatorial supporters was a mixed blessing for Antony. Many resented Cleopatra's influence and frictions arose. That led to defections to Octavian, led by Munatius Plancus, who had been consul in 42 BC and had followed Antony to Egypt, where he did his best to entertain his hosts (Box 2.6). Had he stuck to such talents – few, if any, former consuls possessed them – he might have secured a more lasting place at Antony's and Cleopatra's court. He got the cold shoulder, however, "because of unmistakable evidence of his venal rapacity" and headed for Rome. With him, he brought the knowledge of Antony's testament or, rather, its location, which he promptly divulged to Octavian: the Temple of Vesta in the Forum, where it was kept by the Vestal Virgins. Octavian had no scruples wresting it from them. He could make a case that it was not just a personal will, but a political testament, and he chose to (re)cite from it selectively at a specially staged meeting of the senate, dramatically emphasizing the provisions that he knew would inflame public opinion. They were not hard to find: Antony wanted to be buried next to Cleopatra, even in the event that he died in Rome. Their children were to be his heirs and, yes, Caesarion was Caesar's very own son.

The effect was immediate. Antony's assigned consulate for 31 BC was revoked, as were all his official powers. His possessions, as well those of his followers in Italy, were confiscated unless they switched sides, a move which freed up more land that would be needed for the eventual compensation of Octavian's veterans. When it came to the official declaration of war in October, Octavian was just as savvy: no, this was not another civil war – Antony was not named anywhere – but a war against a foreign enemy, Cleopatra. Rumors had been flying in the meantime that Antony, in the event his side won, was going to give Rome as a present to that Egyptian woman and move the capital to Alexandria. Ever the impresario, Octavian impressively staged the martial declaration in the form of an ancient ritual and spectacle, the hurling of a spear by the Fetial Priest into the territory of the enemy. It did not require a journey to the Egyptian border; practical as the Romans were, they had long ago marked part of the precinct of the war goddess Bellona as foreign territory and the target for the priest's missile. It was, to be sure, a greater show than casting a die.

Soon thereafter, all of Italy became the stage. With the Antonian third of the senate having left the country, pesky questions about Octavian's legal authority had faded away. For all practical purposes, he continued to rule with his triumviral powers; while the Second Triumvirate had terminated at the end of 33 BC, those powers had never been formally abrogated. An easy solution for any concerns would have been his election as consul in 32 after the two original consuls had departed. But in this respect as in others, Octavian foreshadowed the later Augustus by maintaining constitutional

Box 2.6. A Senatorial Talent: Munatius Plancus

"For money, he was ready to be all things for all men. At a banquet, he had played the role of Glaucus the sea god, performing a dance in which his naked body was painted blue, his head wreathed around with reeds, all while he was wearing a fish's tail and crawling on his knees.

"Now, inasmuch as he had been coldly treated by Antony because of unmistakable evidence of his venal rapacity, he deserted to Caesar. Afterwards he even went so far as to interpret the victor's clemency as a proof of his own merit, claiming that Caesar had approved that which he had merely pardoned.... The retort of Coponius, who was the father-in–law of Publius Silius and a dignified praetorian, was not far off the mark when he said, when Plancus, fresh from his desertion, was heaping upon the absent Antony many unspeakable charges in the senate, 'By Hercules, Antony must have done a great many things before *you* left him.'"

Velleius 2.83 (trans. F. Shipley, 1924, with modifications)

(continued)

> There is always time for redemption: Plancus made the motion in 27 BC that Octavian be named "Augustus." His imposing tomb at Gaeta, "a gasometer-like masonry structure with a diameter of 29.50 metres" (so Jocelyn Toynbee described it in her classic *Death and Burial in the Roman World* [Baltimore 1996], 154) was built some seven years later and is one of the best-preserved mausolea from Roman times.

decorum on the one hand and transcending narrow constitutional horizons on the other. He therefore saw to it that two consuls from respected families – comfortable old shoes – were duly elected while he sought his validation in a much larger arena. As he puts it in the *Res Gestae* (25.2):

> All of Italy of its own free will swore allegiance to me and demanded me as the leader in the war in which I was victorious at Actium. The Gallic and Spanish provinces, Africa, Sicily, and Sardinia swore the same oath of allegiance.

As always, too, prudence came before jihadism. Octavian exempted some clients of Antony, such as those in Bononia (today's Bologna), a town that had grievously suffered from the land confiscations for veterans. And in general we may wonder how ready the whole country was, after years of being beaten down, for the fervor of another war. Neither was fervor all they had to come up with; there was another round of gargantuan tax levies, exacting a quarter of every person's annual income and, as we already have seen, one-eighth of the value of a freedman's entire holdings. The result was tax revolts that make the Boston Tea Party and its latter-day mimicries look like an exercise in benign gesturalism. In Rome, however, this was quickly balanced by unprecedented largesses administered by Agrippa. They included a lengthening of the games to 59 days, distribution of free oil and salt, free admission to the baths for both men and women, and even free haircuts. And throughout Italy, the retired veterans who served on town councils were effective in rallying support for the young Caesar's mandate to lead the forces of the west against their eastern opponents.

Actium and Alexandria

And so he did, capitalizing one more time on an adversary's errors of judgment and lack of decisiveness. Antony had amassed an army of over 100,000 legionaries, augmented by 12,000 cavalry and supporting troops furnished by client kings. His navy numbered more than 500 ships, including a large number of behemoths. They were triremes, like many warships in antiquity, but each of their oars was manned by eight or ten rowers. The purpose of these floating fortresses was not maneuverability but to serve as a platform for soldiers and catapults. The security of that fleet soon began to take precedence over planning a decisive strategy and effective tactics for the land army, which had always been Antony's forte. The fleet, therefore, sailed to the west coast of Greece where the large gulf of Ambracia provided ample and protected anchorage, which could be entered only through an inlet at Actium (Fig. 5). Conversely, of course, that was also the only way for the ships to exit. That, however, did not overly concern Antony, who set up his winter quarters at Patrai (modern Patras), which was well to the south, while distributing his troops throughout western Greece and the Peloponnese in order to keep them adequately fed and supplied. He clearly was not planning for an invasion of Italy.

Octavian was tempted by the sitting target and during the winter tried to attack Antony's fleet in its anchorage. The attempt failed because of typically stormy weather in the strait between Italy and Greece; his ships had to turn back and suffered some losses. In the spring of 31 BC, therefore, he transported his land army, which numbered some 80,000 plus 12,000 horsemen, to a point some 120 miles north of Actium so as to stay out of harm's way. His fleet numbered about half of Antony's and was overwhelmingly comprised of smaller and faster ships. Many of them soon operated around the Peloponnese and in the Ionian Sea where they effectively interfered with Antony's supply lines. The food supply, therefore, for his huge army and for his fleet, which kept sitting in the Gulf of Ambracia, became critical. There were shortages and some of his troops were starving and becoming increasingly susceptible to disease.

It is important to realize the prolonged nature of this entire sequence. As with so many other Augustan events, the tendency has been to concentrate on the flashpoint – the actual battle of Actium did not take place till September 2 and was over in four hours – and to isolate it from the larger context of operations in which it was embedded. In this case, the weeks and months dragged on and did not amount to a feverish buildup for the final confrontation.

All this, due in great part to Antony's continuing and atypical hesitation, worked to Octavian's advantage. "Troop strength" has become commonplace, but in this instance we can employ the phrase literally. Antony still had the bodies, but they were attenuated daily by lack of food and disease and desertions were on the rise. By late August, therefore, the number of his ships that could effectively be manned had dwindled to 230, including

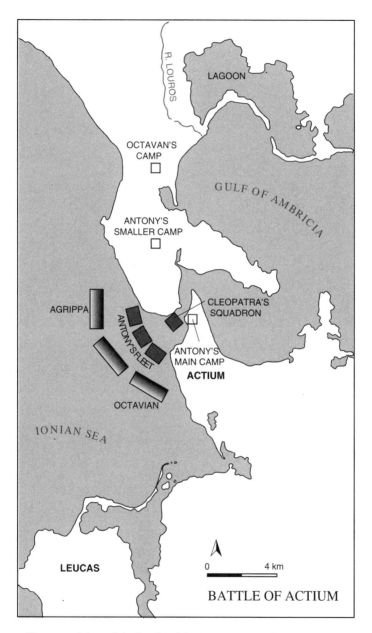

Figure 5. Map of the battle of Actium. Drawing by Deena Berg.

Cleopatra's sixty galleys, giving the numerical advantage to Octavian. On land, things did not look much better: the nineteen legions and several thousand cavalry deployed at the scene had been weakened by attrition and replenished by recruits from the eastern provinces who lacked training and experience. Antony's options, therefore, dwindled correspondingly and narrowed to the single objective of breaking out of the self-imposed containment. He ordered all ships burned that would otherwise be left behind and readied his fleet to punch through Octavian's naval cordon. Several days of heavy storms delayed the operation. Then, on September 2, the storms ceased and a strong wind from the northwest favored the undertaking, but Antony, after weeks of bunker mentality, still kept his ships lined up like a fortress; the two fleets bobbed up and down in the sea at barely one mile's distance. Around noon the engagement finally began, and Cleopatra and her convoy were able to escape through the center and gain the high seas. The rest of Antony's fleet was not so lucky, although he himself transferred to a smaller and faster ship and caught up with her. The day belonged to Agrippa and Octavian; their casualties were not negligible – some 5,000 men – but Antony's were more than twice as large and he had lost most of his fleet. His stunned land forces were in disarray. Some went over to Octavian right away and the rest did so before they had finished retreating through Macedonia.

Actium was not the beginning of the end – it was the end. The next few months were but a sequel. Octavian's pursuit to Alexandria was interrupted, as we have seen, by his need to hurry back to Italy to quell another agitation by some of his soldiers. The victory had not put money in their pockets and Octavian's treasury was broke; the conquest of Egypt would change all of that in a hurry, but not yet. Octavian then set out for the east again; Antony made a final, brave stand and even won a cavalry engagement outside of Alexandria only to be overpowered by Octavian's land and naval forces. He retreated into the city and the accounts of his final days were suffused with melodrama as had been the stories about his behavior since Actium: Antony the manic depressive ruled his contemporaries' and later generations' imaginations just as Antony the general had ruled his troops and military fortunes in better days. Again he tried to commit suicide – there had been an unsuccessful attempt a few weeks earlier – but did not quite finish himself off and hence could be hoisted to the top of the tomb monument that Cleopatra had been constructing and where she was hiding. He died in her arms.

War had been declared against Cleopatra and the dream of any Roman victor was to capture the defeated ruler alive and parade him or her through the streets of Rome in the grandest spectacle of them all, the triumph. However, there was a problem: the vanquished star could steal the show, and her charisma and lore made Cleopatra the ideal candidate (cf. Box 2.7 with Fig. 6). It is not unlikely, then, that Octavian gave her the opportunity to take her own life and settled for a replica of her in his triple triumph of 29 BC. He did meet with her and our sources keep stressing the thirty-nine-year-old queen's charm, insinuating that she was trying to beguile him. In reality, she may have tried to cut one more deal for Egypt to keep it from being swallowed by Rome. Unlike Julius Caesar and Antony, Octavian treated her with great reserve and her suicide followed. Its manner is far from clear; several ancient writers, notably Plutarch and Dio, had their doubts about its serpentine excesses and presented alternative versions. What lived on was her impact on Rome, detailed well by Diana Kleiner, over a wide range of the city's culture from architecture and "Egyptomania" in wall painting to women's hairstyles. It was typical of Augustus and Augustan culture that they appropriated from former enemies – it was a sign of both victory and integration. The Egyptianizing motifs on the walls of Augustan houses are a good example: Egypt was now part of Rome in every way.

In Alexandria the victor both displayed clemency and took no prisoners. The city was not sacked, but Octavian took care to compensate his soldiers for that loss of income with a special payout. Some of Antony's followers were spared, but there was no mercy for the few surviving killers of Caesar who had fled there or for Caesar's son Caesarion. Given the long-standing fascination of Roman generals with Alexander the Great, a visit to his tomb was a must. Octavian's aim to associate himself with that great conqueror and paradigm changer is evident from his earliest portraits (see Fig. 2). Alexander's hair, rising up in the wind to express his youthful dynamism, was stylized into the distinctive forelock which, even if slightly modified here and there, remained a hallmark of all portraits of Augustus along with abiding youth. One spiteful source has it that Octavian, as he laid hands on Alexander's face, knocked off his nose, but otherwise Egypt remained completely intact. For good reason: its wealth wiped out all of Octavian's debts in one fell swoop. The abundant silver and gold in the Ptolemaic treasury was melted down into coinage. Further riches came from a special tax imposed on Egypt's population and from the copious resources provided by anxious client kings as tangible proof of their obeisance to the new ruler. In short, the constant financial woes that had bedeviled Octavian throughout the 30s now came to a sudden end. In addition, the surge of the money supply had the welcome result of bringing interest rates in Italy down from twelve to 4 percent, a development always conducive to a government's popularity. As was so often the

Box 2.7. What Did Cleopatra Look Like?

Figure 6. Marble head of Cleopatra VII. Vatican Museums, Rome.
© Sandro Vannini/CORBIS.

(*continued*)

As Susan Walker (2001, 147) has observed, "Sadly for those who seek the secret of her personal allure, the more we study Cleopatra's surviving images, the less certain we may be of her looks." Not many portraits of her are left in marble; one reason is that Octavian had them destroyed throughout Egypt and replaced them with his own. In Rome, however, he let stand her gilded statue in the Forum of Julius Caesar and the marble head here may be based on that statue. Her image on coins is more "realistic" to the point of sometimes being unflattering, her beaked nose being a trademark.

In short, while not being unattractive, she was not a beauty like Elizabeth Taylor. She did not have to be: our sources are unanimous about her many other charms, such as the sound of her voice and her conversational skills, and she was able to converse in seven languages. Curiously, Latin is not mentioned among them although Troglodyte is, and she was the first Egyptian queen, in the whole Macedonian dynasty of the Ptolemies, to speak the native language of the Egyptian people.

Sources

P. Jones, *Cleopatra: A Sourcebook* (Norman 2006).
D. Kleiner, *Cleopatra and Rome* (Cambridge, Mass. 2005).
S. Walker and P. Higgs, eds., *Cleopatra of Egypt: From History to Myth* (Princeton 2001).

---

case, Octavian was a quick study: Egypt would remain his own province under his direct administration. Even senators who wished to visit there had to get his permission. Far from looting its wealth, Augustus was bent on maintaining it. The income came directly to his own treasury and not the state's, but unlike many a modern ruler, he used it for the benefit of the state; his rebuilding of Rome, for instance, would have been impossible without it.

RETROSPECT AND PROSPECT

We are again at a point where it is good not to be swept away by the moment of ultimate success but to reflect on the road leading up to it and on what might have been. Once more, nothing was preordained and

Octavian's fate hung in the balance time and again – one misstep here and a failed response to another vicissitude there might have altered that balance irrevocably. Octavian benefited from Antony's errors, but his opponent's deficit would not have been enough for him to prevail. Instead, he provided for the positive balance by his own initiatives and and – and herein lies the major difference – by responding not only to whatever crisis was at hand, but by looking and planning further ahead. More is involved than mere calculation; as scholars increasingly have begun to point out, the 30s were not just a decade of mayhem but a productive period of innovations and changes that were further systematized once Octavian became Augustus.

They include, first and foremost, the continuance of the *res publica* and its (unwritten) constitution, mechanisms, and offices. These were not abolished but morphed into what we might call Constitution Plus, meaning the added, leading role of Octavian/Augustus. Further, and perhaps paradoxically at first blush, the triumviral period and its civil wars shaped "Italy's destiny by consolidating the cultural unification of its diverse regions" (Osgood 2006, 173). Roman ways and Latin language spread across the peninsula, abetted by the settlement of colonies of veterans; a similar process, with many regional variations, began to take place throughout the Mediterranean. The addition of the east laid the groundwork for a Greek-speaking Roman empire and its *oikumenē*. *Oikumenē* literally means "the inhabited world," but since the time of Alexander, it had denoted universalism and a cosmopolitan variety of peoples and cultures under the aegis of a ruling power. At the center, the city of Rome was being transformed by the start of numerous building activities, including the restoration of various temples, renovations in the Roman Forum, and, most striking, the huge tomb, soon dubbed "mausoleum," begun by Octavian that signaled his commitment to Rome and, of course, his stature: it was the tallest building to date in the city and his statue at the very top was closer to the gods than anyone else (see Chapter 6). Finally, Octavian took many initiatives in the administration of Roman religion that saw their full development in the "Augustan" age. Besides the renovations of temples, they involved the restoration of ancient rites and priesthoods.

A final commonality is that, just as not everything that happened under Octavian happened because of Octavian, so too not everything that happened under Augustus happened because of Augustus. Clearly, if Antony had won, there would have been a Roman empire, melding east and west, though probably in a different way; we will never know exactly how. Octavian prefigured Augustus by encountering, and not just engendering, events that were already in motion. Often, a parade was already marching. His skill lay in the way he responded to these developments and placed himself at the head of the parade in order to direct its course.

3

THE EXPERIMENT OF
THE PRINCIPATE

RESTORATION: HOW?

Egypt had been conquered – coins with that legend show a crocodile that is perkily snapping its jaws – Antony was dead, and the long, excruciating period of civil wars was over. As the victor put it in the *Res Gestae* (34.1), at the age of thirty-two, he was "in possession of all power." The question was, what now? In particular, how would he govern? There was a wide range of choices, from despotic autocracy to abdicating and returning all power to the senate and the people, with plenty of options between these two extremes.

Not under pressure at last, Octavian could and did take plenty of time to think about it. Several of our sources reflect this and it is best to begin with Augustus himself and a full citation of the penultimate chapter of the *Res Gestae* (see Box 3.1).

BOX 3.1. RES GESTAE 34

1. In my sixth and seventh consulships [28–27 BC], after I had extinguished civil wars, and at a time when with universal consent I was in possession of all power, I transferred the *res publica* from my power to the discernment of the Senate and People of Rome. 2. For this merit of mine, I was named Augustus by decree of the senate, and the doorposts of my house were publicly wreathed with laurels and a civic crown was fastened over my door and a golden shield was set up in the Julian senate house; the inscription on this shield attested that it was given me by the Senate and People of Rome on account of my courage, clemency, justice, and sense of duty. 3. After

(continued)

---

this time I excelled all in influence (*auctoritas*), but I possessed no more official power (*potestas*) than others who were my colleagues in several magistracies.

Figure 7. *Aureus* of Octavian, minted in the province of Asia, 28 BC. British Museum, Department of Coins and Medals, CM 1995,0401.1. © The Trustees of the British Museum.

Within even the constraints of this extraordinarily long inscription, Augustus understandably concentrates on another historical marker, the two senate meetings of January 13 and 16, 27 BC, which ratified the various measures listed by him. It stands to reason, of course, that this was only the final act, or enactment, of decisions and deliberations that had evolved over the previous three and half years since the fall of Alexandria. Until recently, we could only make that assumption, however reasonable, noting that Augustus, too, includes the year which preceded the event; besides, Dio (53.2.5) and Tacitus (*Annals* 3.28) mention that Octavian abolished the unjust regulations of the triumvirate at the end of that year, 28 BC. Glittering confirmation has now come with the discovery of a previously unknown gold coin, an *aureus*, which was minted in the Roman east, probably Ephesus, in 28 BC (Fig. 7). On its front, or obverse, it shows Octavian with a laurel crown and the legend IMP(erator) CAESAR – DIVI F(ilius) CO(n)S(ul) VI. On the reverse, we see him seated in the magistrate's chair, the *sella curulis*, holding a scroll in his right hand, with a document box on the ground to the left. The inscription reads LEGES ET IURA P(ublicae) R(ei) RESTITUIT. It can be translated as "he restored laws and rights *to* the *res publica*" or "he restored the laws and rights *of* the *res publica*"; the ambiguity may well be deliberate.

The "Restored" Republic

What does this coin tell us? More than many others, to be sure. To begin with and in context: Augustus made haste slowly – a characteristic that, in fact, became his motto. He did not rush into setting up a hard and fast mode of governance. After Alexandria fell, he spent several months in the east and passed the winter on the island of Samos; obviously, we are not dealing with a paranoid tyrant who needed to get back to Rome because he felt threatened by upheavals there. He had learned from the fate of his adoptive father, who had died by the daggers of men whose relatives he had pardoned, and he had not taken many prisoners. The times of bloodthirst, however, and *moriendum est* were over. Again, it was not a transformation that could be taken for granted, and many of his contemporaries, who had seen this young murderous killer in action, were understandably far from trusting the appearance of a kinder, gentler version of the same man; push the wrong button and the old Octavian might spring forth again. His previous behavior still weighed heavily and, several decades later, Seneca relativized the "new Augustus" in his treatise *On Clemency,* addressed to Nero (1.11.1). Augustus "was moderate and merciful, but that was, to be sure, after having reddened the Actian sea with Roman blood – after, to be sure, smashing his fleets and those of his enemies in Sicily; and after, to be sure, the human sacrifices and proscriptions at Perusia." Octavian was anything but unaware of this. As early as 36 BC he "burned as many writings as he could that contained evidence concerning the civil strife" (Appian, *Civil Wars* 5.132), and he followed this up by forbidding the publication of the records of the senate, reversing a policy of Julius Caesar. Significantly, he coupled the earlier action with stating his intention to restore the *res publica.*

The exact meaning of that phrase has been the subject of endless discussion. Clearly, Octavian, the product of a small-town Italy and its traditions, did not share Caesar's contemptuous dismissal of the *res publica* as "nothing – a mere name without form or substance" (Suet., *Caes.* 77) nor was he going to repeat Caesar's mistake of appointing himself dictator for life. As we have seen, he never abolished the institutional apparatus of the republic even as triumvir although many of its *leges et iura* were suspended. It was a situation he did not wish to continue; at the same time, there is no question he wanted to stay in power and never relinquish it. The result was a balancing act that evolved over time.

One of the reasons Augustus pulled it off successfully is that he was not an ideologue. Dio, writing for the enlightenment of an emperor some two hundred years later, presented Octavian's choice in terms of the ideological contrast between "democracy" (in the relative terms of republican practice) and monarchy, with Agrippa advocating for the former and Maecenas for monarchy; Octavian certainly had ample time to contemplate the latter during his extended stay in the former Hellenistic kingdoms of the eastern Mediterranean. That famous debate takes up almost an entire book (52) of Dio's *Histories* and although it is unlikely that it ever occurred in this form (see Box 3.2), it reflects the awareness that discussions undoubtedly took place and any choice would be momentous. That choice turned out to be a hybrid, Constitution Plus as I called it earlier, and, as Alain Gowing (2005) has shown, several contemporary and later writers saw a republic headed by a monarch not as a contradiction but as a more perfect form of republic. In what sense, then, could Octavian/Augustus claim to have restored (*restituit*) the republic (*res publica*)?

Box 3.2. What Kind of Rule? Advice to Augustus

Agrippa speaks (Dio 52.2.1–4):

"Be not surprised, Caesar, if I shall try to turn your thoughts away from monarchy, even though I would derive many advantages from it, at least if it was you who held the position. For if it were profitable to you also, I should advocate it most earnestly; but since the privileges of a monarchy are by no means the same for the rulers as for their friends, but, on the contrary, jealousies and dangers fall to the lot of rulers while their friends reap ... all the benefits they can wish for, I have thought it right, in this question as in all others, to have regard not for my own interests, but for yours and the state's....

"For surely no one will assert that we are obliged to choose monarchy in any and all circumstances.... If we choose it, people will think that we have fallen victims to our own good fortune and have lost our senses because of our successes, or else that we have been aiming at monarchy all the while."

Agrippa's argument is consistent with his projection as Augustus' selfless friend and man of the people (see Chapter 5).

Maecenas speaks (Dio 52.17.1–2):

"Now I think you have long since been convinced that I am right in urging you to give the people a monarchical government. If this is the case, accept the leadership over them readily and with enthusiasm – or, rather, do not throw it away. For the question we are debating is not whether we shall take something, but whether we shall decide not to lose it and by doing so incur danger in addition. Who, indeed, will spare you if you thrust the control of the state into the hands of the people, or even if you entrust it to some other man, seeing the many whom you have injured, and that practically all of these will strive to be monarchs instead of you? Yet not one of them will wish either that you should go unpunished for what you have done or that you should be allowed to survive as their rival."

Still, Maecenas does not advocate naked autocracy but stresses that the monarch should rule by example (52.34.1):

"Whatever you wish your subjects to think and do, that you should always say and do yourself. In this way you will be educating them, rather than intimidating them through the punishments prescribed by the laws. The former policy inspires zeal, the latter fear...."

And so (Dio 52.41.1),

"Caesar heartily recommended both him [Maecenas] and Agrippa for the wealth of their ideas and also for their frankness in expressing them. He preferred, however, to adopt the advice of Maecenas."

Trans. E. Cary, with modifications

The place where Romans would see *restituit* displayed most often in public was inscriptions on temples and other buildings that had been rebuilt after some calamity or decay. The important perspective is that they were rarely restored in exactly the same way; there was always some modification or change. The same applies here. It would be wrong to speak of the Republic as if it were a monolith; it underwent change and at least six phases, or republics, have recently been differentiated (Flower 2010). Further, on the coin the phrase *leges et iura restituit*, which may encapsulate the essence of a senate decree passed at his initiative, signals the return to a government based on laws and rights as opposed, for instance, to a government in which Octavian's word simply was law. And overall, he decided diligently to maintain the republican framework: the senate and the assemblies kept meeting and magistrates were elected every year. Octavian was within this framework by being elected consul year after year until 23 BC when a different *modus operandi* was devised. There were and would be alternatives, but Augustus pointedly refers to them in the *Res Gestae* only, and just as pointedly, to conclude each of them with a repeated refrain of refusal: *non recepi* – "I did not accept." For instance, "both the senate and the people offered me the dictatorship" (in 22 BC) – *non recepi*. "They offered me the consulship for life" – *non recepi*. Three times "the senate and the people agreed that I should be appointed supervisor of laws and morals without a colleague with supreme power – *non recepi* any office inconsistent with the custom of our ancestors" (*RG* 5–6).

Even in the early stages, however, it was clear that he was not just any consul. The carefully staged senate meetings in early 27 BC, which were undoubtedly the result of much previous negotiation and discussion, were a perfect and deliberate example. On January 13, Octavian solemnly renounced all his remaining special powers, including his command over the provinces, the armed forces stationed there, and control of the finances. In essence, that meant returning these powers to the disposition of the senate and amounted to a formal restoration of the republic. We may also assume that *res publica restituta* remedied other abuses of the republican system during the triumviral period; in one year, for instance, no fewer than sixty-two praetors had held office instead of the usual eight. Three days later, in just as memorable a ceremony, the senate handed back half the provinces, specifically those where most of the legions were deployed; this meant mainly the provinces on the frontiers. Still, a compromise is apparent: Octavian consented to a limit of ten years for this command (the senate would have to approve renewal), to returning some of these provinces to senatorial control after complete pacification (Augustus lived up to that bargain), and to leaving the senate in control of provinces that were closest to Italy and with command over the legions there. It is clear from Dio's account that not everybody was happy. Neither party got the entire loaf, but the deficit for Octavian was made up by the senate with the truly extraordinary honors he mentions. They deserve a closer look.

"Augustus"

First, "Augustus." Typically – and this is a phenomenon that pervades Augustan art and poetry – the name does not have a single meaning, but evokes several associations. One was a superhuman aura: "More than human," writes Dio (53.16.8), "for all the most honored and sacred things are called *augusta*." *Divi filius* had come into his own right, and Octavian's name henceforth was Imperator Caesar D(ivi) F(ilius) Augustus or any variation thereof (like Caesar Augustus), but always containing "Augustus." Further, its etymological root was *augēre*, to augment or increase, which related it to the central quality on which Augustus claimed his rule was based, *auctoritas*, meaning "influence" or "clout," with the implicit proviso that it is not a statutory power that is abiding. Instead, *auctoritas* constantly needs to be merited and regained by increased (*augēre*) effort. Suetonius (*Aug.* 7.2) also connected "Augustus" with the sacred sphere of augury and, in particular, with what the epic poet Ennius had called the "august augury" of Romulus, who saw twelve vultures in the sky as he was setting out to found Rome, becoming its first king in the process. This last connection is a good example, too, of Augustus' having it both ways, starting with an arrangement that combined both republican and monarchical features. We know that the surname "Romulus" was considered in the discussions leading up to the senate decree because it would emphasize the bearer's second founding of Rome. Wisely, he gave up on it. One reason was that kingship did not sit well with the Romans – as previously mentioned, they prided themselves on founding the *libera res publica* after driving out the last king. Nor was one of the versions of Romulus' end propitious: instead of Romulus' ascending into heaven when a storm cloud plunged the senate chamber into darkness, the senators used that cover to cut him into pieces which they then hid under their togas, making his disappearance somewhat less than miraculous. Augustus, therefore, gave up on outright identification with Romulus but continued an ongoing association that left room for considerable latitude of response – another characteristic quality, as we will see shortly, of Augustan terminology and, again, Augustan poetry and art.

Since the mid-30s, when Octavian had not simply burdened the inhabitants of Italy with expropriations and taxes but rid them of many scourges, such as runaway slaves, robbers, and brigands (Appian, *Civ. Wars* 5.132), he had begun to be honored in exceptional ways and their tide increased after Actium and Alexandria. It reached into every household. In 30 BC, for instance, everybody at private and public meals was to pour a libation for him (Dio 51.19.7), and we know from literary and artistic evidence that the practice was widely followed. The award of the crown of oak leaves and the laurel continued the trend and became emblems on the coinage. The former was a traditional form of recognition for a citizen who had saved another's life. Augustus had saved not just one citizen but all, and the coin legends duly read, "for saving the citizens." While this image situated him in republican traditions of human achievement, the laurel again moved him closer to the gods, Apollo in particular. Not coincidentally, a shining new temple to Apollo had been dedicated in 28 BC on the Palatine, where it stood next to the compound of Augustus' houses. The ensemble was also closely connected with two preexisting temples of Victory and, for that matter, the legendary Hut of Romulus (see Map 2 and Fig. 13).

Return to Constitutional Government

The main significance of the senate meeting of 27 BC and its program was to signal not a return to the pre-Rubicon republic (or its five predecessors) but a distance from the triumviral period when, as Tacitus summed it up, there had been "neither custom nor law" (*Ann.* 3.28). Augustus, then, did not "restore the constitution of the Republic" but rather "restored constitutional government" (Scheid 2007, 89). And it is good to question how many people really wished for a return of that republic – with all its instability, aristocratic jockeying for power, and the government's neglect of the basic needs of people such as the ability to pursue happiness, domestic tranquillity, and a productive life for themselves and their families. Hence, as Dio reports on that occasion (53.11.2), there were members of the senate "who abhorred the republican constitution as a breeder of strife, were pleased at the change in government, and took delight in Caesar." If that was true of senators, it was all the more true of the vast majority of Italians. They were not interested in the politics of the capital, by which they were deeply affected but in which they could not participate unless they went to Rome and voted there. The *libertas* they welcomed was not the liberty *to* engage in cliquish competition for status and office in Rome but freedom *from* the effects of the discord, factionalism, and hardships that system had produced. Hence the end of the *Res Gestae* echoes its beginning where Augustus proclaimed to have liberated the republic from the tyranny of a faction. From all this, yet another reason emerges why Augustus wanted to "restore" the republican system: precisely as a constant reminder of its built-in weaknesses and risks. The republic, without a strong leader, was not the way most people wanted to be governed; there was no nostalgia for its excesses and the economic and political havoc that had resulted. If the system was to work again it required an Augustus. Leaving it to its own devices was to guarantee a return to the bad old days.

Augustus did not hesitate to use that reminder periodically. In 23 BC he let the two censors quarrel, and in 19 BC he stayed calmly in the east while a former praetor, Egnatius Rufus, who had unsuccessfully run for the consulship a year earlier and was popular with the plebs, caused months of violent unrest that ended only when Augustus finally had him tried for conspiracy and executed. For many, such episodes were enough for a taste of the bygone days of the republic, which then was not yet the idealized abstraction it would become in modern times.

Contemporary Responses

The tenor is similar in contemporary responses to the events of 28 and 27 BC. In the *Laudatio Turiae* (cf. Box 2.5), Turia's husband put it simply: "After peace returned to the world and the *res publica* was restored, quiet and happy times were granted to us." Velleius, born in 20 or 19, was more expansive (see Box 3.3). While he itemizes more, the essential meaning of *res publica restituta* in these two witnesses is the same as in Vergil's only use of the phrase in his national epic, which he composed in the 20s. There, quoting his predecessor Ennius, Vergil praises Fabius Maximus, a general in the war against Hannibal, for *restituere rem*, "saving the state" (*Aen.* 6.846). That is what mattered to the Romans.

BOX 3.3. HAPPY TIMES ARE HERE AGAIN

"There is nothing that men can desire from the gods, nothing that the gods can grant to men, nothing that wish can conceive or good fortune bring to pass, which Augustus upon his return did not bestow upon the republic, the Roman people, and the world. The civil wars were ended after twenty years, foreign wars were put to rest, peace was brought back, and the frenzy of arms everywhere lulled to rest; validity was restored to the laws, authority to the courts, and majesty to the senate; the power of the magistrates was reduced to its former limits, with the sole exception that two praetors were added to the existing eight. The old traditional form of the republic was restored. Cultivation returned to the fields, respect to religion, to mankind freedom from anxiety, and to each citizen his property rights were now assured. Old laws were usefully emended and new laws were passed for the general good."

Velleius 2.89.2–3

It would, therefore, be misguided to fixate, as scholars used to do for decades, on the "constitutional" aspects of Augustus' restored *res publica* in the narrow sense of its institutional mechanisms. They were an important part of the unwritten Roman constitution, and Augustus took pains to preserve their "old traditional form," as Velleius notes. Another central function of the *res publica* was the protection of private property, again duly noted by Velleius. Above all, the republican constitution was a system of values and principles. That was behind the senate's awarding Augustus a golden shield on which four cardinal virtues were inscribed: (1) *virtus* itself, which means courage and leadership in both civilian and military life; (2) clemency, which was never absolute but contingent; an example is Augustus' statement in the *Res Gestae* that he preferred to spare, rather than destroy, foreign peoples when they could be pardoned *safely* (3.2); (3) justice, which is essential for any good ruler and good government; and (4) *pietas*, which is the recognition that gods, *res publica*, and family are more important than one's self and that good leaders act accordingly. Renewed emphasis on these and other values, and not legalistic minutiae, was a central aspect of the restoration of the republic.

CHOOSING THE RIGHT TERMINOLOGY

Augustus supplemented the evolving, hybrid concept of republican "Constitution Plus" monarchy with a carefully chosen terminology that defined his role in a nonauthoritarian key and with familiar names. His title was not king or dictator but *princeps*, first citizen. The term had long been in use: the oldest senator who had held office of consul or censor was the *princeps* of the senate and usually one of the first, if not the first, to speak. In the republic, *principes* were known to have been the noblest and most influential members of the aristocracy who, because of their merits and ability to influence others, were held in the highest esteem. That ability was *auctoritas*, another key term and concept used by Augustus. Again it had a traditional ring: the senate – which, it must be remembered, was not a legislative but an advisory body – passed its decrees on the basis and with the force of its *auctoritas*; in Augustan times, the letters S C on the bronze coinage signal that it was issued by decree (*senatus consultum*) of the senate. *Auctoritas* denoted the kind of substance on which real influence is based; Augustus' mother Atia, as we have seen, is a good example. It was a notion with broad and ever-expanding applications, both in private and public life; we already have seen its close connection with "Augustus." It served Augustus to emphasize the distinction, in the final section of the *Res Gestae* (cf. Box 3.1), between the power of a magistrate (*potestas*) and *auctoritas*. The former was institutional but also limited, whereas *auctoritas* was rooted in personal leadership qualities and initiative and actually reached further. *Potestas* was a static power; *auctoritas*, a dynamic and performative one, which therefore, as we have seen, constantly had to be earned anew. This characteristic of never resting even on the laurels the senate had voted him is central to the Augustan mindset.

The Basis of Power: The Army?

It all sounds very high-minded, to be sure. Were Augustus to be interviewed today – a fate from which he was happily spared by the accident of chronology – one of the first questions would undoubtedly be, "What, revered (*augustus*) *princeps*, was the *real* basis of your power?" The point would be to get Augustus to admit that, when all was said and done, his power rested on his control of the army.

There were ostensible limitations at first, as the proconsuls commanding the troops in the provinces that had been allotted to the senate were technically under senatorial control. The *imperium* (executive power of command), however, granted to Augustus was greater than theirs and he could intervene even in the senatorial provinces. The modalities of that system, just like those of the Augustan government in general (see below), underwent several changes and adjustments, but in the end there was no doubt that Augustus was the supreme commander in charge. At the same time, he did not need the army to quell domestic uprisings because there were none.

The decisive reason was not his control of the army. After some hundred years of civil disorder, starting with the assassination of the reformers Tiberius and Gaius Gracchus in 133 and 121, the populace was simply bone-weary and craved a return to some kind of normalcy. Further, even if there was still widespread wariness, Octavian after the conquest of Alexandria turned out to be quite different from his earlier civil-war incarnation. Last but not least, Rome was awash with monies from the east and sizeable benefactions by the new ruler; the economy did strengthen and there was now tangible hope for a better future. Such circumstances are not breeding grounds for political rebellions, even if there were occasional, and ineffectual, conspiracies against his life. In addition, Augustus, as we have already noted, made it a priority to decommission the soldiers who had fought in the civil wars as expeditiously as he could. Overall, the strength of the Roman army was reduced from more than half a million to some 300,000. These troops were engaged in ongoing wars of expansion that aimed at territorial consolidation – *pax Augusta*, as we will see in the next chapter, did not mean the cessation of foreign conquest – nor were they needed, by and large, to suppress ongoing breakaway movements in the provinces, the big Pannonian revolt from AD 6–9 being the proverbial exception. Conversely, Augustus was not a paranoid ruler who holed up in Rome amid a protective cordon. A sure sign of his confidence of being "in control of all affairs" is the many years he spent away from Rome, starting with his departure in the summer of 27 BC for Gaul and an extended military campaign in Spain from where he returned only three years later.

A Material Basis of Power

Republican as things might look, it was obvious that Augustus had special standing, but it was not of the in-your-face kind. It was enhanced by his immense monetary and material resources that increased yet more over time. He was the richest man in the Roman empire but also its greatest benefactor. That process began after his accession as Augustus and was for all to see, including donatives to the urban plebs, (re)building programs, the purchase of land for veterans, and games and shows. His outlays were going to be monumental. Besides his *res gestae*, "the achievements by which he brought the world under the empire of the Roman people" and from which the document has taken its name, the preamble to it continues with the second main heading, "the expenses which he bore for the *res publica* and the people of Rome." The list of those expenses, therefore, takes up a substantial part of the *Res Gestae*.

In sum, his power and *auctoritas* rested on multiple foundations. Similarly, after his final return to Rome from Alexandria, he celebrated a glorious triple triumph in 29 BC for his victories in Illyria and at Actium and Alexandria, a triumph that resonates in one of the most nationalistic passages in Vergil's *Aeneid* (see Box 2.3). It was staged during one of the hottest times of the year in Rome, the middle of August, which today is known as *Ferragosto* and generally marked by an exodus of many Romans to less oppressive venues. In fact, Octavian once more fell ill right in the middle of it but pressed on. Still, that triumph marked another high point of his *auctoritas* because he never celebrated another one and triumphs of others became a rarity during his reign.

Continuing Experimentation

The governmental configuration of January 27 BC was not a detailed hand-book or organization chart but simply provided a framework for moving forward. The abiding issue was the melding of Augustus' role with the republican institutions. It remained a work in progress. The initial solu-tion, naturally, was Augustus' reelection as consul year after year. That worked fine at first but then became problematic. For one thing, Augustus was an absentee consul for some three years while he was in Gaul and Spain. Secondly, his lock on one of the consulships prevented others from attaining Rome's most prestigious office. It is typical of Augustus' experimental bent that he at first floated the idea of expanding the consulate to three. The senate's reaction, alas, was predictable: that sort of arrangement flew squarely in the face of "restoring the constitution" and, besides, government by three smacked uncomfortably of the triumvirate. Typical of Augustus, he did not dig in but looked for alternatives. The solution again was innovative and ingenious, though far less offensive. Midway through his eleventh consulate in 23 BC, Augustus resigned from that office and instead was granted, by the senate, the power of a tribune of the people (*tribunicia potestas*).

This position enabled him, among other things, to convoke the only truly legislative assembly of Rome and initiate legislation. And whereas the tribunes previously had been empowered to convoke the senate (normally the prerogative of the consuls) only on special occasions, Augustus was expressly given the right to do so anytime. The key point, however, was this: Augustus did not actually have to be tribune. Rather, the tribunician power was construed as existing independently of the actual office. Similarly, Augustus did not have to be consul to retain the supreme command position (*imperium proconsulare maius*; tellingly, the codification of that term occurred only after his reign) that gave him power, as we noted earlier, over the armies in all provinces. Neither the tribunician nor the proconsular power was unconstitutional. They were simply used in a new way and exemplified Augustus' mastery of stretching constitutional boundaries – it certainly helped that the constitution was not written down – without transgressing them. In the process, the offices of tribune and consul were not abolished but consuls and tribunes continued to be elected as before. The systems coexisted and the palpable expression was Augustus' taking his place, on a magistrate's chair (*sella curulis*; cf. Fig. 7), between the two consuls at senate meetings.

There had been an interesting prelude earlier that year (23 BC). It began with the trial of Marcus Primus. He was accused of having started a war, without asking the senate for permission, against a Thracian tribe when he was proconsul of the senatorial province of Macedonia. Primus, who was defended by Augustus' co-consul, Terentius Varro, justified his actions by stating that he had received permission from Augustus, which would have contravened the arrangements of 27 BC. Hence Augustus took the unusual step of testifying in court and denied, for the record, that he had granted any such authorization. Primus lost, but not without several of the judges voting in his favor. It was a slap at Augustus' credibility; at the same time, it was harder to say that the old system was not working. Still, Terentius Varro was so upset that he subsequently joined a conspiracy against the emperor. It was discovered, but his sister Terentia, the wife of Augustus' confidant Maecenas, tipped him off, and he escaped. Hunted down by the soldiers, he was killed. Augustus used the consular vacancy to appoint Calpurnius Piso, a true Republican stalwart, which undoubtedly eased the way for the senate's approval of the governmental modifications he was going to seek.

The episode shows that Augustus did not have things in an iron grip, and some free play of forces continued, even involving people quite close to him. Nor, of course, did he have control over his always-fragile health. This time, an illness brought him so close to death that he made arrangements for handing over the government. It was too early for a dynastic succession; the most likely candidate at the time was Augustus' nephew Marcellus, but the demands of the situation, which still was quite unsettled, exceeded the capabilities of another nineteen-year-old – Marcellus was not going to be another Octavian, who had stepped on the stage of history at that age. Besides, he died soon thereafter whereas Augustus recovered, thanks to the ministrations and cold compresses applied by his personal physician, Antonius Musa. Fearing death, however, Augustus had given his personal signet ring, which fittingly displayed the image of the Sphinx, to Agrippa, thus leaving Agrippa in charge of Augustus' personal income and affairs. Dispositions relating to the state, however, including lists of the strength of the army and treasury, were given to the consul Piso, a clear signal that he would be the head of state. That action again spoke to Augustus' republicanism and helped him win favors later in the year. The powers he was granted then basically remained unchanged and were the institutional basis of his rule until his death thirty-seven years later. In contrast to 27 BC, which had signaled the rejection of triumviral government and its excesses, the dispensation of 23 BC could be presented as a commitment, however auratic, to the republic. Deliberately, therefore, Augustus himself counted the official beginning of his reign as 23 BC. The adroit maneuvering and tenacity displayed here were the same as those that had characterized Octavian and brought him success.

Pater and Pontifex

In terms of political and institutional power, therefore, Augustus solidly was "in control of all things"; as for the vicissitudes of life, that is another

Box 3.4. The Prima Porta Augustus

Figure 8. Marble statue of Augustus from Prima Porta. Tiberian copy of ca. AD 15, based on original from after 20 BC. Vatican Museums, Rome. Alinari/Art Resource, NY ART 33464.

(continued)

This is probably the most famous statue of Augustus. It is a marble copy found at the villa of Livia at Prima Porta (outside of Rome) where she lived after Augustus' death. The original was made of bronze and may date to c. 20 BC.

Augustus is shown as addressing the troops (an act known as an *adlocutio*). The scepter is a modern restoration; originally, he held a spear in his left hand. The type of mantle that is slung around his hips is found on statues of Caesar. Other restorations have placed a spear in his right hand and a laurel branch in his left. His bare feet may be an indication of his divinity.

The pictorial program of the cuirass combines history and mythology and, as so often in Augustan art (cf. the Ara Pacis at Figs. 10 and 11), encourages the viewers to make their own associations. In the center, a representative of Rome (Mars or Tiberius) receives the military standards from the Parthian king that Rome had lost in 53 BC and recuperated in 20 BC; the seated female figures on the right and left represent regions that Rome has brought under her control. The event resonates: a new day is beginning, personified by the sun god driving his chariot underneath the gaze of the sky god at the top of the cuirass. The goddess of dawn and another female deity, possibly Venus, precede him. Now is the time for the gods to return to Rome, hence Apollo and Diana are shown on the far right and left side beneath the central scene. At the bottom of the cuirass, corresponding to the sky god, reclines the figure of bountiful earth, Tellus, with the cornucopia that presages the return of prosperity.

Like many sculptures in Greece and Rome, this statue was colored. For an attempted reconstruction, see, for instance, http://www.washingtonpost.com/wp-dyn/content/photo/2008/05/02/PH2008050203201.html.

story to which we will turn later. It was typical of him to accompany this newly minted supremacy not with ostentation but reserve. The inoffensive terminology of *auctoritas* and *princeps* reached its culmination in 2 BC when, in the words of the concluding chapter 35 of the *Res Gestae*, "the senate, the equestrian order, and the people of Rome all together hailed me as 'father of the country' and decreed that this title should be inscribed in the forecourt of my house, the Julian senate house, and in the Augustan forum." *Pater patriae* again had multiple resonances: a Roman

Figure 9. Statue of Augustus from the Via Labicana. Rome, Museo delle Terme, inv. 56230. DAI-Rom 1965.1111 (Koppermann).

pater familias was a caring father figure but also had power (*potestas*) over his family; the senators were called *patres*; *pater* was a byword for Romulus, the founder, and for Camillus, the savior of Rome from the Gauls; just as Jupiter was father of the gods, so Augustus was father of men (Ovid, *Fasti* 2.132). Besides, this appellation of Augustus was not a novelty but had been eased in, as is shown by inscriptions from Italy and the provinces, over the previous years. Along with this went the restrained use, in official sculpture, of Augustus as a martial figure; the famous statue, for instance, from Livia's villa at Prima Porta with its elaborate cuirass is placed in a private setting (see Box 3.4 with Fig. 8). Instead, Augustus is shown in priestly garb time and again (Fig. 9). Whereas, as we have seen, he made it a point to refuse any extraordinary political offices like the dictatorship, such reserve did not apply to his unprecedented accumulation of priesthoods that he mentions with great pride in *RG* 7.3: he was a member of all four of the state's major priestly colleges and, after waiting out Lepidus' death, became chief priest, *pontifex maximus*, in 12 BC. Not by coincidence, Augustus' ancestor Aeneas is styled in the same way: he has come to Italy, he says, not to seek a kingdom, but to establish (literally: "give") gods and religious rites (Vergil, *Aen.* 12.190, 192): *nec mihi regna peto ... sacra deosque dabo.*

A Roman *pater familias* was not an autocrat but consulted with friends and family. Likewise, the *pater patriae* had his kitchen cabinet. The key members were Livia (more about her in Chapter 5), Agrippa, and Maecenas. Agrippa, whom we already have encountered on several occasions, was born in the same year as Augustus and their mutual trust and friendship reached back to their teens. He became Augustus' indispensable right-hand man who got things done, whether in military affairs, urban reconstruction, or civil administration (cf. Chapter 5). Maecenas, who prided himself on regal Etruscan descent, brought different talents to the team: he excelled at reconciling, negotiating, and personal diplomacy. In addition and due to his personal wealth, he was a great patron of the arts and the poets; "Maecenas" has become a byword for cultural philanthropist. His divergent personality provided more attractive fodder for ancient writers than Agrippa's. A good example is Velleius' (2.88) summary: "Of sleepless vigilance in critical emergencies, far-seeing and knowing how to act, but in his relaxation from business more luxurious and effeminate than a woman." It is, to be sure, a good example of stereotyping, too.

Self-stylization: Civilis Princeps

In his interactions with the populace, including the senators, Augustus played the role of the non-autocratic ruler, *civilis princeps*, consummately. Suetonius (chapters 52–6) provides example after example. The first episode he cites is telling: Augustus did not want be called "Lord," not even at home (see Box 3.5). Decades later the emperor Domitian called himself "Lord and God"; he died by assassination. It was not until some 300 years after Augustus that Diocletian and his co-emperors would officially title themselves *domini* and the Dominate replaced the Principate in tone as well as substance; Diocletian's tough-guy countenance in his portraits is a vivid illustration. Suetonius goes on to relate examples of Augustus' personal kindness to commoners (he relaxed a nervous petitioner) and senators: "When a senator named Gallus Cerrinius, whom Augustus knew only slightly, went suddenly blind and decided to starve himself to death, he came to visit him and consoled so much that Gallus changed his mind." In addition, he let senators scream and yell at him all they wanted at meetings of that august body, even while wearing a protective jacket under his toga – he had no desire to choose Julius Caesar's path to heaven – and leaving the meetings in exasperation more than once. As Suetonius notes, free speech, which had always included a heavy dose of libel in Roman politics, was not suppressed. Additionally, Augustus genuinely liked popular entertainments – many of the kind Caesar had shunned – and sponsored an enormous number of them. Small surprise, then, that Suetonius went on to conclude, "[T]he degree of affection that Augustus won by such behavior can easily be gauged." At the same time, everybody knew the steely nature underneath that surface. Sometimes it even shone through his eyes; "it gave Augustus profound pleasure if anyone at whom he looked piercingly dropped his head as though dazzled by looking at the sun" (79.3). The overall impression is that of a man very secure not only in his external surroundings – some conspiracies continued without influencing his behavior – but, more important, in himself.

Box 3.5. Augustus – Not "Lord"

"He always felt horrified and insulted when called 'My Lord' (*dominus*) [a form of address used by slaves to their owners]. Once, while he was at the games and watching a mime play, one of the players spoke the line 'O just and generous Lord,' whereupon the entire audience rose to their feet and applauded. An angry look and a peremptory gesture soon quelled this gross flattery, and the next day he issued an edict of stern reprimand. After this he would not even let the children or grandchildren in his household use the obsequious word, even when they were joking and talking just among themselves."

Suet., *Aug.* 53.1, trans. Robert Graves

Wide Horizons

The deeper reason for Augustus' success, however, lay not only in creating an atmosphere that was blissfully different from that of the 30s but in his response to the social and cultural changes that had taken place in Rome and the Mediterranean in the previous decades. This is but another example of the contrast between Augustus and the mindset of the oligarchic senatorial regime of the Republic. As we have seen, their focus was on Rome and its politics. Syme therefore, as we have seen, famously defined Augustus' victory as the victory of the nonpolitical classes of Italy, but the Augustan horizon and vision went further. They comprised the entire Mediterranean world.

That world had changed greatly due to the Roman conquest. Its effect was not simply military and administrative, but there was a plethora of interactions – cultural, religious, economic, and social – that were reciprocal, had their own dynamics, and increasingly originated outside of Rome and Italy. Their human agents were what one scholar has called "diaspora Romans" (Purcell 2005). The term here, of course, does not connote a forced exit from the homeland. Instead, they were the large and increasing number of entrepreneurs who availed themselves of the opportunities Rome's expansion offered. They were a heterogeneous group, including Roman citizens who had emigrated and their descendants, freedmen (and their descendants), and locals who had been granted Roman citizenship. They were an important constituency – not necessarily the glue that held the empire together but clearly a binding link and vital connection between these lands and Rome. Their ethnicities and cultures reflected those of the entire Mediterranean; one of the things that made them "Roman" was their relation to the powers that were at Rome, which gave them privileged status. The presence of a monarch provided a much clearer focus for that relationship, and Augustus evolved into the patron of patrons. We are looking not at a tight administrative structure but at a dynamic system that is akin to what we would today call networking. A case can be made that the true locus of action had shifted to the diaspora because "it was in that world that the political outcomes of the age were determined"; it was no accident that Caesar "had spent formative years in the currents of the diaspora" (Purcell 2005, 104).

So did Augustus. He was at Apollonia when Caesar was assassinated and, before and after the conquest of Alexandria, spent months on Samos, a central networking point in the eastern Mediterranean. Soon after his ascension to Augustus, he governed the Roman empire for almost two years from Tarraco in Spain. His presence there was not mandated by military operations, which proceeded fitfully anyway. And we find him again in Greece and the east, including several months on Samos, from 21 to 19 BC, all in connection with civil administration. The Mediterranean and its diaspora Romans were an essential gallery that needed to be attended to.

The emperor did not wait for them to come to Rome; he came to them. The recognition of their role, in every way, led to increased cohesion of what had been a collection of conquered territories that had often been treated as mere appendages to Rome (cf. Chapter 7).

Power: The Knowledge Dimension

Similarly, Augustus built on a second major shift that had been in the making by the time he appeared on the scene. It had to do with power, but not simply political power. The loser again was the former ruling class, and that development, too – not just the loss of power in the polit-ical arena – is behind the laments about the "decline" of the Republic. The issue involved the control of knowledge in just about every major area of Roman cultural activity: religion, the calendar, public speaking, law, and the proper use of Latin, to mention only the most significant. In all these areas, the control of knowledge – and it is well recognized that knowledge is power – had passed from the Roman aristocracy to profes-sionals, who were then conscripted by Augustus. The phenomenon has been called "the Roman cultural revolution." Let us look briefly at one or two examples.

One key area was control over the calendar. More is involved than a mere reckoning of time: the calendar determined the flow of public life as it differentiated between festival days, business days, and days the govern-ing bodies could meet. In addition, annual lists, *fasti*, marked identity by singling out individuals for the offices they held and their activities. There was a great deal of latitude for those who knew how to handle such mat-ters or, at any rate, handled them. They were, of course, mostly members of the nobility and they often proceeded at will; the calendar for the next month was announced often only a few days in advance.

The calendar reform of Caesar marked the arrival of expert profession-als. They brought their knowledge to bear on regularizing a haphazard system – at the time of the reform, the Roman calendar and real time were some three months out of sync – and they were employed and appropriated by the new leader of the state. The process continued under Augustus with the additional dimension that, like control over the calendar, *fasti* were not a privilege anymore that was limited to the aristocracy, but sprung up all over for local festivals, magistrates, and functionaries, including freedmen and slaves. In Andrew Wallace-Hadrill's succinct formulation: "In slipping from the nobility, Roman time becomes the property of all Romans" (2005, 74). Far from being isolated, this occurrence is part of a broader phenom-enon to which we will return: one of the defining aspects of the Augustan reign was precisely the opening up of formerly restricted opportunities to a much larger segment of the populace. Paradoxical as it may seem, a shift to autocratic government is accompanied by the authentic civic involvement of much wider strata of the population. Everyone, not just the city of Rome and the consuls, gets to publish their *fasti* now, whether monthly calendars and annual lists of functionaries, or in combination. We find them in towns like Praeneste, for the officials (*vicomagistri*) of the approximately 265 neighborhoods in Rome who were freedmen, the slaves of an imperial villa, and many more. Augustus certainly led the way by reshaping the official *fasti* of Rome with a veritable invasion of anniversaries and commemorations relating to himself and his family.

Another poignant and central example of how Rome's culture changed is the control over the very language of Rome, Latin. There is a certain irony: as the Roman nobility engaged in its wars of conquest and enlarged Rome's territories, it could not maintain the traditional way that knowledge of Latin was passed on. In earlier days, the model was by customary practice (*consuetudo*) emanating naturally from the ranks of Latin speakers in the capital. Needless to say, inhabitants of faraway regions and even those in much of Italy could not partake in this process. For them and for others, Latin would need to be regularized and systematized according to "rational" rules (*ratio*). Once more we find Julius Caesar in the forefront, composing a treatise *On Analogy* in the midst of his Gallic wars. The real practitioners of this new systemization, however, were emerging professionals, the *grammatici*, who established themselves as "guardians of language." They took control, and their services were accessible to broad groups of people in ways the Roman aristocracy itself had never been.

Some of Augustus' actions become fully understandable in light of this paradigm shift. Let the senators hanker after their privileges, consulships, provincial commands, and other honors – Rome had become a different society whose culture could no longer be controlled by them anyway. Developments had had their own dynamic. Augustus had not started them, but he recognized this changed environment and took charge of it.

A pivotal question remains. Now "having power over all things," did Augustus exercise power for its own sake, or did he use it as the means to an end? The answer is, quite unambiguously, the latter. Its various manifestations will occupy us through the rest of the book, but it is useful to conclude with an early example because it opens up this perspective and, at the same time, provides another illustration of the experiment of the early principate. That was his attempt to introduce legislation, around 27 BC, to make marriage mandatory. There were several reasons for this, which I will take up in the next chapter, moral zealotry being the least of them. The measure was not designed to gain him popularity; a howl of protests arose and Augustus pulled back, only to push for it again, this time successfully, a few years later. The point is that he was trying to do more than just stay in power or even bring back material prosperity. He was not, as we have seen before, an ideologue, but he had a definite vision of where he wanted Rome to go.

4

THE CHALLENGE OF
PAX AUGUSTA

Some myths die hard. The issue, in the Augustan context, is not the myth of the Golden Age itself, but the myth of the Augustan Golden Age. The entire period of Augustus' reign has often been characterized with this label which, as most labels, is convenient rather than precise. On that view, the last ripples on the Augustan sea were those of the battle of Actium. Calm then prevailed, prosperity returned, problems receded if not evanesced, splendid new edifices arose, and the arts flourished. Especially in ever-increasing retrospect, it was a blessed time that led later ages, notably in France, England, and Saxony, to appropriate the seal of an Augustan Golden Age for themselves (cf. Box 8.2).

As always, the reality was more complicated. We already saw in the last chapter that there were choppy waters on which Augustus needed to navigate. Things fell into place neither automatically nor providentially after Actium and Alexandria. And how could they? The decades of disarray, amounting to almost a century, had left deep marks and fissures. A return to stability would require considerable time and always be a work in progress. That is, in fact, the mindset we find in many of the contemporary sources: not facile self-congratulation, but awareness of the need for ongoing effort. Vergil's *Aeneid* is a sterling example. It is about the founding of Rome, but not in the physical sense. In the national epic, Rome is of course not built in a day – in fact, it is not built at all. That will come later; the emphasis is on the exertions *(labores)* and struggles of the founding father.

While the contributions of the poets and others amount to more than simply being "on message," we can assume that Augustus had much to do with setting the tenor of the discourse. He did, as we have seen, celebrate a spectacular triple triumph after his victorious return from the east in 29 BC, but it is equally telling that he did not celebrate another triumph for the remaining 43 years of his reign. Triumphalism had its limits. In lieu of a triumph in 25 BC, the *princeps* accepted the privilege of wearing garlands and triumphal dress on the first day of every new year (Dio 53.26.5), but that did not signal that he was going to rest on his laurels. Instead, we can see that an ethos of struggle, and of seeking out and meeting challenges, was the unsurprising result of the experiences that had shaped his character since his youth. Like Achilles, to whom he compared himself in one of his early speeches in Rome (Appian, *Civ. Wars* 3.13), he could have chosen an easier life just by refusing, as advised by his well-meaning stepfather, to become Caesar's heir. Further, there was the constant coping with his physical frailties – no cause for triumphant exultations there either. Thirdly, as we have seen, much of his success was due to acting (or, in current parlance, being proactive) and looking ahead rather than simply reacting. All these characteristics did not vanish once he had gained supreme power. Instead, they shaped the character of his reign and provide a useful perspective for surveying some of its aspects and developments.

Pax: Meaning and Practice

In his *Res Gestae*, Augustus himself defined *pax* very succinctly: it was "born of victories" (*parta victoriis pax*; 13.2). It is a very Roman notion (and that may be one reason it does not appear in the Greek text): victory and conquest come first and then there is a pact (*pax* is etymologically related to Latin words meaning "to make firm," "to make an agreement or pact," etc.). That pact, *pax*, was reciprocal: it obligated both the subjected people and the Romans. Sure, panegyrists who sang the praises of empire, *laudes imperii*, often overstated the case with fulsome rhetorical exuberance, but at bottom was a pact that in return for relinquishing their sovereignty, the conquered now came under the protection of Rome, enjoyed security, wider opportunities for commerce and trade, participation (including social mobility) in and access to a larger network, religious freedom, and a normative system of justice; as for the latter, the Romans, as in most other areas, left native systems alone so long as they did not contravene generally accepted standards and reserved only capital crimes for their jurisdiction. Taxes, therefore, were amply justified in the Romans' view even if their collection could be an irritant for both sides.

When we speak of *pax* in the Augustan context, an essential distinction is necessary. Augustus brought peace domestically, in the sense of ending the civil wars. They had frayed the psyche of the nation and their end caused the outpouring of relief and gratitude cited in the previous chapter. The most potent symbol of the cessation of war was the solemn closing of the door of the Temple of Janus. That happened rarely, as Rome was engaged in warfare against foreign foes virtually without letup. That ceremony was elaborately staged after the conquest of Alexandria; the official enemy in that war had been the foreign queen and not Antony. Hence Vergil could appropriate it for the sonorous prophecy of Jupiter with which his prologue to the *Aeneid* culminates (1.291–6):

> Then shall the age of violence be mellowing into peace:
> venerable Faith and Vesta, with Quirinus and Remus,
> shall make the laws; the grim, steel-welded gates of War
> will be locked; and within, on a heap of armaments, a hundred
> bronzen knots tying his hands behind him, shall sit
> unholy Furor, grinding his teeth and howling with bloody mouth.
>   (Trans. C. Day Lewis, with modifications)

The image clearly refers not to foreign wars but to the ruinous, fratricidal discord in Rome, starting with Romulus (Quirinus) and Remus. That was the real fury and it had finally been tamed. The end of civil strife was the *sine qua non* for any recovery, economic or other. Only a jaundiced critic like Tacitus (*Ann.* 1.2) would denounce the resulting domestic tranquillity as the kind of leisure (*otium*) and freedom from worries by whose "sweetness" Augustus "seduced one and all" to lull them into apolitical torpor. More relevant, the doors of the real Temple of Janus were opened up again soon enough because of ongoing warfare that aimed at "peace born of victories."

That was the other face of *pax Augusta*, openly stated in the heading of the *Res Gestae*: "The achievements of the deified Augustus by which he made the world subject to the *imperium* of the Roman people." True, at the end of his reign he is said to have formally advised his successor "to keep the empire within its present boundaries" (Tacitus, *Annals* 1.11; cf. Dio 56.33.5). That sentiment, despite legitimate doubts about its authenticity, has played well with historians because it is kindred to George Washington's famous injunction, in his farewell address, to "avoid foreign entanglements," which again is something that did not quite happen. At any rate, foreign wars of conquest were a constant feature of the Augustan reign. In that regard, too, Augustus could present himself as a worthy successor to the republic and its generals; in the end he added more territory to the *imperium Romanum* than anyone before him and took pride in it. How did he do it and what does it tell us about the man?

An overriding characteristic is one we have already encountered: pragmatism came before ideology. The goal was not simply unlimited expansion and it might, therefore, be better to take Jupiter's famous pronouncement in the *Aeneid* – "I have given [the Romans] empire without end" – in a temporal rather than territorial sense. Restrictions applied: Augustus, for reasons we saw earlier, reduced the civil war armies of 500,000 soldiers to 300,000 – not a large number for safeguarding an empire that stretched from the Near East to the North Sea, and from North Africa to the Danube. Furthermore, the troops were not deployed solely for defensive purposes or quelling rebellions, but a large part of them continued to be engaged in wars of expansion. Conquest, while incessant, was handled with prudence, tenacity, and a flair for presenting, in the then current media, even modest successes, or successes obtained by other means, as victories. And why not? The best example is the "victory" over the Parthians that did not cost the life of one Roman soldier. The Parthians, as mentioned earlier, had inflicted a major defeat on the invading army of Crassus in 53 BC. There was an ongoing howl in Rome to take revenge for that embarrassment; Caesar readied an army against them, with Octavius as his *magister equitum*, before he was cut down and later Antony marched into Parthia, only to be defeated.

The voices, highly audible even in poets like Horace and Ovid, which called for a grand military undertaking were incessant. Augustus proceeded otherwise. He did proceed, physically, to the east in 20 BC and used the impact of his presence to work out a settlement with the Parthian king, including arrangements in the kingdom of Armenia. An accord was reached about mutual spheres of influence. The enemy returned the legionary standards they had captured in 53 BC and the surviving Roman POWs. Augustus maximized the use of these highly charged assets for public posture and consumption. The whole event was styled, and spun, as a momentous victory. In the *Res Gestae* (29.2), he speaks of "compelling" the Parthians "to give back to me spoils and standards of three Roman armies and to come to me as suppliants and request the friendship of the Roman people." Coins showed the Parthian king groveling on his knees as he was handing back the standards. The standards were destined to be deposited in the inner sanctum of the temple that dominated the Forum of Augustus, which was under construction at the time (see Map 2). That Temple of Mars the Avenger originally was vowed in commemoration of Octavian's revenge on the murderers of Caesar and now took on the added meaning of revenge on the Parthians. Another resonance of the event and its publicity is the cuirass of the most famous statue of Augustus, the posthumous one from Livia's Villa at Prima Porta, where the Parthian surrender of the standards is the center of the pictorial program (see Box 3.4).

Savvy of the use of such messages, including visuals, had, of course, already been a hallmark of Octavian. So had tenacity, which Augustus again kept displaying in plenty. The conquest of the previously unconquered regions of Spain, for instance, was slow and protracted. It was costly in lives and was not concluded until 13 BC. In Germany the objective was expansionist. The campaign there did not serve the purpose of consolidation, as was the case in the Alpine regions, but to show the flag, and more, beyond the Rhine River; the goal may have been the Elbe. In the course of such an expedition, the Roman army suffered one of its worst setbacks during Augustus' reign as three legions were ambushed and just about annihilated in the hills and forests near Kalkriese in AD 9. Three legions out of twenty-eight was a considerable loss and the hyping of the event especially by patriotic Germans has a basis in Suetonius' vignette (*Aug.* 23.2) that upon getting the bad news, Augustus cried "Quinctilius Varus, give me my legions back!" and then roamed the palace for months disheveled and refusing to shave, a sort of precursor to Richard Nixon, who was rumored to have talked, with slurred speech of course, to the pictures of his predecessors in the White House in the depth of his despair. Reality interposes itself: Augustus rebuilt the lost legions and increased the total number of legions in Germany from five to eight, first under the command of Tiberius and then of Germanicus, both high-profile members of the imperial house (see Chapter 5). While the intent to conquer was never given up officially, the main purpose of continuing incursions across the Rhine was a show of force and demonstration that Roman troops could operate freely in the enemy's territory. The word was that Rome could have subjugated Germany in a year if it had wanted to (Strabo 7.1.4). Another precaution that Augustus took was to replace his German bodyguard because the leader of the assault, the German prince Arminius ("Herman the German"), had served as an officer in the Roman army and acquired equestrian status before committing treason.

These examples, which could be extended, show Augustus' flexibility, determination, and pragmatism, including instances of cost/benefit analysis (Lintott 2010, 160). Different circumstances required different actions – it would be wrong to speak of "responses" because that implies reaction rather than active initiative. A good definition might be that Augustus was determined to be pragmatic. The overall goal, however, still was to "enlarge the boundaries of the Roman empire" (*RG* 26.1) although in a pragmatically determined way, and to portray that extension, even when and where there were prudent limits to it, as an actual conquest for the greater glory of Rome and himself. Hence Germany is duly included in the list of these conquests in the *Res Gestae* (26.2) – to the mouth of the River Elbe, no less.

It is clear from the small size of the Augustan army and its prevailing engagement in wars of expansion that uprisings within the empire were generally not an issue. The proverbial exception, besides the usual brushfires, was the massive revolt in Pannonia (roughly today's Hungary; see Map 1) that lasted from AD 6 to 9 and really put the empire to the test. At its height, no less than a third of the Roman army had to be deployed there, straining resources elsewhere. It was not, however, the signal for an empire-wide rebellion, which could have altered the shape of things considerably. Germany, for instance, stayed quiet, and Arminius somehow bided his time until a few days after the final Roman victory over the Pannonian insurgents. Why the relative calm? Augustan rule was based on soft power as well as on hard power and many natives accepted the fact of Roman *imperium* because of the advantages that resulted from a larger and more stable network, such as security and greater opportunities for trade and commerce; I will return to this in Chapter 7. Another Roman strategy, more immediately relevant to the present context, was psychological warfare. It cost less than the alternative, increased troop strength, and was mostly effective. The main agents were terror and intimidation – mess with the Romans and revenge, however excessive, would be forthcoming even if, because of a stretched-out army, it might take a while. As Susan Mattern has noted (1999, 122), a "central aspect of Roman strategy was image." So, as we have seen, was much of Augustus' foreign policy – the two were natural, and deliberate, complements.

So were two other factors that were part of the mix. Augustus' ongoing agreement with the senate was to resubmit, every five to ten years, the extension of his supreme command over the legions (especially those in the frontier provinces) for ratification. Such extensions had to be justified by the need for continuing pacification (interestingly enough, so far from being laden with negative associations the term occurs even in Vergil's "Messianic" *Eclogue* [17]; cf. Box 4.2). The problem was that successful pacification would mean, at least technically, reversion to senatorial control of such provinces and, more importantly, the legions stationed there. Hence the need to present the work of pacification as ongoing – a neat mirror image of the strategy of declaring "victory" over the Parthians. The impression had to be given that danger persisted and required military attention and activity. In many cases, such a situation may genuinely have existed, but at times it was easier to make the case by outright forays into enemy territory, as on the German frontier. In so many words, an overall strategy, even if evolving, existed and it was dual: military and political. Both parts coalesced into the consolidation of both the empire and Augustus' powers.

This tells us a lot about the man, as does his way of dealing with the domestic repercussions of the Pannonian revolt. The huge army contingent in Pannonia had to be supplied and since the rebels used the strategy of scorched earth, much of the grain supply in Rome had to be diverted to the front. That caused famines and uprisings; among other drastic measures, Augustus expelled all foreigners from the city, with the exception of physicians and teachers. He reorganized the administration of the grain supply in Rome, breaking with the republican tradition of having two senators in charge, and similarly systematized the fire brigades. These were bread and butter issues. So was the provision of retiring soldiers with land. It was replaced in 13 BC with a cash payment that Augustus at first financed from his own treasury. That changed in AD 6, when a separate military treasury (*aerarium militare*) was established and a new, and wildly unpopular, inheritance tax was introduced to help fund it. In addition, a legionnaire's service was lengthened to twenty years and freedmen, including many slaves who had been freed solely for that purpose, were conscripted into the army during the Pannonian emergency. Other signs of stress during those years were electoral unrest (elections were more than a formality under Augustus); the admission in court of evidence obtained from slaves by torture; a falling out between Augustus and his grandson Agrippa Postumus (so-called because he was born after Agrippa's death in 12 BC) and the latter's exile; and a conspiracy against Augustus that also led to the exile of his granddaughter Julia and the poet Ovid. In addition, Augustus' actions led to a flood of calumnies and slanderous pamphleteering.

GOLDEN AGE REALITIES

Was this the vaunted Golden Age? Hardly. Events like these are ample demonstration that the Augustan reign was full of ongoing challenges and there was no attempt by the Augustans to create contrary illusions by resorting to an imagery that would gloss over such realities. Both contemporaries and later authors were cognizant of them. A good example is the Elder Pliny's stark catalogue of the trials and tribulations of Augustus' life. It is an important passage and therefore is quoted almost in its entirety in Box 4.1. The list of incidents, including both factual and tabloid material, is longer than I have room to discuss in this book, though most have already been mentioned. The point is that Augustus was seen not only as man of great success, but also as an exemplar of misfortune. Another point, just as important, is that he coped with it and that is one of the reasons he was so successful.

Box 4.1. Augustus' Trials and Tribulations

"In the life of the now deified emperor Augustus even, whom the whole world would certainly agree to place in this class [i.e., of those who were considered particularly fortunate], if we carefully examine it in all its features, we shall find remarkable vicissitudes of human fate. There was … the hatred produced by the proscription; his alliance in the Triumvirate with some among the very worst of the citizens, and that, too, with an unequal share of influence, given the oppressive the power of Antony; his illness at the battle of Philippi; his flight, and his having to remain three days concealed in a marsh, though suffering from sickness; … his shipwreck on the coast of Sicily, where he was again under the necessity of concealing himself in a cave; his desperation, which caused him even to beg Proculeius to put him to death, when he was hard-pressed by the enemy in a naval engagement; his alarm about the rising at Perusia, his anxiety at the battle of Actium; the extreme danger he was in from the falling of a tower during the Pannonian war; seditions so numerous among his soldiers; so many attacks by dangerous diseases.

"Also, the suspicions which he entertained about the intentions of Marcellus; the disgraceful banishment, as it were, of [his grandson] Agrippa; the many plots against his life; the deaths of his own children [i.e., his grandsons Gaius and Lucius], of which he was accused, and his heavy sorrows, caused not merely by their loss; the adultery of his daughter, and the discovery of her parricidal designs; the insulting retreat [to Rhodes] of his son-in-law, [Tiberius] Nero; another adultery, that of his granddaughter; to which there were added numerous other evils, such as the lack of money to pay his soldiers; … the pestilence that raged in the City; the famine in Italy; the design which he had formed of putting an end to his life, and the fast of four days, which brought him within a hair's breadth of death.

"And then, added to all this, the disastrous defeat of Varus; the base slanders whispered against his authority; … and, last of all, the machinations of his wife and of Tiberius, the thoughts of which occupied his last moments. In sum, this same god, who was raised to heaven – I am at a loss to say whether deservedly or not – died, leaving the son of his own enemy his heir" [Tiberius' father had been a partisan of Antony's; see p. 41].

Pliny, *Nat. Hist.* 7.147–50, trans. H. Rackham, with modifications

This is one of several factors as to why there was no trumpeting of a return to an old-style Golden Age during those long years. The conventional notion was that there was a cycle of ages, all named after metals – golden, silver, bronze, and iron. In addition, the Roman mentality was declinist; Horace, for instance, memorably concludes his six "Roman" Odes, which have Roman virtues as their theme, on the note that "Our parents' age, worse than their parents', has brought forth us, who are yet more worthless, and will soon produce a more depraved offspring yet" (*Odes* 3.6.46–8).

There was hope in the traditional mythological scheme: after reaching an iron-age nadir, the system would cycle back to the age of gold, even if only to begin over again. That hopeful notion found its strongest expression in Vergil's Fourth or "Messianic" *Eclogue* (see Box 4.2), written around 40 BC, which presaged the birth of a wondrous child and the return of paradise – no human effort required. And that is precisely what changed. In his next poetic work, the *Georgics*, Vergil speaks of the recuperation of the golden age through unceasing human toil, personified by the Italian farmer. Finally, in the *Aeneid*, we reach the next stage: in one of the only three passages where he mentions Augustus, the poet has Aeneas' father Anchises prophesy (in real time for Vergil's contemporaries) that

---

Box 4.2. A Golden Age Utopia: Vergil's "Messianic" Eclogue

"For you, child, shall the earth, un-tilled, pour forth
her first small gifts: wandering ivy with cyclamen everywhere
and Egyptian lilies blended with smiling acanthus.
Goats of their own free will shall bring home their udders
filled with milk, and cattle shall not fear mighty lion.
Unasked, too, your cradle will pour forth caressing flowers.
The serpent will perish, and perish, too, will the treacherous
poison-plant; Assyrian spice will spring up all over.
But once you can read the glories of the heroes
and your father's deeds and understand the nature of true valor
then the plain will begin to grow yellow with soft spikes of corn,
from wild thorns shall hang the reddening grape
while the tough oak will distil dewy honey.

"Next, when strengthened age has made you man,
traders shall quit the oceans and no more shall pine-built ships
exchange their wares; all lands will bring forth all things.
The earth shall not suffer the hoes, nor the vine the pruning-hook;
Then, too, the sturdy ploughman will loose his oxen from the yoke.
Wool will no more deceive with varied dyes, but on his own
the ram shall change his fleece in the fields,
now to sweet-blushing purple, now to saffron yellow;
spontaneously scarlet will clothe the grazing lambs.

"The time will soon be here. Enter on your great honors,
beloved offspring of the gods, mighty progeny of Jupiter!
Look how the vaulted mass of the universe nods –
The lands, the expanses of the sea, and heaven's depth!
Behold how all things rejoice as the new age dawns!"

Eclogue 4, 18–30, 37–45, 48–52

Scholarship on this poem has been immense – it exceeds that on any other Latin poem – as have varieties of reactions to it. The main reason is that in its associative and evocative manner it taps into many strands of imagination and strikes many responsive chords. That was certainly true at its own time against a background of decades of war and destruction: there was a tremendous yearning for an end to it all and for better times. This basic issue has been needlessly overlaid by incessant speculation about the identity of the child; it is easy to see why it was appropriated to presage the birth of Christ. Quite simply, the child is the new age. Given the multicultural environment of Rome, inspirations from both east and west have been discerned; here again, strict proof is not possible. As for the Augustan Golden Age, Vergil's over-the-top imagery, such as color-changing rams, clearly was not a blueprint.

"Augustus Caesar, son of the deified, will bring once again
ages of gold to Latium, to the land where Saturn reigned
in early times." (6.792–3)

The Latin word for "bringing back" (*condet*), however, also contains the notion of "closing down," because the new golden age is not just a return

Figure 10. Female deity with symbols of fruitfulness. Relief from the Ara Pacis, Rome. DAI-Rom 1986.1448 (Schechter).

to the old. Instead, it will be, in keeping with Augustan realities, an age of expansion, conquest, and warfare, and Vergil even resorts to hyperbole:

> beyond the Garamants [near the Sahara] and Indians will he extend *imperium*; over far territories north and south of the zodiacal stars, the solar way, where Atlas, heaven-bearing on his shoulder turns the night-sphere, studded with burning stars. (6.793–7)

"Empire without end" indeed – the passage harks back to Jupiter's prophecy about Augustus in the first book (1.279; see above). It is not, however, a comfortable golden age of paradisiac indolence but rather the *pax Augusta*, and it requires ongoing effort.

The arts convey the same message. Take the most resonating representation of the *pax Augusta*, the Altar of Augustan Peace: the goddess of blessings, surrounded by vegetation and contented farm animals, is paired with the goddess Roma, who sits proudly on a pile of conquered arms (Figs. 10 and 11). Similarly, the cuirass of the Prima Porta Augustus expresses the message of peace based on conquest: the

Figure 11. Roma seated on arms. Reconstruction of relief from Ara Pacis, Rome. Rome, Museo dell'Ara Pacis Augustae. Photograph Archivio Fotografico dei Musei Capitolini.

central scene is the Parthian surrender and, as a result, the goddess Tellus appears in the register below with a cornucopia, the symbol of plenty (see Box 3.4).

Global Leadership and Moral Leadership

One of the hallmarks of Augustus, which made his time so distinctive, was to go beyond the restoration of the material sphere and military success. An imperial people, in his view, had obligations to conduct itself in a way that validated its claim to world rule. In other words, the basis had to be moral and ethical. That was one of the underlying reasons for one of his most remarkable and ambitious initiatives, his so-called moral legislation. It was, no doubt, an invasion of the private sphere on a scale that, so far from being problematic for our modern sensibilities, already had many Romans recoil in protest. Tacitus regarded it as the height of the state's interference with personal freedom and "the end of fair law" (*Annals* 3.25). The continuing debate these laws stirred up – they remained in effect for over two hundred years – is also evidenced by their attracting more comment from Roman jurists than did any other laws, including capital punishment. Their pursuit is yet another example of Augustus' tenacity and, after restoring stability, aiming for more than a feel-good package of peace and prosperity.

What was involved? Mainly, compulsory marriage, especially for the upper classes. Augustus seems to have pushed, as we have seen (see pp. 82–3), for this kind of legislation already in 27 BC but had to bide his time for almost a decade until he got the laws passed – they were called the Julian Laws as he, exceptionally, was the sponsor – in 18 BC. They mandated marriage and remarriage for men from ages twenty-five to sixty, and women between twenty and fifty, widows and widowers included. Of course people could choose not to comply, but there were penalties. They could not, for instance, choose heirs outside their family nor did they receive preferential treatment for civil careers or for seats in the circus and theater (probably the more important issue to many people). Conversely, there were rewards for those who had three children or more. Companion laws cracked down hard on adultery and included a provision that protected women. The custom had been, when a woman had been raped, to deal with the incident within the victim's family, who often suggested to her, gently or not so gently, to rid the family of that shame by committing suicide; modern analogies abound. The most famous ancestral example, of course, was Lucretia, the wife of Collatinus, who had been forced by the son of Rome's Etruscan king, Tarquinius, to have sex with him. She killed herself despite her innocence and the incident led to the overthrow, led by Brutus and Collatinus, of the Etruscan kings and the beginning of the Roman Republic (see Box 4.3).

BOX 4.3. LUCRETIA

"[Sextus Tarquinius] waited until everyone in the house seemed to be asleep. Then, when all was quiet, he drew his sword and made his way to Lucretia's bedroom, determined to rape her. She was sleeping. Laying his left hand on her breast, 'Lucretia,' he whispered, 'not a sound! I am armed – if you utter a word, I will kill you.' Lucretia opened her eyes in terror; death was imminent, no help at hand. Sextus urged his love, begged her to submit, pleaded, threatened, used every weapon that might conquer a woman's heart. But all in vain; not even the fear of death could bend her will. 'If death will not move you,' Sextus cried, 'dishonor shall. I will kill you first, then cut the throat of a slave and lay his naked body by your side. Will they not believe that you have been caught in the act with a servant – and paid the price?' Even the most resolute chastity could not have stood against this dreadful threat. Lucretia yielded. Sextus' libido won out and he rode away, fiercely proud of having triumphed over a woman's honor.

"In her grief over so great an evil Lucretia sent a messenger to her father in Rome and her husband in Ardea, urging them to return at once with a trusted friend – and quickly, for a frightful thing had happened.... They found Lucretia sitting in her room, in deep distress. Tears rose to her eyes as they entered, and to her husband's question, 'Are you well?' she answered, 'No. What can be well with a woman who has lost her honor? In your bed, Collatinus, is the imprint of another man. My body only has been violated. My heart is innocent – death will be my witness. Give me your solemn promise that the adulterer will be punished: he is Sextus Tarquinius.'

"The promise was given. One after the other they tried to comfort her. They told her she was helpless, and therefore innocent; that he alone was guilty. It was the mind, they said, that sinned, not the body; without intention there could never be guilt.*

"'What is due to *him*,' Lucretia said, 'is for you to decide. As for me, I am innocent of fault, but I will take my punishment. Never shall Lucretia provide a precedent for unchaste women to escape what they deserve.' With these words she drew a knife from under her robe, drove it into her heart, and fell forward, dead" (Livy 1.58; trans. A. de Selincourt, with modifications).

* This emphasis reflects contemporary legal opinion. Anachronistically, Livy has Lucretia's family adopt that standard which would have applied in an Augustan court. As a side note, Augustine (*City of God* 1.19) blamed Lucretia for adding the wrong of suicide to an offense of which she was not guilty; the Augustan procedure happily obviated, if not anticipated, such Christian strictures.

The resurgence of the Lucretia story, therefore, in Augustan times was not accidental. But, as in the case of the golden age myth, the point was not simply a restatement of received notions because adultery and Lucretia cases now had to be dealt with by the courts. The same blend of invocation of past examples with innovative adaptation to contemporary realities is precisely what informed Augustus' legislation on marriage and morals. Here is he how put it in the *Res Gestae* (8.5):

> By new laws (*legibus novis*) passed on my initiative I brought back into use many exemplary practices of our ancestors that were disappearing in our time, and in many ways I myself transmitted exemplary practices to posterity for their imitation.

Legibus novis – that phrase would make many a Roman shudder because the expression for "upheaval" or "revolution" was simply "new things" (*res novae*). Augustus uses it deliberately: laws that upended the status quo were needed precisely to bring back a commitment to some of the old ways.

We do not have to look far to see how and when some of these "exemplary practices" had fallen into disuse. The purpose of the laws was to foster social responsibility. For understandable reasons, many Romans in the last decades of the Republic did not want to have children – pointless to bring them into a world of starvation, turmoil, and violence. Hence they did not feel compelled to get married, as the purpose of marriage and sex was always defined as procreation rather than recreation. That created a boom, especially among the affluent, of gold diggers and gigolos, though their social comportment could be quite civilized. Older singles would naturally rely on these helpful companions and then amply reward them in their wills. Fortunes that had always been in a family, however extended, thus could easily dissipate beyond it and end that family's wealth. Augustus' legislation was meant to put a stop to that situation, too.

Mostly, however, it was aimed at bringing back the exemplary practices and traditional Roman virtues of not putting yourself first and instead making sacrifices for others. Purposely, the hero of Rome's national epic is a sterling example and his chief quality, *pietas*, means social responsibility and dedication to the welfare of others rather than "piety." And what better place, as we all know, to learn and practice these virtues than within a family, where daily cooperation and effort are required for the sake of the common good; poets like Horace, therefore, went so far as to decry immorality, especially within the family, as the root cause of civil war.

The legislation, however unconventional, formally called forth those traditional ideals while jettisoning others such as a woman not marrying again after the death of her husband (*univira*); Dido in the *Aeneid* is a good example. And it responded to a school of thought, including that of Stoic philosophers, that a people who wanted to rule over others should not just be stronger, but also better, including ethically better. Global leadership entailed moral leadership. We are looking, as so often, at a mix of intentions. Such multiplicity of dimensions is typically Augustan and we encounter it everywhere, including in poetry, art, and architecture.

The Romans were not impressed. They kept protesting against the imposition of these laws. Hence there were some revisions in AD 9 – a time of considerable duress, as we have seen – to ease the time requirements for remarriage. Overall, however, Augustus did not back down. He was a strong leader precisely because he defined the salient issues, even if unpopular, and appealed to ideals and values.

THE ROLE OF RELIGION

The legislation was a keystone of Augustus' domestic program. The importance he attached to it also explains why he waited until after its enactment to proceed, in 17 BC, with a stirring religious festival, which could be celebrated only once every one hundred years (or more). That was the Secular Games; the name comes from *saeculum*, which denotes such a period and whose equivalent is found in languages such as French (*siècle*) and Spanish (*siglo*). One reason for their institution – some traditions date them to the fourth century BC – was that they were clearly meant to serve as a marker: a people would do well to reflect on past events at periodic intervals and even do penance, symbolically of course, for its faults. The traditional celebration, therefore, was centered on underworld deities like Pluto (Hades) and Proserpina (Persephone) and their appeasement; the rituals, appropriately, took place at night.

As always, Augustus combined tradition with innovation. As ever, too, he loved to stage a spectacle and he and Agrippa were heavily involved in the preparation of the solemn festival and its rites; at the same time, it was a grand occasion for the entire population of Rome to come together as a community. In preparation, Augustus and other members of the college of priests in charge distributed to all citizens means of purification, such as sulfur and tar, with which they needed to cleanse themselves in a private ritual. The celebration went on for three days and nights and, typically, a forward-looking dimension was added to it. Replacing the rulers of the underworld were deities such as the "all-creating Fates" and "the childbearing goddesses of childbirth" – clearly a reference to the marriage legislation – along with Mother Earth, Jupiter, Juno, Apollo, and Diana. It was an impressive and elaborate ceremony with new features such as sacrifices on the Palatine near Augustus' residence and the performance of a special hymn by Horace (see Box 4.4). It marked not only a remembrance of the past, but, Janus-like, a call to action for the next *saeculum* and its underpinnings, such as striving for social harmony, peace, and plenitude, and taking responsibility for families, all with the help of the gods. Again, typical of Augustus, there was nothing celebratory in the sense of "look how far we've come domestically and how successful we have been with the *imperium Romanum* (the Parthians had 'surrendered' two years earlier) – let the Golden Age begin." Instead: "Yes, we have come a long way, but this is only a beginning and a longer road still needs to be traveled."

Box 4.4. Four Stanzas from Horace's *Carmen Saeculare*

"Gods, give good customs to a teachable youth,
gods, grant the aged tranquil peace;
to the race of Romulus grant riches and offspring
and all glory and honor.

And what the glorious scion of Anchises and Venus
entreats of you with a sacrifice of white steers,
may he obtain it, triumphant over the warring enemy,
but lenient to the fallen.

Already the Parthian fears our might on land and sea
and he fears the Alban axes.
Already the Scythians, haughty not long ago, ask for
our directives, as do the Indians.

Already Faith and Peace and Honor and time-honored
Decency and neglected Virtue dare
to return, and blessed Plenty appears
with her full horn."

Verses 45–60

These stanzas contain several of the themes underpinning the Augustan celebration of the Secular Games. A corner has been turned: the Roman *imperium* has reestablished its hegemony (a signal event was the recovery of the lost army standards from the Parthians in 20 BC). At the same time, Rome has recuperated her moral standards of old (the Augustan moral laws were enacted in 18 BC), making her a safe place again for the gods. Both events will lead to happier times, but there is still a way to go; hence the prayers to the gods for their help in the future.

The Secular Games were only the most prominent example of Augustus' revitalization of Roman religion at large by the use of both tradition and new departures. It started with the outward face of religion, that is, sanctuaries, temples, and shrines. After long decades of economic duress and civil strife they presented anything but an uplifting appearance. It is one thing for a utilitarian building to look run down, but quite another for the house of a god. Rome had always prided herself on her close association with the deities, and Rome's success was widely attributed to her respect (*religio*) for them. "You rule (*imperas*, related to *imperium*), Roman," wrote Horace, "because you keep yourself lesser than the gods: with them all things begin, to them refer each outcome" (*Odes* 3.6.5–6). In the same breath he bemoans the dilapidation of the temples. To many it signified decay in general.

In Rome, as we saw earlier, there was no separation between religion and state. The religion of the state was a civic or civil religion. It did not center on personal salvation or questions of the afterlife but supported the stability of the *res publica* and its values. It therefore was an integral part of the *res publica* and, perforce, of Augustus' restoration of the *res publica*. Hence visible rebuilding was a priority and Augustus wasted no time: in his *Res Gestae* he proudly announces the rebuilding of no fewer than 82 temples that he had already begun in 28 BC "on the authority of the senate, neglecting none that required restoration at that time" (*RG* 20.4). Many of them were far from grandiose and built of simple materials like wood or even clay. In terms of image and perception, which mattered greatly, their rebuilding was a tangible demonstration of Augustus' commitment to time-honored *religio* and respect for the gods (another aspect of *pietas*); in addition, such shrines were repositories of cultural memory. At the same time, the city, in his own words (Suet., *Aug.* 28), was transformed from brick to marble. The standard bearers of that transformation were some twelve temples, also duly mentioned in the *Res Gestae*, that were either newly built or included the renovation of prominent and large structures, like the landmark Temple of Castor and Pollux in the Roman Forum. They were sheathed with the luminescent white marble from the quarries at Carrara, discovered in 55 BC, which were to provide Michelangelo with his material and are still operating today. That kind of splendor, too, showed respect for the divine protectors of Rome and their rightful place amid the magnificence of a capital that now truly aimed, in Vitruvius' words (*Pref.* 2), at the majesty (*maiestas*) befitting a world city.

In sum, Roman religion, always an essential pillar of the commonwealth, was not only restored and restabilized by Augustus' actions, but also reformed and revitalized. That applied to priesthoods, cults, rituals, and buildings. Even Tacitus gave him credit for "accommodating certain relics of horrid antiquity to the spirit of the present" (*Annals* 4.16). Just as fundamentally, if not more, this updating involved a vast expansion of opportunities for participation, especially for non-elites. Political avenues remained limited, but participation in cults and religious associations now provided an ever-increasing civic alternative, which in turn provided status and recognition. We will look at some empire-wide examples in Chapter 7; as for the capital, the cult of the crossroad deities (*Lares Compitales*) is a paradigm.

It was a neighborhood cult. Often, these neighborhoods had been hotbeds of social unrest, especially as a large part of Rome's population, consisting of freedmen and slaves, was given no meaningful outlet to participate in the *res publica*. Political enfranchisement, of course, was out of the question. The alternative was civic enfranchisement and it was effected by the reorganization of the cult in the wake of the organization of the city into 14 regions with some 265 neighborhoods, which also had the result of making the city more knowable to all. The focal point of each neighborhood (*vicus*) was an altar of the protective deities of the main crossroads and the cult was elaborated, and it became a matter of civic pride. Its top functionaries were plebeian *vicomagistri*, aided by freedmen or slave *vicoministri* (Fig. 12). Their status paralleled that of the consuls: on the days of ritual performance, they were accompanied by a lictor and, most visibly, the list with their names was displayed in the Forum right along with that of the consuls. There was more: in addition to the Lares, the cult was dedicated to the *genius* (not meaning "genius" in the modern sense, but something like "innate spiritual essence") of Augustus and Augustus is as present on several of the surviving altars as he was in real life when he visited the neighborhoods.

Figure 12. Compital altar with four *vicomagistri* sacrificing. The lictor with his bundle of rods is shown in the background on the left. Musei Capitolini, Centrale Montemartini, inv. 855. DAI-Rom 1935.0388 (Faraglia).

Are we looking at a personality cult? To some extent, definitely. Further enhancements converged on the same result. Quite in contrast to his stated rejection of excessive and, therefore, un-republican governmental positions, he prided himself on his unprecedented membership in the four major priestly colleges and three more religious brotherhoods (see p. 78). Also, the anniversaries of many restored temples were changed to significant Augustan dates such as the conquest of Alexandria on 1 August, the month which the senate had renamed after him in 27 BC, though, typically, Augustus waited prudently with the actual implementation. He proceeded similarly with the formal assumption of the office of highest priest (*pontifex maximus*) until its absentee holder Lepidus finally died in 12 BC.

All in all, this constant cultic association was the carefully modulated counterpart to the empire-wide civic cult of Augustus that we will analyze later. But the underlying reason is the same: in contrast to ever-changing republican magistrates or an abstract constitution he provided a personal, unifying figure of continuity, stability, and identity – "the *res publica* is Caesar," as Ovid put it (*Tristia* 4.4.15). Especially in Rome and Italy, there were no colossal statues of him – Egypt, naturally, followed native traditions – as there were to be for later emperors and potentates up to our time. Augustus consummately played the role of the *civilis princeps*, maintaining dignity and his unique status – after all, he was "The Sublime" – as well as closeness to the people. In contrast to his multitasking adoptive father, the man from Velitrae thoroughly enjoyed the lowbrow entertainments that were the rage of a marginally literate populace. Suetonius devotes three entire chapters to that subject, giving example after example (*Aug.*, 43–5). As for the games in the Circus Maximus, for instance, "he watched the proceedings intently; either to avoid the bad reputation earned by Julius Caesar for reading letters or petitions, and answering them, during such performances, or just to enjoy the fun, as he frankly admitted doing." Whether dumb shows, mime performances, gladiatorial games, animal hunts, or athletic or theatrical contests – the emperor was there for all to see. Style points did not matter: "His chief delight was to watch boxing, particularly when the fighters were Italians – and not merely professional bouts, in which he often used to pit Italians against Greeks, but slogging matches between untrained toughs in narrow city alleys." His visits to the neighborhoods, then, could be more than ritualistic. He was a visible presence as a man – not necessarily of the people, but among the people – and as a man with a divine aura who would be a god one day, *praesens divus*, as Horace called him (*Odes* 3.5.2). The Greek equivalent for *praesens* in such a context was *epiphanēs*, hence epiphany.

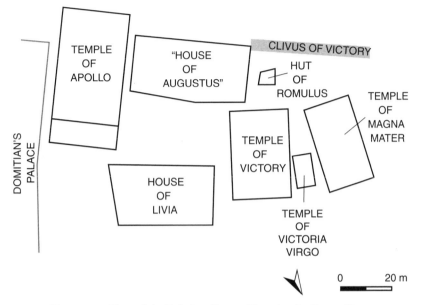

Figure 13. Plan of the Palatine, Rome. Drawing by Deena Berg.

Augustus had no intention to reach heaven the way Caesar did, but the goal was clear and he carefully cultivated that aura. Having divine patrons was part of it. His association with Apollo has sometimes been overstated in light of inventions such as Apollo being his real father. Still, on the Palatine his closeness to the god was demonstratively palpable, as Augustus' compound was connected with the newly built (28 BC) marble temple of Apollo that sent its white gleam over Rome. No less important, however, was the proximity of Augustus' residential complex to two temples of Victoria (see Fig. 13). For good reason, Victoria became the most visible deity of Augustus' reign. She and her symbols are ubiquitous in public and private art, including in utilitarian implements such as table props and lamps. After all, "peace was born of victories" and both peace and victories were ongoing. An oil lamp from Carthage (Fig. 14) is a representative specimen as it replicates the many official representations of Victoria holding the Shield of Virtues (see p. 70). They and others were busily reproduced in private art and on consumer objects and the emperor's favorite images were welcomed into the private realm without any pressure from above. Art objects and utensils displaying them simply were big sellers, and while Victory may not have had a thousand fathers, she certainly had tens, if not hundreds, of thousands of followers.

Figure 14. Terracotta lamp with figure of Victory holding Augustus' shield of virtues (*clupeus virtutis*). Musée de Carthage. Used with permission of the museum from T. Hölscher, *Victoria Romana* (1967) 13.2.

The innovative revival of religious practices, the building and rebuilding of temples, the use of religion for social policy, the resonance of religious imagery among the people – all these were phenomena of a stabilizing *res publica Augusta*. They were largely the result of Augustus' statecraft. But how religious was Augustus himself?

So far as we can tell, very. Roman religion was not just a matter of cult, but emanations of the divine were to be found anywhere, including as omens and other premonitory signs. As Suetonius reports, Augustus regarded them as "absolute certainties" and considered occurrences which we might consider trivial or accidental today as prodigies (see Box 4.5). Phenomena like thunder and lightning also instilled *religio*, awe. In this respect and others, Augustus evinced the sensibilities of someone who had lived in small-town Italy and its countryside. So far from being a mere filling station for basic material needs, the Roman house had always been a locus of the family religion. It was typical of the Roman house, too, that its private and public functions interacted. And it was typical of Augustus that he moved this conjunction to a new level. The worship of Vesta, the goddess of the hearth, was integral to family observances almost on a daily basis. When Augustus became *pontifex maximus*, he did not relocate to the priestly residence in the Forum, next to the Temple of Vesta. Instead, he remained on the Palatine and converted a part of his residence to house a shrine to Vesta. What was public here and what was private? In essence, that is the answer to our question about Augustus' private religiosity: public and private were inseparable. He was a very religious man in both realms.

Box 4.5. Augustus' Superstitions

"Augustus had absolute faith in certain premonitory signs: considering it bad luck to thrust his right foot into his left shoe as he got out bed, but good luck to start a long journey or voyage during a drizzle of rain, which would ensure success and a speedy return. Prodigies made a particularly strong impression on him. Once, when a palm tree pushed its way between the paving stones in front of his house, he had it transplanted to the inner court beside his family gods, and lavished care on it. When he visited Capri, the drooping branches of a moribund old oak suddenly regained their vigor, which so delighted him that he arranged to buy the island from the city of Naples in exchange for Aenaria. He also had a superstition against starting a journey on the day after a market day, or undertaking any important task on the Nones [the seventh or ninth day] of a month – although, in this case, as he explained to Tiberius in a letter, it was merely the unlucky 'non' sound that affected him."

Suetonius, *Aug.* 92, trans. R. Graves

Succeeding Augustus

One other central issue required his adroitness. That was the question of a possible successor. It would, of course, not have been a question if the Augustan *res publica* had indeed been a full return to the Republic (with a capital "R") because there were, after all, two duly elected consuls every year. Such a scenario, however, would have entailed a return to republican discontinuity of leadership and lack of long-term planning. Hence Augustus' balancing act. On the one hand, he was motivated by the responsibility, and not simply authoritarian urgings, to continue with a sense of direction and to provide stability and, therefore, not to surrender the enterprise of the state to short-term leadership, however experienced. On the other hand, he wanted to avoid, so far as that was possible, even the impression of seeking to establish a hereditary dynasty. And, true enough, there never was a declaration to that effect. Nor, as time went on, did there need to be one. The boundaries between republic and principate were far less distinct to Augustus' contemporaries than they are to us today in the bright light of retrospect. Everybody knew, however, or at least could sense that things were changing, with the result, in Augustus' own words, of a new state (*novus status*) of affairs. The principal challenge, as always, was how to articulate that change.

In this instance, and quite in contrast to the marriage legislation, Augustus chose to leave much unsaid. Critics might consider this dissimulation, but most people at the time probably appreciated the ambiguity and indirectness. Caesar was reputed to have loudly proclaimed that the Republic was a dead body, only to become one himself. We can be sure that most contemporaries knew what Augustus' aims were but appreciated his tactful restraint of not being explicit. When he was close to death in 23 BC, as we have seen, he engaged in the perfect balancing act: he handed over some of the responsibility to a consul, who was an elder statesman, and other tasks to Agrippa, who was his right-hand man but had not yet married into Augustus' family. That was, of course, just four years after his beginnings as Augustus. The important point is that, contrary to much expectation, then, Augustus in 23 did not choose the dynastic route by designating his young nephew Marcellus as his heir. At the same time, the considerable degree of speculation about Marcellus indicates that people early on were expecting a hereditary principate and, as time went on, any decision by Augustus to move in that direction would hardly elicit surprise or opprobrium. And move he did, even if not by official proclamation. In due course, Agrippa received substantial special powers parallel to Augustus' own, as did Tiberius later. The criteria were competence and proven experience rather than cronyism, and that certainly helped smooth the way to acceptance. A contributory factor was the general desire to maintain the obvious stability the new system was providing for all.

Another, more tragic factor, was the untimely death of Augustus' two grandsons, Gaius and Lucius, at the ages, respectively, of twenty-three and nineteen. He absolutely doted on them (I will discuss Augustus' relations with his family in the next chapter) and gave them preferential public roles even while they were still in their teens. What would have happened if one or both had survived? Would Augustus have waited until they acquired as impressive a résumé as that of Tiberius? Would there have been major, if any, objections to their designation as successors despite their relative lack of experience? That was unlikely, at least for Augustus – who, after all, had been only eighteen at Caesar's death – as he mentions them specifically in the preamble to his will almost as his first choice: "Since cruel fortune has deprived me of my grandsons Gaius and Lucius, Tiberius shall be my heir" (Suetonius, *Tiberius* 23); obviously, the intent of the sentiment, however honest in expressing a grandfather's grief, was not designed to bolster Tiberius' self-esteem. No matter: when Tiberius was announced as Augustus' heir in the will, there was no question in anyone's mind that this meant political succession, too. There had been such questions when Caesar named Octavian. But this was fifty-eight years later and the senate promptly declared Tiberius as the second *princeps*. The total lack of any attendant controversy was a testament, in its own way, to the psychological skill with which Augustus had handled the issue of the continuation of the principate.

His ongoing effort in this regard is a salutary reminder, too, that activity and initiatives never ceased throughout his reign. Naturally, the heady mood of renewal that characterized the early years did not last for decades, but challenges – including many that Augustus deliberately sought – continued and the atmosphere even of the last decade was not simply one of torpor or dominated by personal reverses like the death of the grandsons and the exile of the Julias (see next chapter). Augustus continued to provide both programmatic substance and leadership skills of the kind we have discussed in this chapter. He was an agent of change in both meanings of that phrase: he took control of changes that were already under way and, at the same time, he initiated change. The *res publica* was not only restored but also transformed.

5

AUGUSTUS AT HOME
Friends and Family

"As Augustus' public fortune had been successful, so that of his household was unfortunate," intones Tacitus in his account of the recall from exile, under Tiberius, of Decimus Silanus, one of lovers of the younger Julia, Augustus' granddaughter (*Ann.* 3.24.3). Both ancient writers and modern academics are fond of such dichotomies and there is certainly some truth to Tacitus' statement. Its stark absolutes, however, need to be given more contours; we have seen, for instance, that even Augustus' public life was not a simple sequence of benign Fortune smiling on him, but a continuing series of challenges, tests, and ongoing exertions. The physical setting of this chapter, Augustus' house (not to be identified with the current "House of Augustus" on display), itself provides an appropriate perspective: the Roman upper-class house combined public and private functions. That is all the truer of Augustus' residence because, as we have seen, it incorporated the public cult of Vesta and her shrine.

We can connect this theme with the truism that our greatest strengths often are also our greatest liabilities. While Augustus' unrelenting persistence had much to do with his success in public life, it also shattered the fortunes – emotional, psychological, and physical – of some of his closest family members. Pursuit of happiness for them was not Augustus' objective. Instead, they were shuffled around as pawns in a dynastic game that took its toll on them and him. Amid all this, life went on with its usual contradictions: our sources stress Augustus' penchant for wit, humor, and hilarity – Macrobius offers a Top Eighteen list (*Sat.* 2.4) – while, at the same time, family members were torn asunder and some of them rotted in dismal exile, being deprived of human contact and more. Not all, of course: he was close to others and they were close to him. Here, Fate could cast its dark shadows as several of them died at an early age. Welcome, then, to the private world of Augustus, which was inextricably intertwined with his public one.

LIVIA: WIFE AND CONSIGLIERE

To start on a positive note: Livia Drusilla, the not quite twenty-year-old who was pregnant with her husband's child and whom Octavian could not wait to marry (see p. 41), became his mainstay throughout his life. Infatuation changed into trust and a long-lived partnership. On his death-bed, his last words to her were: "Livia, live on remembering our marriage and be well!" (Suet. *Aug.* 99). The sentiment reflects their strong and enduring relationship. As we saw earlier, she had been tested by considerable hardships and upheavals before linking up with Octavian and she stood by him through more of the same in the violent decade of the 30s BC. We know that throughout his life he turned to her for advice, and quite systematically so: he often wrote out memos – none have survived – in preparation for their discussions of weighty matters, just as he would when consulting with other important advisers. Her capacity as a true helpmeet made up for their disappointment in not having children. Livia did get pregnant early in their marriage, but the infant daughter was still-born. Both she and Augustus, of course, had offspring from their previous marriages and many of our sources are consumed with the resulting issues, as we shall see throughout this chapter.

The real emphasis deserves to be placed elsewhere. Upon Octavian's ascension to Augustus, she became Rome's first First Lady (Fig. 15); in fact, a Roman author, who addressed a (rather long) poem of consolation to her after the death of her son Drusus, calls her just that: *Romana princeps* (*Consolatio ad Liviam* 356). It was an experiment, just like the principate. Just as there was no precedent for Augustus' role, so was there no precedent for hers. And just as Augustus shaped his role successfully, so did she proceed with shaping hers. In her case, that meant deliberate public restraint. Again, the parallel holds: Augustus, too, took pains to deemphasize the pomp and circumstance of a monarchic appearance and instead styled himself as *princeps*. Still, his public role and image were ubiquitous whereas Livia kept herself in the background. She did not appear on coins in Rome nor in her husband's *Res Gestae*, and her sculptural presence in Rome did not remotely match Augustus'. Instead, the instances where she was given profile were targeted carefully. Only one year after the senate bestowed inviolability (*sacrosanctitas*) on Octavian in 36 BC, Livia (together with Augustus' sister Octavia) was granted the same extraordinary privilege along with exemption from the standard legal requirement for women to have a legal guardian (*tutor*). They also were given the right, unprecedented for living women, to have statuary, which, as can be seen, did not lead to excess (Dio 49.15.1). Instead of quantity, the focus was on

Figure 15. Sardonyx cameo with portrait of Livia, ca. 20 BC. One of Livia's finest extant portraits, it features exceptional details, such as the double braid on top of her head and the silky texture of her hair. Gems of this type were collector's items rather than mass-produced. Geldmuseum, Utrecht.

quality: not only is Livia represented, with other family members, on the quintessential emblem of the Pax Augusta, the Augustan Altar of Peace (see Fig. 20) but its dedication and anniversary date coincided with her birthday, January 30. In the provinces it was different. Especially in the Greek east, where paying homage to royal couples had been standard procedure, there developed a plethora of honorific inscriptions along with prominent statuary, and Augustus put her image on his coins in Egypt.

What was Livia's actual role in decision-making? Again, discretion prevailed and while it is clear that she had such a role, our sources have to be content with being able to cite only a few bona fide instances aside from scandalmongering. The instances include pleas for special status for the inhabitants of Samos, for granting a Gaul citizenship, and for recalling Tiberius from Rhodes. Augustus acceded to some with modifications and rejected others. Further, Livia, who often accompanied Augustus on his travels while keeping a typically low profile, developed a network of friends around the Mediterranean. It included Salome – not *the* Salome, but the sister of Herod the Great to whom she gave some dynastic marriage counseling. Livia, in short, clearly was a woman of substance and influence and Augustus respected her judgment. However, it is precisely because most of her daily interactions with Augustus cannot be documented that Tacitus sweepingly characterizes her as dominating her husband. The actual picture is more telling: Augustus – and we assume she, too – strove to portray any such give and take of advice as taking place within the domestic sphere and not encroaching on institutional territory. Livia was a trusted confidante, but not part of the imperial org chart.

For lack of precise information on this important role of hers, some of our major sources, Tacitus and Suetonius in particular, compensate with an orgy of lurid details about the wicked stepmother on the Palatine. It was an easy picture to paint because Greco-Roman literature is replete with the clichéd portrayal of the evil proclivities of stepmothers. It entered even into the realm of metaphor; witness the tragedian Aeschylus' pronouncement that a reef was "a stepmother to ships." There really was not much else to do for a writer who was looking to captivate an audience with Livia's deeds. Sexual escapades were not an option because her marital behavior was unexceptionable; unlike her stepdaughter Julia, she was the living embodiment of the traditional wifely virtue of *pudicitia*. The resulting stories, therefore, center on her maneuvering to promote her sons, Tiberius and Drusus, and her adversarial relations with Augustus' kin. Whenever any of the Julian males – whether the nephew Marcellus or the grandsons Gaius and Lucius – emerged as pretenders to the throne, Livia the poisoner would spring into action. Never mind that Gaius died far away in the east on a military expedition – Livia's long arms would reach even there. Similarly, Livia was said to have hastened Augustus' death by feeding him some poisoned figs and then to have falsified his will. Further, she promptly conspired to have Augustus' remaining grandson, Agrippa Postumus (so named because he was born after his father's death), executed by the guards on the island to which he had been exiled. All this to make sure that her own son Tiberius would be the unchallenged successor.

What was these writers' motive – rivetingly translated into the TV series *I Claudius* – for this denigration of Livia (and I heartily invite the reader to turn to them for the full treatment)? Besides the stepmother complex, which was more of a means to the end, it was simply the palpable unease of Roman aristocratic males at the prospect and, yet more, the presence of a powerful woman. Hence, too, the tirades against Cleopatra, one of Caesar's and Augustus' most gifted contemporaries, whose impact on Rome, as Diana Kleiner has shown, was substantial in many ways; for that matter, Livia and Cleopatra even wore the same hairstyle. A somewhat different compensatory strategy had to be pursued for her *pudicitia*: Livia became a willing and eager procuress for her husband. These were, it seems, one-siesta stands – young virgins preferred, as the always-helpful Suetonius points out (*Aug.* 71).

There are some more realistic glimpses of her life. As the female head of the Palatine household and compound, she was involved with a large number of family members and others living there, from relatives to Antony's offspring and children of Near Eastern rulers, who were provided with a free education while serving as insurance against their fathers' potential lack of loyalty to Rome. An expression of more than loyalty was the choice of Drusus' widow, Antonia, to live with her mother-in-law rather than marry again; this information, typically, comes from a source other than Tacitus or Suetonius (Valerius Maximus, 4.3.3). Antonia's son Claudius, the future emperor, suffered from some grotesque and embarrassing disabilities, but even Suetonius singles out Livia's special care for him. And she gave material support to the younger Julia, her husband's granddaughter, in her exile, although Tacitus again depicts this as part of her scheming. As for the operation of the household (*domus*), we have unembroidered and yet fascinating evidence from inscriptions relating to her staff of several hundred. Besides accountants, seamstresses, carpenters, and shoemakers, they included a sizeable medical staff, supervised by a *supra medicus*. Livia was unusually obsessed with her health (but then she lived to the exceptionally old age of 86) and there are even two medical recipes ascribed to her, one for sore throat and the other, probably much in demand, for nervous tension (see Box 5.1). The real surprise, however, is the number of artisans on her staff who specialized in luxury items: a goldsmith, a pearl setter, and a *colorator* (probably for furniture) among them. Augustus took pains to project, quite literally, an image of homespun simplicity: "Except for special occasions he purposely wore common clothes for the house that were made by his sister, wife, daughter, or granddaughters," and his furniture was such that most of it "would hardly be considered the mark of private elegance" (Suet., *Aug.* 73). Obviously, greater variety prevailed in the *domus Palatina*.

Box 5.1. Livia's Prescription for Nervous Tension

"Salve for chills, tiredness and nervous pain and tension, which when applied in winter prevents any part of the limbs from being chilled. Livia Augusta used this:

Ingredients:
1 sextarius of marjoram

1 sextarius of rosemary
1 lb of fenugreek
1 congium* of Falernian wine
5 lbs of Venafrian oil

"Apart from the oil one should steep all the ingredients in the wine for three days, then on the fourth day mix in the oil and cook the medicine on a moderate coal, until the wine vanishes, and the next stage is to strain through two layers of linen and to add half a pound of Pontic wax while the oil is warm. The medicine is stored in a clay or tin vessel. It is effective when rubbed gently into all the limbs."

Because of her interest in such medicines, it was not hard to defame Livia as a poisoner.

* Congium is a liquid measure (about 3 quarts); one sixth of its dry equivalent is a sextarius.

Source: Marcellus Burdigalensis, *De Medicamentis* 35.6,
ed. M. Niedermann, trans. J. Kollesch and D. Niebel,
Corpus Medicorum Latinorum 5 (Berlin 1968)

Unsurprisingly, then, Livia has many dimensions. She was a major force in Augustus' life, but fuller knowledge about her personality and activities eludes us. Quite probably, she would hardly object.

AGRIPPA: RIGHT-HAND MAN AND VICEROY

No one contributed more to Octavian/Augustus' success than Marcus Vipsanius Agrippa. Their friendship started when they were both in their youth: we find Agrippa at Octavian's side at Apollonia when the news of Caesar's assassination reached him. The rest is history: Agrippa the victorious strategist at Naulochus and Actium; Agrippa consul with Augustus in the key years of 28 and 27 BC; Agrippa in charge of military and administrative operations in the east and the west; Agrippa receiving virtually the same powers of *imperium* as Augustus in 18 BC; and, last but not least, Agrippa fathering five children with Julia, the emperor's sole daughter. He died, quite unexpectedly, in 12 BC. Augustus' grief was immense. He held the funeral oration (see Box 5.2) and had him buried in his mausoleum on the Campus Martius (see Map 2), which had been the site of many of Agrippa's building activities.

BOX 5.2. FRAGMENT FROM AUGUSTUS' FUNERAL ORATION FOR AGRIPPA

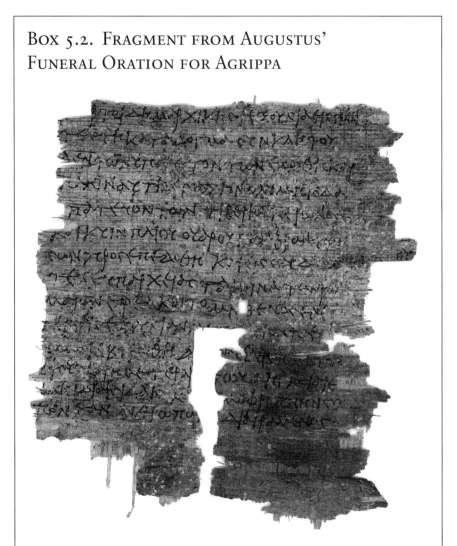

Figure 16. Papyrus Köln 249. Photograph courtesy Papyrological Collection, University of Cologne.

"The tribunician power was granted you for a period of five years by decree of the senate in the consulship of the two Lentuli, and it was granted you again, for another quinquennium, in the consulship of Tiberius Nero and Quinctilius Varus, your sons-in-law. Moreover, it was ratified by law that no one, in any of the provinces into which the public affairs of the Roman people should call you, would have greater *imperium* than you. You were raised to the highest position with our support and through your own virtues by the agreement of all men."

Source: A fragment from a papyrus (P. Koeln 249).
The text is a Greek translation from the Latin original –
the challenge is to reconstruct that original phrasing
and, especially, its terminology of Agrippa's powers.

Yet, and even more so than in Livia's case, much information about Agrippa is lacking. It begins with his birth and family: we do not know his exact birth date – he was born in 64 or 63 BC – nor where the Vipsanii came from. They were not, as we saw earlier, members of the Roman nobility, and, therefore, these aristocrats always looked down their noses at him. What irritated them even more is that he paid no attention to their snobbery, as his abilities and accomplishments easily eclipsed theirs. Julius Caesar had begun the process of selecting trusted operatives, on the basis of ability, from nonnoble backgrounds. Gaius Oppius and Lucius Cornelius Balbus, a Spaniard who acquired Roman citizenship, took care of business in Rome during his many absences and became important advisers to Octavian (see p. 26). To an even greater degree, Agrippa embodied the rise of the expert, which was the central phenomenon of Rome's "cultural revolution" that ended the nobility's traditional monopolies (see pp. 81–2). What the aristocrats found even harder to swallow was that this was not a paradigm shift in the power of knowledge (of the use of Latin or the calendar, for example) but of executive power. As in his own case, Augustus did not need to validate the flow of Agrippa's power through traditional channels like the consulship, which Agrippa did not hold again after 27 BC. Let nobles hold those yearly offices and others they coveted; Agrippa was in it for the long haul, so he kept building his record and, as a result, became Augustus' co-regent.

Velleius' and Dio's thumbnail characterizations of the man are what one would largely expect (Box 5.3). He had Octavian/Augustus' absolute trust. When Agrippa's house burned down – a very common occurrence in Rome – Augustus had him stay at his own house while Agrippa was building another residence. Augustus never had to fear that Agrippa would be a rival because Agrippa's nonaristocratic background served as enough of a brake. Significantly, therefore, when he was close to death in 23 BC,

Augustus handed control over his private affairs to Agrippa but handed the oversight of his public functions to the consul Piso. Had the situation recurred a few years later, when both had been granted equal powers by the senate – and we should not forget that these powers, proconsular *imperium* and tribunician power, had to be renewed periodically by the senate – Agrippa might have deferred to Tiberius; we will never know.

Box 5.3. Agrippa's Qualities

Velleius (2.79.1):

"He was a man of the noblest excellence (*nobilissimae virtutis*), unconquered (*invictus*) by toil, loss of sleep, and danger. He was well disciplined in obedience, but to one man alone, yet quite eager to command others. In whatever he did, he knew no such thing as delay, but with him action went hand in hand with deciding on a plan."

Dio (54.29):

"Such was the end of Agrippa, who had shown himself the noblest of the men of his day and had used the friendship with Augustus with a view to the greatest advantage both of the emperor himself and of the commonwealth. For the more he surpassed others in excellence, the more inferior he kept himself of his own free will to the emperor; and while he devoted all the wisdom and valor he possessed to the highest interests of Augustus, he lavished all the honor and influence he received from him upon benefactions to others. It was because of this in particular that he never became obnoxious to Augustus himself nor invidious to his fellow-citizens; on the contrary, he helped Augustus to establish the monarchy, as if he were really a devoted adherent of the principle of autocratic rule, and he won over the people by his benefactions, as if he were in the highest degree a friend of popular government. At any rate, even at his death he left them gardens and the baths named after him, so that they might bathe free of cost, and for this purpose gave Augustus certain estates. And the emperor not only turned these over to the people, but distributed to the populace four hundred sesterces apiece, making it understood that Agrippa had

---

so ordered.... Augustus felt his loss for a long time and hence caused him to be honored in the eyes of the people.... The death of Agrippa, far from being a merely private loss to his own household, was at any rate such a public loss to all Romans that portents occurred on this occasion in such numbers as usually happens to them before the greatest calamities."

Loeb Classical Library translation, with modifications

Dio then goes on to mention owls flitting about, lightning strikes, a comet, and more.

Agrippa's abilities were, and are, unquestioned. Where he acquired the knowledge to build and train Octavian's fleet in a thoroughly innovative way we again do not know. As can be seen, therefore, both Dio and Velleius emphasize that Agrippa's real nobility lay in his ability and accomplishments. The word Dio uses, *aristos*, could connote both excellent pedigree (hence "aristocracy") and excellence of deeds, which is reinforced by *aretē* in the next sentence. The Latin equivalent of *aretē* is *virtus* (literally, "a man's excellence," though Romans used it for women, too). Pointedly, then, Velleius characterizes Agrippa as a man "of most noble excellence." The echoes reach back into the late republic when the so-called new men, such as Cicero and Octavian's father, started working their way into the senate and challenged its traditional aristocracy on the basis of nobility of *virtus*. Alas, many of them did not live up to that claim, but Agrippa was the real thing and more. And since he came from an untraditional background, he could do what a Roman noble would never have done: descend from the pinnacle of the consulship, which he held for the first time in 37 BC, to the much lower office of aedile. An aedile (the word is derived from *aedes*, i.e., "building") in Rome was in charge primarily of public works and order, games, and the water supply. At Octavian's behest, Agrippa took on the job with relish in 33 BC. It was the beginning phase of the showdown against Antony and, as we have seen, a time of great deprivation and unrest in Italy. It was simply imperative that the urban populace be kept happy, no matter what it took. Agrippa energetically fixed up the tottering infrastructure, including the restoration of Rome's big sewer, the Cloaca Maxima, to functionality. To celebrate that achievement, he proudly sailed on its channel to where it flowed into the Tiber (Pliny, *Nat. Hist.* 36.105). To win hearts, minds, and bodies, he sponsored lavish games, paid for free haircuts, and distributed free olive oil and salt. With the home front secure,

Agrippa the aedile once more became Agrippa the admiral whose superior skills prevailed at Actium. Fittingly for this innovative man, he had been given an innovative emblem, the naval crown of ships' beaks, after his victory at Naulochus (see Box 2.3). Along with his subsequent engagements across the reach of empire, his building activity in Rome continued and was instrumental in reshaping the city (see Chapter 6); the Pantheon still bears his inscription (Fig. 17, Box 5.4).

Box 5.4. The Pantheon

Figure 17. The Pantheon, Rome. Photograph by Canali Photobank, Milan, Italy.

The original building was built by Agrippa as part of his master plan for the Campus Martius. It was very different from the present building, whose construction began during the time of Hadrian (AD 117–138) or, as scholars have claimed more recently, under Trajan (AD 98–117). Its dome, one of the marvels of Roman construction and inspiration for St. Peter's, was not part of Agrippa's building. Here is Dio's account (53.27.1–4); he also comments on its name:

"Meanwhile Agrippa beautified the city at his own expense.... He also completed the building called the Pantheon. It has this name perhaps because it received among the images that decorated it the statues of many gods, including Mars and Venus; but my own opinion of the name is, that because of its vaulted roof, it resembles the heavens. Agrippa, for his part, wished to place a statue of Augustus there also and to have the structure named after him. But when the emperor would not accept either honor, he placed in the temple itself a statue of Julius Caesar and in the anteroom statues of Augustus and himself. This was done, not out of any rivalry or ambition on Agrippa's part to make himself equal to Augustus, but from his hearty loyalty to him and his constant zeal for the public good; hence Augustus, so far from censuring him for it, honored him all the more."

It is interesting to see Augustan memory-management at work in the presentation of Agrippa for posterity. Which of his many *res gestae* should be highlighted? Which were to predominate for the creation of his image? There was much to choose from, including his high-level diplomatic and personal relations with potentates such as Herod the Great. He immortalized himself by constructing a map of the world that was exhibited in the Porticus Vipsania, built by his sister. As can be seen, however, from several later writers, including Velleius and Dio, the emphasis is on Agrippa as a man of the people. His "ignoble" (Tacitus) and unknown background – blue collar rather than blueblood – was turned to his advantage: here is Agrippa, the benefactor of the people. As the people's friend, he advocates democracy versus Maecenas' espousal of monarchy in Dio's fictional debate of Octavian's counselors (Book 52; cf. Box 3.2). And he insists that private art collections should be accessible to all instead of being kept "in the exile of villas" (Pliny, *Nat. Hist.* 35.26). Of all those who emerged successfully from the civil wars, Agrippa was the only one, claims the younger Seneca, who was "happy only for the public good" (*Letters* 15.94.46).

Neither does it hurt that image to learn that Pliny the Elder characterized him as a man who had "country rather than sophisticated tastes" (*Nat. Hist.* 35.26).

Clearly, there was a lot more to Agrippa. But like Livia, he never tried to eclipse the principal player. He may have been born with his feet first – that is one conjectured meaning of "Agrippa" – but the head surely followed.

Julia: Chattel and Rebel

Julia's behavior was different. A biographer of Livia has aptly observed that "Livia was in a sense everything that Julia was not" (Barrett, 50) and it is easy to reverse the equation. For good reason: Julia was the only offspring of the *princeps* and she knew it. That status, however, cut both ways. On the one hand, she cherished the privileges it afforded; witness her response to "a serious friend" (*gravem amicum*) whom Augustus sent to impress upon her the simple lifestyle of her father: "He forgets that he is Caesar, but I remember that I am Caesar's daughter" (Macrobius, *Sat.* 2.5.8). The other side was that Augustus used her as his premier dynastic instrument and her marriages were made not in heaven but by him. While such arrangements were not atypical of Rome's aristocratic class (and, of course, monarchies throughout history), Augustus' ruthless modus operandi goes a long way towards explaining Julia's rebelliousness, which ultimately got her exiled. Despite repeated pleas from many sides, her unforgiving father never recalled her. He had two difficult daughters, he kept saying: the *res publica* and Julia (Macrobius, *Sat.* 2.5.4). Both certainly were high maintenance.

Julia, we may recall, was the daughter of Scribonia whom Octavian divorced immediately after Julia was born in 40 BC. As usual, nothing is known about her early childhood. It seems likely that she lived in her father's Palatine complex after turning five; there were, as we have seen, plenty of other children there, including her cousin Marcellus and stepbrothers Tiberius and Drusus. She took to the good education she received there, and Macrobius singles out her love of literature and *eruditio*. There was no fierceness in her character, he continues, but a kind *humanitas* – no surprise that she was very popular (*Sat.* 2.5.2). Anecdotes are plentiful about the difference between her and Livia's lifestyle and, in particular, her love of fashion, and she was always ready with a witty answer (see Box 5.5). Nor does it seem to have been impossible for her to slip away from the Palatine to go into the city or attend shows. On those occasions she was noted for her entourage of lively young people.

> ## Box 5.5. Julia's Repartee to Her Father and Stepmother
>
> "She presented herself to Augustus in a rather daring dress. It offended his eyes, but he kept silent. The following day, she changed her outfit to something more severe and embraced her father, who was happy to see her that way. He, who had controlled his grief the day before, was unable to control his joy and said: 'This way to dress is so much more fitting for the daughter of Augustus!' She was not lacking for a defense: 'Today I dressed up for the eyes of my father; yesterday, for those of my husband.'
>
> "Also known is this example of her quick wit. When Livia and Julia attended gladiatorial games, the spectators were struck by the dissimilarity between their two entourages. Livia had surrounded herself with serious-looking men whereas Julia was sitting amidst a group of young and chic people. Her father admonished her in a letter about the difference between the two leading (*principes*) women. She elegantly wrote back: 'These, too, will become old folks with me.'"
>
> Macrobius, Saturnalia 2.5–6

Roman women married early – we need to keep in mind that the average life expectancy was around 35 years (see Box 1.2) – and Julia was married to Marcellus, the son of Augustus' sister Octavia, in 25 or 24 BC. Their union was squarely intended to consolidate the Julian line. Fate did not cooperate, as Marcellus died in 23. Vergil set a monument to him by concluding his parade of future Romans in *Aeneid* 6 with Marcellus' untimely death (860–86) as another powerful reminder that Rome's destiny included not only achievement and success, but also loss and sorrow. When Vergil recited these verses to Augustus' family, their effect was such that Octavia fainted. In contrast to the accounts of her ongoing grief, we hear nothing about Julia's reaction.

Augustus chose her next husband. It was none other than Agrippa. In one of the enlivening twists that were seemingly endemic to Augustan weddings – remember Livia's ex-husband giving her, who was pregnant with his child, away to Octavian (see p. 41) – Agrippa had actually presided over Marcellus' and Julia's ceremony because of Augustus' absence in Spain. Further, Agrippa was already married – to Marcella, Marcellus' sister, but

Figure 18. *Denarius* with portraits of Julia with Gaius and Lucius Caesar. Rome mint, 13 BC. New York, American Numismatic Society, ex Richard Hoe Lawrence Collection. Photo: American Numismatic Society, New York, 1937.158.390.

the divorce was obtained smoothly and, apparently, without any rancor from the still grieving Octavia. The marriage, which took place in 21 BC, lasted until Agrippa's death nine years later. Despite Agrippa's many absences from Rome – it is never spelled out how often Livia and Julia accompanied their husbands abroad, although at least one visit of Julia to the east is attested – the union produced the desired result, namely three boys and two girls. It was reassuring to see that they all bore some likeness to their father; in response to curious inquiries, Julia quipped that she was not taking on any customers unless the cargo hold was already full. As so often in Rome, the age difference between the two spouses was neither uncommon nor problematic. An ancient house, found under the Renaissance Villa Farnesina by the Tiber in Rome and identified today as Agrippa and Julia's, is an example of elegant taste at its best. Its wall paintings reveal considerable sophistication and point up the contingent nature of Pliny's comments on Agrippa's rusticity. Augustus doted especially on the two oldest boys, Gaius (born 20 BC) and Lucius (17 BC). As he sometimes would, he broke with tradition by adopting them when they were mere infants. In 13 BC, their likenesses were placed on a denarius, with Julia's in the middle (Fig. 18). Livia, by contrast, never was so singled out, as we have already noted.

The real turning point in Julia's life came after Agrippa's death. We saw earlier that Augustus carefully avoided proclaiming a dynasty, but clearly, dynastic succession was a priority and most Romans by that time would have expected it. The loss of Agrippa was critical and the grandsons were still too young. Hence the rush to have Tiberius fill the gap and become part of the Julian family. Julia's own wishes were not a factor nor were those of Tiberius, who happened to be married most happily, in this marriage carousel among friends and relatives, to the eldest daughter of Agrippa, Vipsania Agrippina. He was forced to divorce her and his distress was palpable.

I will discuss Tiberius shortly; suffice it to say that he was not quite the bundle of negatives – moroseness, diffidence, and perversion being most prominent – as which especially Tacitus and Suetonius packaged him for posterity. But temperamentally, he and the free-spirited Julia were far apart indeed. They tried to put up a good face and soon had a son together, but, as so many Roman children, he died soon after his birth. Then, in 9 BC, came the death of Tiberius' brother Drusus to whom Tiberius had been very close. The frequent military campaigns and absences of Tiberius took their toll, too, and Suetonius reports that the couple kept sleeping apart. The final break came in 6 BC when Tiberius had a major falling out with Augustus, resigned from all his offices and moved to Rhodes, where he stayed for seven years (see below). Julia remained in Rome. Unlike her aunt Octavia, however, who had moved to the Palatine *domus* with her children after Antony left her for Cleopatra, Julia was not ready for a celibate life. It is here, of course, that our sources have a field day and equip her with a fantastic sex life.

The usual perspectives are present here. In the case of a man, philandering was taken as a sign that he still had a pulse, and such stories are a staple of the writing about prominent Roman males, including Augustus. Besides Livia's gratifying her husband's lechery with young girls, scenarios (all provided by Suetonius, who admits that some of these stories came from Antony's camp) for the young Octavian in particular include his sleeping with his enemies' wives for purposes of reconnaissance and hustling a consul's wife from the dining room to the bedroom in that consul's very house (Suet., *Aug.* 69). Now, there is no reason to assume that Augustus was strictly monogamous, even after his early years, but, as a wise Oxford scholar (and lifelong bachelor) has put it, "If the fetid indelicacy of Roman imagination could think of no greater scandals than these with which to tax him, it may be safely assumed that ... he was a reasonably moral man" (Balsdon 1962, 68–9).

Different standards applied to Julia, as they did to Roman women in general. Her sexual activity outside of a nonexisting marriage – and Augustus wanted for her and Tiberius to stay in that marriage – was sensationalized as the epitome of promiscuity. Understandably, Julia had lovers, without perforce degenerating into a nymphomaniac. As in the case of Augustus' adulteries, we need to factor in routine exaggeration. Instead of a helpless consul's bedroom, for instance, we are presented with the speaker's platform (the Rostra) in the Roman Forum as a locus for Julia's nightly cavorting. And contrary to lurid descriptions that she was taking on all comers, it is reasonably clear that most of her lovers were members of her entourage of aristocratic peers.

That, in turn, has led to speculation that politics was involved, too. Some of the accounts mention that she and her companions congregated daily (or nightly) in the Forum by the statue of Marsyas. He was a satyr who had been skinned by Apollo and his statue, for various imaginative reasons, had become a symbol of popular liberty. Julia is even said to have crowned that statue. Was this a political gesture aimed at bringing back the old-time *libertas* of the Republic and defying the man who cultivated a special bond with Apollo, including a splendid temple to the god in his domain on the Palatine? One has to be careful here: rebellious gesture, yes; political program, no, unless in the limited sense of a return to the competitive cronyism that had been the hallmark of the republican nobility and a major reason for its failure. Yet, one of the paramours was a son of Antony, Jullus Antonius, and the liaison smacked uncomfortably of Antony's revenge. Little surprise, then, that some of our sources go so far as to claim that Julia plotted parricide. In any event, she was not a poster child for her father's legislation on morals and marriage.

The event – a thunderclap, really – that provides much of the basis for ancient and modern speculations was Augustus' impetuous and horrendously public decision, in 2 BC, to ban Julia from Rome forthwith. In tones that he regretted later – "none of this would have happened to me, if either Agrippa or Maecenas had been living" (Seneca, *Ben.* 6.32) – he scathingly denounced Julia to the senate. The writ, delivered by a quaestor, included a list of her lovers and the public venues of her nightly debaucheries. He did not grant her a trial but summarily condemned her to exile, first on the island of Pandateria and, some five years later, near Rhegium in the far south of Italy. Her mother Scribonia accompanied her voluntarily. Jullus committed suicide, other lovers were exiled, and the absent Tiberius was granted a divorce.

The conditions of Julia's exile went from harsh to manageable to dreadful. On Pandateria, she lived in solitary confinement without visitors or other contacts aside from Scribonia; Augustus even denied her wine and good food. In Rhegium, things were better: she was allowed to go into the city and socialize, and Augustus granted her an allowance. When her ex-husband succeeded Augustus, all this changed radically. She became a prisoner in her house, was forbidden access even to her mother, and quickly starved to death. This occurred within weeks of Augustus' own death.

Tiberius: Competent and Taken for Granted

Unsurprisingly, actions like his treatment of Julia have cast a long, dark shadow over Tiberius. Much of it comes from his behavior during his twenty-three-year reign during which our major sources portray him as diffident, embittered, sexually perverted, and remote in more ways than one – he withdrew to Capri for his final thirteen years. This is not the place to discuss those vicissitudes. Rather, we need to focus on his career under Augustus and the relations between the two.

Suetonius has it right when he summarily states that "his childhood and youth were beset by hardships and difficulties" (*Tiberius* 6). The reference is to Livia and her first husband being on the run from Octavian (see p. 41), and the 30s, for obvious reasons, were anything but a blessed time for a child to grow up (Tiberius was born in 42), even for a stepson of Octavian. The usual scant data follow: a funeral oration for his father in 33 and in 29, his participation in the splendid triumph of his stepfather: he rode the left trace-horse of the triumphal chariot whereas Marcellus, Octavia's son and therefore a member of the Julian family, rode the right. The triumph was one of Rome's greatest spectacles and it must have been a heady occasion for a twelve-year-old. There followed some routine tasks that elevated his profile, such as presiding over games in the city, and others that were not routine – reorganizing the grain supply, for instance, which was a perennial headache. Mainly, however, Tiberius from an early age started carving out a military career for himself that would make him, after Agrippa's death, Rome's premier general and all the more so after the death of his brother Drusus, which hit him hard, in 9 BC. The Augustan empire and reign are unimaginable without Tiberius' generalship.

His effectiveness rested not only on strategic and tactical abilities but also on his treatment of the troops and his closeness to them. No remoteness here: he slept on the ground with them, shared their hardships, and made his own special resources, such as physicians and food, available to them when they were sick (see Box 5.6). There is no reason to disbelieve Velleius here; as a ranking officer in the Pannonian campaign, he saw Tiberius from up close and there were enough contemporaries around to set any false record straight. The key, as Suetonius confirms, too, was Tiberius' extraordinary care and solicitude for his soldiers. He was detail-oriented not only in matters of military planning and the like but in his concern for their safety – Varus, who was an experienced commander, lost three Roman legions through carelessness, but Tiberius never ran the risk. At the same time, he expected and enforced utmost discipline. The reasons for Velleius' admiration of the man, gushing as it may be at times (see Box 5.6), are found here. Tiberius inspired his soldiers not by charisma, but by these qualities, "preferring efficiency to show" (Velleius, 2.113.2). He looked the part, too: strongly built, tall, with broad chest and shoulders, and, interestingly enough, hair that came down over the neck (Suet., *Tib.* 68).

Box 5.6. Tiberius as General

"And now for a detail. It does not lend itself to grandiose telling, but it stands out for the true valor (*virtus*) of the man and its practical aspects, and for being a most pleasant experience and unique for its kindness. Throughout the whole period of the German and Pannonian war, there was not one of us, or of those either below or above our rank, who fell ill without having his health and welfare looked after by Caesar with as much solicitude indeed as though this were the chief occupation of his mind, preoccupied though he was with heavy responsibilities. There was a horsed vehicle ready for those who needed it, his own litter was at the disposal of all, and I, among others, got to enjoy its use. Now his physicians, now his kitchen, now his bathing equipment, brought for this one purpose for himself alone, ministered to the comfort of all who were sick....

"Let me also add the following trait: ... Caesar alone of the commanders was in the habit of always traveling in the saddle and, throughout the greater portion of the summer campaign, of sitting at the table when dining with invited guests."

Velleius 2.114.1–3

"What armies of the enemy did we see drawn up for battle in the first year! What opportunities did we avail ourselves of through the foresight of the general to evade their united forces and rout them when they were divided! With what moderation and kindness did we see all the business of warfare conducted, though under the authority of a military commander! With what judgment did he place our winter camps! How carefully was the enemy so blockaded by the outposts of our army that he could nowhere break through and that, through lack of supplies and by dissension within his own ranks, he would gradually be weakened in strength!"

Velleius 2.111.4 (Loeb trans., with modifications)

History, as we all know, is full of ironies. The present example is that Augustus, who originally was of "ignoble descent" and therefore prized talents such as Agrippa's, acted completely differently toward Tiberius. Now that he had live descendants, the grandsons, in the Julian family line into which he had been adopted by Caesar, noble pedigree trumped merit – even Julia, the ostensible devotee of Marsyas' populist liberty, had sniffed that she did not consider Tiberius as her equal (*imparem*). Two developments, then, coalesced to produce the perfect storm that led to Tiberius' stunning rupture with Augustus in 6 BC. One is that Augustus marked out Tiberius simply as Agrippa II or, as Jochen Bleicken has put it (1998, 635), ersatz Agrippa. The forced marriage to Julia was one aspect; the other, seemingly prestigious in its own right, was the bestowal of honors and powers on him that were almost identical to Agrippa's, making him the virtual co-regent with the *princeps*. What, then, was the problem? It lay, to put it briefly, in the cold expediency that was written all over this arrangement. It did not amount to a real vote of confidence in Tiberius, let alone a psychological boost. This was painfully obvious, and here is a second determining factor: Augustus' showing excessive favoritism to Julia's oldest sons, who were barely into their teens. Typically, however, Augustus never gave up on this sentiment even after their deaths. The first sentence of his will, read out to the senate in AD 14, let everyone know that "since cruel fortune deprived me of my (grand)sons Gaius and Lucius," Tiberius was to be his heir (Suet., *Tib.* 23). Moreover, Augustus enshrined the same wording in his *Res Gestae*, where an entire chapter (14) is dedicated to the honors the youngsters received.

These honors were as substantial as they were, for the most part, premature. We already saw that Augustus broke with all precedent by adopting them as infants. When Gaius was twelve and participated in military exercises for the first time, the troops received a special donative, and silver and gold coinage used for their pay in Gaul started bearing his likeness. A year later, he was placed in charge of prestigious games in Rome when Tiberius had to depart suddenly to quell a disturbance in Germany. A high point or, from Tiberius' perspective, the last straw, came in 6 BC when the electoral assembly of the people chose Gaius to be consul at the age of fourteen. That would have beaten Octavian's record by a full five years and Augustus, who may or may not have been in on the plan from the start, then had Gaius' election changed to consul designate in 1 BC while granting him other privileges. It didn't take much for Tiberius to conclude that he was merely warming the seat for Gaius. While most observers might have seen it that way, it was not enough for Julia, who was a driving force in intriguing for her sons, and for Gaius' supporters to whom the accumulation of Tiberius' powers seemed threatening. In this contentious atmosphere Tiberius simply quit – "amid an abundance of success and in the prime of life and health," as Suetonius poignantly puts it (*Tib.* 10). He announced that he was going to Rhodes, an island known for its good climate and even better school of philosophy. Augustus was shocked and openly complained in the senate, Livia begged him to stay, and Tiberius went on a hunger strike. They had to let him go and, leaving almost all of his friends behind, he sailed off and was not to return from his sabbatical until seven years later.

It was an amazing turn of events, by all standards. Here was the second most powerful man in the empire, who had been conspicuously elevated by Augustus, trading his military and civil boots for the proto-Birkenstocks of Greek philosophy professors whose lectures and discussions he assiduously attended and, in Greek garb and all, leading an ostensibly inconspicuous life in private far away from Rome. He was not stripped of his powers nor did he officially resign them, but he simply did not exercise them. There was one telling exception: once, when he joined, as every so often, in the argument between two philosophers, another member of the audience berated and abused him for taking sides. Tiberius thereupon returned to his house, only to reappear with his official attendants. He ordered the man to be taken to court, over which he presided, and gave him a jail sentence. He otherwise kept a low profile, though Roman officials who were on business in the eastern Mediterranean made it a point to pay him their respects.

The situation became precarious when his powers gradually expired. At that point, like Octavian initially, he was only a private citizen, though not one protected by mercenaries. He started sending feelers to Rome about a possible return, which Augustus resolutely denied him. Livia kept interceding and so did fate: Julia had been packed off to exile and Gaius Caesar was away from Rome, at the head of a military command in the east. He let it be known that he was not concerned about a rival. Tiberius slunk back to the capital (in AD 2) and was ordered to live quietly in a secluded villa. A few days later, Lucius Caesar died (of natural causes) in Marseilles while on the way to Spain and in February of AD 4, Gaius died of a wound he suffered during the siege of a city in Lycia.

Tiberius' time had come again and Augustus wasted none of it. He adopted him into the Julian family and saw to it that he was granted the tribunician power, renewable after ten years like Augustus', and an all-encompassing power of command (*imperium*). As if on cue, there had been no major unrest in the empire during Tiberius' self-exile – the expeditions of Gaius and Lucius were expansionary and consolidating in scope rather than defensive – but this situation ended soon enough, requiring experienced leadership. Tiberius had not missed a beat, as is clear especially from his handling of the Pannonian revolt in AD 6–9 that earned him Velleius' raves.

At last, Augustus even granted him a triumph and his tribunician power and *imperium* were duly renewed after ten years. When the sole surviving grandson, Agrippa Postumus, whom Augustus had adopted at the same time as Tiberius, tried to stake his claim at the age of eighteen in AD 6 – by comparison, Gaius and Lucius had been only fourteen and eleven in 6 BC – Augustus was in no mood for a repeat of those events. Instead, he made a 180-degree turn: Agrippa was declared to have a "troublesome" and "difficult" temper and exiled. Tiberius' succession never really was in question.

Yet, when Augustus' will was opened, it presented him as successor almost by default. A sense of alienation must have pervaded Tiberius' relations with Augustus, relativized as it was by Augustus' letters to him that expressed admiration for his outstanding military capabilities (Box 5.7). They were sorely needed and the emperor knew that. One of the best known artifacts of that time, a large cameo called Gemma Augustea, is a visual testament to Tiberius' role and the emphasis on almost incessant campaigning even in Augustus' late years (Fig. 19, Box 5.8).

Box 5.7. Some of Augustus' Letters to Tiberius

1. "Fare well, Tiberius, most charming of men, and may success go with you, as you do battle for me and for the Muses.* Fare well, most charming and valiant of men and most conscientious of generals, or may I never know happiness."

* The text is uncertain here (Augustus, as so often in his correspondence, is interspersing Greek phrases with the Latin text), but the reference may be to Tiberius' literary tastes.

2. "I have only praise for the conduct of your summer campaigns, dear Tiberius, and I am sure that no one could have acted with better judgment than you did amid so many difficulties and such apathy of your army. All who were with you agree that the well-known line* could be applied to you: 'One man alone by his vigilance has saved our country from ruin.'"

* The original line, in the epic *Annales* of the Latin poet Ennius (c. 239–c. 169 BC), is about the Roman general Fabius Maximus Cunctator, whose delaying tactics slowed down Hannibal's progress in Italy: "One man alone by his cautious ways has saved our country from ruin." Vergil cites it almost verbatim at *Aeneid* 6.846.

(continued)

An interesting contrast is provided by Dio (55.31), who writes that Augustus suspected Tiberius during the Pannonian campaign of "delaying purposely, in order that he might be under arms as long as possible, with the war as his excuse." Augustus, then, may have written the letter to correct his earlier criticism of Tiberius.

3. "When I hear and read that you are worn out by constant hardships, may the Gods confound me if my own body does not wince in sympathy; and I beg you to spare yourself, that the news of your illness may not kill your mother and me, and endanger the Roman people at the top of our rule."

4. "My state of health is of little importance compared with yours. I pray to the gods that they will keep you safe and sound for us unless they hate the Roman people utterly."

Suetonius, *Tib.* 21

Box 5.8. The Gemma Augustea

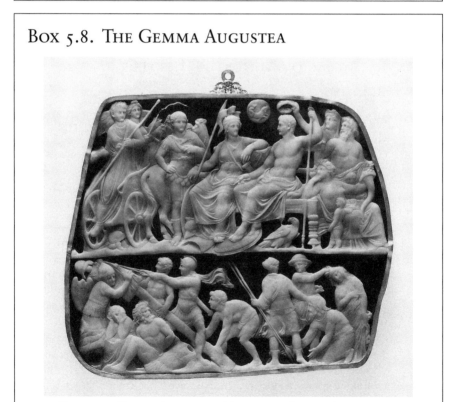

Figure 19. Gemma Augustea, c. AD 10. Kunsthistorisches Museum, Vienna, Inv.-Nr. IXa 79. Museum photograph.

This large (7.5 × 9 in.) cameo of double-layered Arabian onyx stone was probably made near the end of Augustus' reign. It does not celebrate a golden age; rather, more than three quarters of the decoration is taken up by references to war. In the lower part, there is a generic scene of Roman soldiers erecting a trophy amid defeated barbarians, including a female captive who is dragged by the hair. In the upper portion, Augustus and the goddess Roma are seated on a throne and hold the spear and scepter of imperial power. Above them is the sign of Capricorn. Further, Roma rests her left hand of her sword and Augustus is crowned by Oikoumenē. Oikoumenē had been the personification of global empire since Alexander the Great and her appearance is typical of the Augustan synthesis of Greek and Roman. The crown is the Roman *corona civica*, awarded to citizens who saved the life of others and hence, to Augustus for saving the Roman people. To the left is a young prince, probably Germanicus, in military dress while the triumphing Tiberius descends from a chariot, driven by the goddess Victoria. But the emphasis is not on celebration: she is impatiently urging on her horses to take him to the next campaign, a realistic reflection of his and Germanicus' almost constant campaigning in the last decade of Augustus' reign. Corresponding to the pair of Tiberius and Victoria on the left is that of Neptune and Italia on the right. It is telling that Italia's cornucopia is empty, as famines and poor harvests were not infrequent.

Cf. Galinsky (1996) 120–1

MORE ON THE GRANDCHILDREN

As we have seen, the lives and fortunes of Gaius and Lucius were intertwined with those of Tiberius, and only a few details need to be added. The essential point is that Augustus simply doted on them. Understandably, he promoted them yet more conspicuously after Tiberius' flight to Rhodes. Both in 5 BC and 2 BC, when, respectively, Gaius and Lucius assumed the *toga virilis*, a rite of passage that signified they had come of legal age, Augustus let himself be elected consul again in order to mark the significance of the event. Adding to it was the new title bestowed on the two, *princeps iuventutis* (leader of the young), which was obviously patterned on his own title – they clearly were meant to be his successors. The point was not lost on Ovid, who hailed Gaius as "now a prince of young men and destined to be prince of the old" (*Art of Love*, 1.194), although this may also be a typically sly allusion to Gaius' mother Julia's famous retort that the young men with whom she, as one of the two *principes* women, was surrounding herself would turn into oldsters in due course (see Box 5.5). Further, as could be expected, Augustus hurried to arrange a suitable marriage for Gaius before he departed for the east in 1 BC. The chosen bride, who at least was of the same age as Gaius, was the daughter of Tiberius' brother Drusus and Antonia Minor, a daughter of Augustus' sister Octavia. It reconfirmed the union between the Julian and Claudian branches of the imperial family. The official recognition of the two princes cascaded, and their images became ubiquitous throughout the empire on coins and in statuary, reliefs, and honorific inscriptions. And they were part of the imperial family on one of the premier monuments of the time, the Altar of Augustan Peace (see below).

How did the boys react to all this, including the exile of their mother? We catch only glimpses. Suetonius reports that Augustus acted as their teacher for "simple tasks" such as riding and swimming as well as writing: "He made it a point to make them model their handwriting on his own" (*Aug.* 64). No surprise, then, that the front hair locks of their portraits were also modeled on his, signifying both their descent and claim to succession. He also saw to it that they were present when he hosted dinners and they accompanied him on his travels.

They were not simply clones, of course. Unlike their mother, they did not rebel, but the attention they received and their status could go to their heads, to grandfather's chagrin. As Dio comments explicitly (55.9.1):

> Augustus was vexed when Gaius and Lucius were by no means inclined of their own choice to emulate his own conduct, as was fitting for young men who were being reared as members of the imperial house. They not only indulged in too great luxury in their lives, but were also inclined to insolence.... They were being flattered by everybody in the city, sometimes sincerely and sometimes to curry favor, and consequently were being spoiled more and more.

And he continues that, "wishing in some way to bring Gaius and Lucius to their senses still more sharply," Augustus provided Tiberius with the powers I detailed earlier, and that is when, according to Dio, the rivalry escalated. Be that as it may, when Gaius died – a letter written by Augustus on his sixty-fourth birthday testifies to their special bond (Box 5.9) – Augustus went into an orgy of grief. Public business in Rome was suspended for months.

Like Lucius, who had died a year and half earlier, his ashes were placed in the Mausoleum. Both their names were included in one of Rome's oldest ritual hymns, that of the Salian priesthood. An arch was to be built in their honor in the Forum, Julius Caesar's basilica there was to be renamed after them, honorific decrees in Italy (a splendid example comes from Pisa) and the provinces reached another crescendo, and a temple in Nîmes was dedicated in their honor. Today, it is the site one of the best-preserved temples from Roman times, the Maison Carrée; the present building is most likely a slightly later restoration of that original temple.

Box 5.9. Augustus Writes, on His Birthday, to Gaius

"Hello, dear Gaius, my sweetest little donkey. I always miss you when you are away from me. But especially on days like this one, my eyes look for my Gaius, and hope wherever you have been today, you will be happy and healthy as you celebrate my sixty-fourth birthday. For, as you can see, I have escaped the common Climacteric of old men,* my sixty-third year. Now I beg the gods that we may be allowed to spend whatever amount of time is left in good health and with the country being in a most fortunate condition, while you boys perform like heroes and wait to take on my watch."

Aulus Gellius, *Attic Nights* 15.7.3

* Age sixty-three, the result of multiplying nine times seven, was reputed to be a major juncture in a man's life. Every seventh year was called a "climacteric," and sixty-three became the Grand Climacteric.

There remained Agrippa Postumus. It is best to start with the beginning of his end: as we have seen, he was exiled in AD 6. Why? Our sources speak of some kind of personality disorder. Suetonius' terms are rather sweeping: he had a "sordid and fierce disposition." After one year of exile near Sorrento he grew even "less manageable" and "more out of his mind by the day" (*Aug.* 65). Hence he was transferred to the small island of Planasia, near Corsica, and kept under military guard. Velleius (2.112.7) chimes in by moralizing about his "reckless ways" and "strange depravity of mind and disposition" by which he "alienated himself from Augustus' affection." Dio (55.32) adds the detail that he "didn't act like a free-born person" but spent his days fishing and therefore called himself Neptune. Further, he was in dire need of anger management, kept saying bad things about his step-grandmother, and blamed Augustus for not giving him his part of his father's inheritance. Therefore, "when he could not be made to moderate his conduct," he was shipped off into exile.

It all sounds a little fishy, reminiscent of the grounds for consigning dissidents to mental institutions or jail. Hence, too, the sob story of Augustus' secretly visiting Planasia just before his death and tearfully making up with his banished grandson. At any rate, the "first heinous deed" (so Tacitus) of the new regime was to murder Postumus because he of the Julian line could be an obvious rival for Tiberius and there had been popular demonstrations for his recall and that of his mother and sister (on whom see below). Augustus crustily and venomously rejected any such calls for mercy, calling these relatives "my three boils and carcinomas" (Suet., *Aug.* 65). As in just about all things Augustan, there have been endless arguments about Postumus' banishment and the perpetrators of his death. Clearly, there must have been some personality issues, exaggerated as they come across in our sources. Augustus chose not to groom him for military operations, quite in contrast to the new and rising star Germanicus, who was three years younger than Postumus and (along with the future emperor Claudius) a brother of Livilla's, the only daughter of Drusus and the younger Antonia. In addition, as noted above, Postumus felt slighted because of Augustus' disparate treatment of him from that of Gaius and Lucius. At some point there was nothing further to work out and Augustus was unsparing.

That left the two granddaughters, Julia the Younger and Agrippina, and their fates could not have been more different. Probably as a result of Postumus' relegation, Julia became involved in a conspiracy against Augustus in AD 8. It was typical of most of such plots against him. They were *ad hoc* rather than the result of systematic opposition, and the phenomenon in general has been characterized as "scattered, isolated, ineffective, and, overall, minimal" (Raaflaub and Samons 1990, 454); Tacitus gripes that this was because Augustus "had seduced one and all by the dolce vita of leisure" and bemoans the disappearance of "ferocious individuals" who had made republican times so exciting. As for Julia, instead of being treated like the empress in waiting, she must have felt disadvantaged as the non-Julian Tiberius clearly was on the ascendant. Her husband, Aemilius Paulus, came from one of Rome's aristocratic families but was no heavyweight. Instead of a well-organized and broadly based overthrow attempt, it was another episode of flailing about in personal rebellion. It turned out that she had cuckolded her husband and Augustus cashed in on her promiscuous mother's reputation, although only one lover could be identified, the Silanus whom we encountered at the beginning of this chapter. He simply had to absent himself from the city as the emperor "renounced his friendship," a mild slap on the wrist compared to Julia's condemnation to banishment. This time the chosen place was a small island in the Adriatic, Trimerus. Livia was able to provide enough support to keep her from starving though Tacitus, as usual, could not bring himself to seeing anything good in her motives. Like her mother and brother, however, she never was recalled and died twenty years later. In modern times, the whole episode has received added attention because the poet Ovid somehow was caught in the imbroglio and exiled to the Black Sea; our ancient sources, except for Ovid himself, apparently did not feel it was worth mentioning.

Agrippina, by contrast, thrived as the wife of the age's last and rising star, Germanicus. Born in 15 BC, he was the son of Tiberius' younger brother Drusus and Antonia Minor, the daughter of Augustus' sister Octavia (and Mark Antony, but that was an issue only for her brother Jullus Antonius, who was, as we saw earlier, driven to suicide in the scandal involving the Elder Julia). Hence the couple had plenty of Julian lineage. In addition, Agrippina had inherited her mother Julia's procreative genes: the couple produced nine children, all of whom Augustus proudly displayed before an assembly of equestrians who were wailing about his marriage laws. The poster children had arrived at last, even if one of them turned out to be Caligula. Germanicus received early honors, though not on the same scale as Gaius and Lucius had previously, and became commander of the Roman army in Germany in AD 13, hence his name. But Augustus, who by now was well into his seventies, clearly was not going to stir up things by promoting him as a possible rival of his uncle Tiberius, with whom young Germanicus worked closely in the field.

"We Are Family": The Altar of Augustan Peace

All in all, then, Augustus' family was a very mixed bag of individuals, problems, conflicts, tensions, successes, joys, sorrows, tenderness, and calculation. That is, of course, hardly atypical of most families, save the exceptional harshness (or, for that matter, ability) of the *pater familias* to exercise his *potestas* and relegate inconvenient relatives to island prisons. Our sources, of course, love to dwell on disruptive incidents and behaviors. One reason for that emphasis may well be a reaction against the family's public representation and image.

For the creation of that image, Augustus went even further than with that of his own, which remained timelessly youthful and unruffled. In any family, and especially those that are the result of several marriages, the connections that are created do not automatically translate into mutual resemblance, let alone resemblance to the head of the family. That would not do for Augustus. As Diana Kleiner has astutely demonstrated, he "yearned for greater symbiosis and skillfully fabricated a fictional family" (2005, 212).

One aspect, as we already have seen, was the casting of Gaius and Lucius as miniature Augustuses throughout the empire. In general, a male member of the Julio-Claudian family could be identified immediately by his distinctive hair locks, a circumstance that has been very helpful to modern scholars. In one of the quintessential monuments of and to the Augustan reign, however, the process is far more sophisticated. That is the Altar of Augustan Peace (Ara Pacis Augustae; cf. p. 94). It is one of the high points of Augustan art due to its deliberate richness of associations and evocative appeal to the viewers to make their own connections within the framing idea of what constitutes *pax* under this *princeps*. We will look at some of these aspects later; what matters in the present context is its function as a monument to Augustus' family. That was itself another new departure because the Ara Pacis was the first public monument in Rome to include women and children. They are represented on the long sides of the altar enclosure as being part of a procession that converges on the sacrifice of Augustus. Their figures are anything but stiff; monotony, which creeps easily into such representations, is avoided; some are chatting with one another and the children wiggle as they generally do during lengthy ceremonies (Fig. 20). But amid all this individuality, "real and imagined semblance is the goal, melding the imperial family into a unified ruling elite that, in its indivisible concord, ensure the stability and flourishing of Rome. The portraits of Augustus and Livia serve as prototypes and all members of the procession are potential surrogates for one another. The message ... is that they are all for one and one for all" (Kleiner 2005, 216). No sign of discord, of course, which by the time of the altar's dedication in 9 BC had not yet fully exploded. Thereafter, it was time to conjure up the idea of concord anew. That was done by the reconstruction of the Temple of Concord in the Roman Forum and its explicit rededication to Concordia Augusta by Tiberius in AD 10.

Figure 20. Ara Pacis, 9 BC: south frieze. Procession with imperial family: Agrippa is the first from the left; Livia, the second. Rome, Museo dell'Ara Pacis Augustae. Photograph Archivio Fotografico dei Musei Capitolini.

AUGUSTUS AT HOME

How are we supposed to imagine Augustus amid some of this family turmoil? How did it affect him? As always, we do not have a diary or more than sporadic testimonies. Obviously, events of this kind upset him greatly and he could lose it, as is clear from his reaction the Elder Julia's misdeeds. And the lack of forgiveness is stunning – would the exile of three family members not weigh on anyone? But life went on and Suetonius offers some details. Augustus had good friends, gave frequent, though not sumptuous, dinner parties, and loved gaming, literally rolling the dice for hours. And that not just on holidays, as Suetonius reports with astonishment, but on working days. His dinner parties could be very entertaining. A highlight was a blind auction: each guest was given vouchers with greatly different values and expected to bid on paintings that had their faces turned to the wall (*Aug.* 75). In general, Augustus had a penchant for being lighthearted and for making even shy or awed people feel at ease to join in. Even a few days before his death, while he was on the Bay of Naples, he gave a banquet for young men where he "not merely allowed, but expected them to play jokes" (*Aug.* 98) and had them engage in a scramble for sweets and other goodies. In short, "he indulged in every sort of fun."

He could make a joke as well as take it (see Boxes 5.10 and 5.11). It led Macrobius, who lists the lot (*Sat.* 2.4.1–31), to generalize that "there is more merit in patience than in ease with (witty) words" and he admired Augustus for that quality, especially as some of the barbs directed at him did not lack bite. What emerges once more from these interactions is the emperor's accessibility. The vignettes are vivid: a Greek constantly singing Augustus' praises (and hoping for a reward) whenever he came down from the Palatine; a veteran of Actium shaming Augustus into being his advocate in the Forum rather than leaving the job to one of his aides; Augustus having a meal in someone's humble abode "because he rarely rejected anyone who invited him"; and others. The contrast with his treatment of relatives like Julia and Postumus thereby stands out all the more starkly.

BOX 5.10. TWO INSTANCES OF AUGUSTUS' WIT

"When many of those accused by Cassius Severus were absolved from his slanders and the architect of the Forum of Augustus once more dragged out the expected completion date, Augustus made this joke: 'I wish Cassius would accuse my forum, too' (and the job would be absolved)."

Macrobius 2.4.9

Background: Cassius Severus himself was known for his caustic wit. In his speeches and writings, "he defamed distinguished men and women" (Tacitus, *Ann.* 1.72). That attracted Augustus' ire, and the senate banished Severus to a small island in Greece. There is no evidence that these "libelous writings," which were ordered to be burned – subsequently earning Augustus the reputation as a book burner in modern times – were directed against the *princeps* and his family rather than illustrious Romans of the past. It is precisely these that were displayed in the "Hall of Fame" in the Augustan Forum, which took decades to complete.

"When he heard of the enormous debt (some 20 million sesterces) that a Roman knight had been able to hide before he died, he ordered someone to buy his pillow at the auction of the knight's possessions. When some wondered why, he was ready with this reason: 'That must be good pillow for getting sound sleep if a guy with so much debt could sleep on it.'"

Macrobius 2.4.17

According to Suetonius (*Aug.* 78), Augustus often had trouble sleeping.

Box 5.11. Augustus, Birds, and Their Cheeky Owners

"He put up with snubs or, rather, temerity, even when they came from a soldier. He was at a house in the country and did not sleep well there because of the frequent hooting of an owl. So he ordered the owl to be captured. A soldier, who was an expert bird catcher, carried out the task and hoped for a big reward. The emperor complimented the soldier and had 1,000 sesterces paid to him.* That one dared to say: 'I'd rather let the bird live' and set him free. Who would not be astounded that Caesar let this arrogant soldier leave without showing offense?"

Macrobius 2.4.26

* By comparison, the annual pay of a Roman legionary was 900 sesterces.

"He returned to Rome in all the glory of his Actian victory. Amid the congratulating crowd a man ran up to him who was holding a raven, whom he had taught to say: 'Hail Caesar, victor, imperator.' Amazed, Caesar bought the obliging bird for 20,000 sesterces. A partner of the bird trainer, who had not benefited from this generosity, assured Augustus that the man had a second raven and asked that he be commanded to bring him, too. Once there, the bird uttered the words he had learned: 'Hail, victor, imperator Antony!' Augustus did not get upset but left it at ordering the man to share his booty with his associate."

Macrobius 2.4.29

The "House of Augustus"

When our sources speak of the *domus* of Augustus on the Palatine, they refer not to just one house but to a residential complex made up of a number of dwellings. Octavian's agents bought up several such properties, some of which retained their names, such as the House of Hortensius and the House of Catulus. Due to an inscription with her name on a lead pipe, we can identify the house that Livia used after Augustus' death. It survived the fire of AD 64 that enveloped the Palatine. The remains of most of the other Augustan buildings are lost to us today, being buried beneath the subsequent buildings of the Flavian emperors (see Fig. 13).

A conspicuous exception is a well-appointed house that started being excavated in 1961 and is now known as the "House of Augustus." Its wall paintings are vivid and the decoration is well planned, including a room on the upper level, which accords with the references in our sources to Augustus' study. The motifs of some of the paintings, such as Victories and a cone associated with the cult of Apollo, are easily relevant to Augustus. The largest room is remarkable for its decoration with theatrical masks, enabling us to make the leap forward to Augustus' famous dying words: "Have I played my role well?" Further, there are Egyptianizing motifs that became fashionable especially after Actium. All this is not inconsistent with Suetonius calling Augustus' house "modest." That may only mean that it was not ostentatious; in fact, the criterion Suetonius uses is the absence of ornate marble floors and none have been found. Further, as recent excavations have shown, a more grandiose extension to the house, which was in progress until 36 BC, was scrapped and reworked into a public portico in front of the new Temple of Apollo that was vowed that year and dedicated in 28 BC. "Modest," then, may mean relative to its originally planned grandeur. A parallel in the literature of the time is Horace's use of *paupertas*, which literally means "poverty" but basically denotes the absence of luxury.

An obstacle to the identification of this house as the "House of Augustus" is Dio's notice (55.12.4) that a fire destroyed "the palace" in AD 3 whereas the style of wall painting in the house dates from earlier decades. Dio uses the term *palation*, which in Latin (*Palatium*) had come to designate the entire Palatine complex. Dio obviously referred to only a part of it, but which? The actual dwelling of Augustus? In the end – and the issue is a good example of how many questions are still open merely about Augustan material culture – there is no probative evidence that the "House of Augustus," which has been open to the public since 2008, was his actual residence for most of his life. What is unquestioned is the preeminence to which he raised the Palatine. His furnishings may have been unprepossessing and his clothes homespun, but the complex was grand as is indicated, too, by the list of Livia's craftsmen working there. It was not just a "palace" but an ensemble of residences with streets and alleys between, a splendid new temple gleaming with white Carrara marble, porticos, and a Greek and Latin library. In the Secular Games of 17 BC, therefore, the Palatine Hill was established as a venue equal to that of the Capitoline. It is in that ambiance that Augustus lived, not as a pretentious potentate but as *princeps*.

6

CULTURAL VITALITY

The Augustan period was a time of outstanding creativity. The recuperation of peace and stability certainly was conducive – we may compare the creative burst of fifth-century Athens after the trauma of defeat and destruction had been banished; for good reasons, Augustan Rome looked back to the Athens of Pericles, its architecture and art in particular. But there was more. A major element in the dynamic of Augustan culture – besides, of course, the ideas, ideals, and values Augustan projected – was the characteristics of Augustus' style of governing. They were not simply transferred to the arts, let alone mandated by him from the top down. Instead, and as can be readily imagined, what he did and the way he reshaped things engaged the imagination of his contemporaries and stimulated many responses. Parallels, then, are evident. They do not comprise the entire, rich spectrum of the arts under Augustus, but I will foreground them in this book, which centers on Augustus and his impact.

"AUGUSTAN" CHARACTERISTICS: OVERVIEW AND SOME EXAMPLES

Augustus' evolutionary principate, as we have seen, was marked by experimentation and innovation. There was a framework of guiding principles, but their execution was undoctrinaire: if one road did not work, there would be another (and in the end they all would lead to Rome and Augustus). The past was invoked but at the same time recast; diverse traditions were melded. One result was that most Augustan phenomena are, by design, many-sided; a representative sample is the varied meanings of *libertas* and para-constitutional terms such as *auctoritas*, the range of associations evoked in the first sentence of the *Res Gestae*, the purposes of the "moral" legislation, and the very name "Augustus." They all have multiple dimensions, are rich in associations, and therefore elicited involvement and response.

When we look at Augustan poetry, art, and architecture, the same qualities stand out. A paradigm is an icon of Augustan literature, Vergil's *Aeneid*. It was a bold experiment to modernize Homeric epics – the *Iliad* and the *Odyssey* had been composed some 700 years earlier – and adapt them to Roman values. There had been nothing like this for centuries. Vergil's contemporary Propertius, who was a very different kind of poet, said this much (2.34.65–6): "Move over Greek and Roman writers: something greater – and I can't quite define it – than the *Iliad* is born." While paying his respects to that tradition, Vergil changed it thoroughly – in style, substance, and the use of myth. The innovations begin at the very beginning (see Box 6.1): Vergil speaks in the first person – "arms and the man *I* sing" – which Homer never did. And instead of invoking the Muse right away, he waits for several verses and then introduces a key theme from Greek *tragedy*: here is a decent man having to endure the injustice of a god. Further, instead of asking the Muse to "sing" or "speak" to him, the Roman poet calls on her to "bring to remembrance" (*memora*) the story of Aeneas. Reflecting its defining role in Roman culture, memory is essential to the *Aeneid*; the epic is a poetic (re)construction of Roman cultural memory. Another of its many innovations is, in fact, Juno's relentless persecutorial hatred of Aeneas. It is not found anywhere in the previous tradition. And there is always more than one dimension: Vergil's most extensive ancient commentator, Servius (fourth century AD), observed that the very first verb in the *Aeneid*, "I sing," can have at least three meanings: to praise, prophesy, and sing. Servius opted for the last, but the other two remain present in the semantic spectrum. It is left to the reader or listener to determine the exact mix.

Box 6.1. Vergil Begins the *Aeneid*

"Arms and the man I sing, the first to come from Troy's coasts,
displaced by fate, to Italy and the Lavinian shores.
Much was he tossed about on land and sea
by the powers above because of Juno's unforgetting rage.
Much, too, he suffered in war until he could found a city
and bring his gods to Latium. From there rose the Latin race,
the Alban fathers, and Rome's high walls.

(continued)

"Muse, bring to my memory now the reasons, what injured godhead
and what affliction made the queen of the gods drive
a man of such devotion to go through so many misfortunes,
to enter on so many travails? Can divine hearts know such anger?"

Aeneid 1.1–11

Besides the aspects mentioned on p. 145, Vergil's proem (as the preface to an epic is called) is replete with themes and resonances that are then developed in the poem. Here, succinctly, are five major ones: (1) "Arms and the man" is a reference to Homer's *Iliad* and *Odyssey*; (2) "displaced" would strike a chord with many Romans who suffered that fate in the 30s; (3) in contrast to that chaos, "fate" here stands for divine plans; (4) the building of a nation and the effort necessary for it are stressed throughout; and (5) Aeneas' endurance of Juno's willful anger is modeled on that of Hercules, one of the most popular heroes in Greece and Italy; he ultimately was deified.

This kind of concentration is typical of Vergil, whose pace of composition was approximately three verses a day. The *Aeneid* became an instant success not because of imperial patronage but because of the broad, topical appeal of such themes and Vergil's craftsmanship.

The first lines of the *Aeneid,* then, are a programmatic microcosm of these characteristics. They pervade the epic and have contributed in large part to making it a "classic" – not a static one, but an innovative and dynamic classic that could, and did, have many different receptions over time.

To turn to an entirely different area: architecture and architectural ornament. A paradigm is the Temple of Castor (and Pollux) whose three tall extant columns are a landmark of the Roman Forum today. The temple was restored under the patronage of Tiberius and rededicated in AD 10. "Restored," as we saw when we looked at the analogy with the "restoration" of the *res publica* (see p. 65), did not mean rebuilding the structure in its exact previous form. Many details were changed, such as the shape of the column bases, the configuration of the capitals, and the decorative elements of the entablature (the structure above the columns between the capitals and the roof). They exhibit plenty of innovation and experiment. It may suffice to quote the conclusion of two expert architectural historians (Strong and Ward Perkins 1962, 28):

It is true that from one point of view, Augustan architecture in general, and architectural ornament in particular, may seem to be remarkably conservative, harking back as it so often did to earlier classical models. But such a view is apt to disregard another and hardly less important aspect, namely its great variety and the extraordinary amount of detailed experiment that took place within the broad framework of conventional classical practice. Some of the new ideas never really caught on; others ... had to wait half a century or more before passing into general use. But seeds of so much of the later development are to be found already present in the architecture of the Augustan age that it may without exaggeration be claimed as the great moment of original experiment in the field of Roman architectural ornament.

Clearly, then, there was a return to classicism, conveying order and stability after the excesses of the Republic, and that point was reinforced by Augustus' ordering at least one extravagant private residence to be torn down. We are not looking, however, at the kind of sterile neoclassicism displayed in government buildings of the nineteenth and early twentieth centuries. There was free play and plenty of it. That was a legacy of the Augustan age not only for later Roman architecture but the uses of classicism up to our time. Palladio, Jefferson, and Schinkel are among the exemplars of that tradition, which is continuing creatively. In the well-chosen words of the architect Robert Stern (1988, 283): "Classicism offers the architect a canon as a guide, but what a liberal and tolerant canon it is. It proposes models of excellence in composition and detail. It does not set out on a singular route, but points out various ways." The same can be said about Augustan poetry.

In essence there was a creative synergy between the conditions and ideas generated by Augustus and the cultural life of his age. An example is Ovid's masterwork, the *Metamorphoses*. Chronologically speaking, Ovid, born in 43 BC – the "Augustan" poets Vergil and Horace were born in 70 and 65, respectively – is the true Augustan poet. The civil wars were over by the time he reached his early teens, and thus he knew only the *pax Augusta*. The *Metamorphoses* is about change, and change was the hallmark of the Augustan principate. Of course the *Metamorphoses*, and, for that matter, Vergil's *Aeneid* and Livy's *History of Rome*, would have been written differently if Augustus had been the author, but that is not the point (though for many scholars, it still is as they solemnly determine "Augustanism"). Rather, Ovid engages with a central issue of his time and treats it from many different perspectives. Vergil, who belonged to the generation that lived through the civil wars, did the same in a totally different way in the *Aeneid*. His central theme is not change, but the yearning for stability and permanence. It is important to keep in mind that this "national epic" was written in the first decade of the Augustan reconstruction or, rather, Augustus' attempts at reconstruction. Too often this grand poem has been viewed, in retrospect, as a paean on Augustus' achievements and his "golden age." In fact, as we have seen, the 20s were still a very precarious time and much hung in the balance. Vergil expresses relief about the end of civil discord, but takes nothing for granted; the tenor of the poem is cautious hope and anxiety rather than glorification. "So great a task it was to build the Roman nation," he says (1.33) and he is referring not just to past struggles, but present ones as well – the task is ongoing and success is no more certain than failure. It is for reasons such as these that many voices have been discerned in this unique epic.

AUGUSTAN PROPAGANDA?

There was nothing monolithic about Augustan culture. It was not Augustan in the sense that it was steered from the Palatine by "ideology" or "propaganda." Maecenas, who has sometimes been compared to modern managers, if not ministers, of propaganda because he sponsored some of the principal poets, was in fact highly unorthodox in terms of his personal habits and literary tastes.

What, then, about Augustus' own preferences? Suetonius (*Aug.* 89.3) makes the global statement that "he encouraged talented individuals of his time in all ways" and attended recitations from their works "with good will and patience." Both qualities were probably needed frequently. We do know that he was most interested in the progress of Vergil's *Aeneid* and that at one of the readings his sister Octavia fainted when Vergil, who excelled at such readings, recited the passage about her son Marcellus' death (*Aen.* 6.860–86). Moreover, Suetonius continues, Augustus looked for "precepts and examples that were salutary for public and private behavior" in the writings of Greek and Roman authors. By contrast, the tone of the surviving snippets of correspondence between him and Horace is entirely lighthearted. He tried to persuade Horace to become his private secretary, an offer the poet could refuse without repercussions unless we consider Augustus' characterization of him as "the purest penis" as such. Horace, a confirmed bachelor, was known to have a mirrored ceiling over his bed, the better to observe his interactions with prostitutes. The Augustan moral legislation did have its glass ceiling.

Suetonius devotes an incomparably larger chunk of the *Life of Augustus* – three chapters in all (43–5) – to the *princeps'* predilection for, and lavish sponsorship of, mindless *spectacula*, the many hours of his attendance there (see pp. 104), and his concern especially for the conduct of pantomime players. That is no accident: the pantomime was a genuinely new cultural product of the time. It transformed myth and tragedy into the nondemanding and glitzy fast food of show business. Scenes were selected for their sensational value (for example, Oedipus poking his eyes out or Ajax's suicide) and performed to musical accompaniment by a single actor who did not speak a word but mimed the action. For a mass audience, whose brush with literacy was rather occasional, this type of performance became the rage; it helped, too, that the length of each scene was comparable to that of today's half hour hit shows on television, minus the commercials. But we would be looking in vain for any propagandistic function.

Another popular phenomenon had a more complex dynamic. Emblems associated with Augustus, such as Victoria (see Fig. 14), laurel trees, the sphinx (the symbol on his signet ring; she also appears on the shoulder flaps of the Prima Porta statue; see Fig. 8), and even his hairstyle were rapidly appropriated into the private sphere. Excepting his hair lock, these symbols appear on everyday items such as lamps and table supports; on urns, tombs, and private funerary altars; on the mass-produced Arretine tableware; and even on gladiators' helmets. The reason, as Paul Zanker has authoritatively demonstrated for this aspect and others of Roman private art, was not a propaganda apparatus that mandated such manufacture and purchases. Instead, they constitute autonomous responses of private taste and the market. Again, there was no monolithic schema, and these responses can be interpreted in various ways: for instance, as demonstrations of loyalty, as mostly aesthetic preferences for something new, or as an opportunity for adaptation to private messages; the Victoria lamp, for instance, was transformed into a decor for New Year's wishes. Such images, then, were depoliticized and internalized in the process of continuing engagement.

It was a process that fostered creative variety rather than uniformity. Sure, Augustus pushed an agenda. In architecture – and I will take up his rebuilding of Rome shortly – that meant emphasis on the classical style whose *auctoritas* provided a dignified foundation and framework within which, as we have seen, innovations could easily take place. Similarly, classicism shaped much of official Augustan sculpture, again to be adapted autonomously into the private realm. At the same time, however, there flourished a culture of the fantastic, the paradoxical, and the marvelous. Its most palpable manifestations are found in wall painting. In vivid colors, the walls are populated not only with griffins and other fantastic winged creatures but deliberately project an air of unreality by presenting vegetal creations, such as floral stalks, rather than solid columns, supporting the structures painted on the walls. In Vitruvius' classical handbook on architecture, such "aberrations" had no place (see Box 6.2). In the houses of the Augustan family, they did.

Box 6.2. Vitruvius' Strictures

"Imitations based upon reality are now disdained by the improper mores of the present. On the stucco are monsters rather than definite representations taken from definite things. Instead of columns, there rise up stalks; instead of pediments, curled leaves and the tendrils of plants. Likewise, candelabra hold up the images of aediculae [painted pavilions]; on their summits, clusters of thin stalks rise from their roots in tendrils with little figures seated upon them at random. In the same fashion, slender stalks with heads of men and of animals attached to half the body. Such things neither are, nor can be, nor have been. On these lines the new mores have brought it about that bad judges condemn good craftsmanship."

On Architecture 7.5.3–4

Vitruvius, who dedicated his *Ten Books on Architecture* to Octavian, is not quite the conservative classicist he has been often made out to be; in fact, considering architecture as a liberal art, he allows for experiment and innovation. As can be seen, however, there were limits. Vitruvius couches his censure in terms of *mores*. Always a key concept in Roman life, it was extensively used by Augustus, too; consider *Res Gestae* 8.5 (cited on p. 98) where Augustus says that he was bringing back disappearing *mores* by *new* laws – a nice paradox. Here, Vitruvius seizes on the unsettling connotations of "new" – the *mores* he castigates are not traditional ones. Augustus did not follow him in this instance; as we know, he could be unorthodox.

For more on Vitruvius, see I. D. Rowland and T. N. Howe, eds.,
Vitruvius: Ten Books on Architecture (Cambridge 1999).

Above all, a central impulse for the creativity of the age was Augustus' vision or agenda for Rome. It ranged beyond the restoration of material well-being but addressed itself to Roman ideals and values. In short, Augustus generated ideas. Not only that, but "it is clear from the poems that Augustus was a poetically exciting idea" himself (White 1993, 207). He launched a national conversation and was not the only one to participate in it. It stands to reason that, after decades of self-destruction, many thoughtful people, and not just Augustus, reflected on how Rome had gotten to that point and what was the way out. The discussion of that subject alone is rich and varied in our contemporary sources. Perspectives range from the original sin of Romulus' killing of Remus (Horace) to the gloomy assessment that "we have reached the point where we can suffer neither our vices nor the remedies for them" (Livy). As for Vergil, he eschewed the easy – and expected – road of writing an epic on Augustus, an *Augusteid*, perhaps incorporating the story of his ancestor Aeneas by flashbacks. Instead he reversed the perspective: the building of Rome lies in the future and requires the unceasing effort of generation after generation. In this way, Vergil captured the Augustan ethos far more authentically.

Another type of response is that of the love poets, such as Propertius and Tibullus. They are not partisans who simply reject or espouse Augustan ideals in the "real" world (except for Propertius' protest against the marriage legislation), but they appropriate such themes for their private, poetic world and take them up in that context. Augustan topics such as war, peace, the Troy myth, old times versus new, *pietas*, and importance of family thread through their poetry. In that world, the lover is as brave as any Augustan warrior, and he adheres to the Roman and Augustan ideals of faithfulness and trust (*fides*); even while opposed to compulsory marriage, Propertius does not advocate promiscuity. Similarly, Ovid's poetic version of the Roman calendar and its festivals, the *Fasti*, interacts with the Augustan world at every step. It could not but, given Augustus' massive remake of the real *fasti* by inserting many commemorations of events relevant to him and his family (see p. 82). It is tricky business for both Ovid and his modern interpreters: is Ovid's stance political or aesthetic or both? And to what degree? And can these spheres be neatly separated? One issue is Ovid's persistent interspersion of frothy and even risqué stories, such as the comic sexual adventures of Pan and Faunus, into the official sequence. It certainly raises the entertainment value of what could be a rather straightforward narrative, but how are we to assess it? One answer is that Ovid is unifying the calendar, which in republican times was a collection of unconnected festivals, by these themes just as Augustus did by means of Julian themes. In other words, Ovid is following Augustus' procedure in his own way.

In sum, there were many ways in which poets engaged with Augustan ideas and subjects. There was a wealth of new material here, and "it was irresistible" (White 1993, 207). Another commonality is that these poetic responses, and Augustan poetry in general, resist stereotyping, pigeonholing, and monolithic categorization as readily as do the historical and political aspects of the Augustan age.

THE REMAKING OF ROME

Another, and clearly more visible, imprint of Augustus was his rebuilding of the city of Rome. It was the literal equivalent and material manifestation of his rebuilding and restoring the *res publica*, just as his claim to have rebuilt Rome from a city of brick to one of marble was meant to be taken both literally and as a metaphor for his rebuilding of the state. The principal dimensions of this process for Rome the city mirror those of the remaking of Rome in the larger sense.

The first such commonality is that order supplanted disorder. While not uniformly so, Rome presented a shabby and exhausted appearance due to years of neglect and lack of resources that had been siphoned off by civil wars. Caesar, as we have seen, initiated a massive public works program, but another civil war interfered and most of his projects, like his own Forum, were in fact completed by Augustus. Rebuilding and restoration, therefore, were extensive and carried out in the typically Augustan manner, one that Diane Favro has called "enhanced familiarity": traditional forms were maintained, but their dimensions were often quite literally heightened and enriched in the way exemplified by the Temple of Castor (pp. 146–7). Other building types were involved besides temples, such as arches and basilicas. As it did for the state in general, rebuilding meant transformation. In the case of the Basilica Aemilia, for instance, in the Roman Forum it was so successful that Pliny the Elder some decades later singled it out, along with the newly built Forum of Augustus, as one of the most beautiful buildings in the world (*Nat. Hist.* 36.102).

Another aspect of order was the reshaping of the cityscape. There were existing markers such as the Forum, the Capitoline, and the recently built Theater of Pompey, but they were embedded in a tangle of streets. Rome had grown by accretion and not on the basis of regularized plan. World cities, such as Alexandria, presented a different appearance. The resulting approach again was typically Augustan. Radical change was out; Julius Caesar, contemptuous of "the dead body" of the republic, had practiced it with regard to his Forum, destroying a neighborhood. For his own Forum, by contrast, Augustus patiently bought out the property owners and even sacrificed symmetry of design, a holy writ of classical architecture, when one of them simply would not budge. More generally, he respected tradition and, therefore, did not simply straighten out urban quirkiness. Rather, his approach was, once more, evolutionary. Restored structures, which asserted themselves, and new buildings, which were inserted when the opportunity presented itself, became new markers and the resulting sight lines created an experience that suggested order. It was reinforced by creating ensembles, often by means of connecting porticos, out of formerly discrete buildings, strengthening overall cohesiveness. Last but not least, Augustus saw to the maintenance and addition of plenty of green space.

The second major dimension, as in the life of the state, was the architectural presence of Augustus himself. Nowhere was this clearer than in the development of the previously open space of the Campus Martius (see Map 2). Here architects and planners had a free hand. The most imposing monument was the Mausoleum, begun after the conquest of Egypt (see below). It became the tallest building in Rome and therefore served as another connective landmark. On axis to the south was the Pantheon (see Box 5.4), flanked by the enormous enclosure for the electoral assembly, the Saepta Julia. Measuring some 37,000 square meters, it was also used for gladiatorial games. Midway to the east stood the Augustan Altar of Peace. Aligned with it at the center of the monumental expanse was an obelisk, taken from Egypt, with a globe on top. It was part of a meridian that marked the changing length of days and nights during the year. A meridian line ran directly north-south with a surrounding pavement large enough to accommodate the obelisk's longest shadow on the shortest day of the year – the winter solstice in the sign of Capricorn (see Box 1.1). Caesar's calendar reform had at first been implemented incorrectly, with a leap year every three rather than four years. Once he became *pontifex maximus* in 12 BC, Augustus was able to establish the correct order. The meridian – several scholars insist that it was really a sundial (*horologium*) – symbolized that adjustment; there now was order in the heavens just as there was on earth, as signified by the Ara Pacis; both monuments were built contemporaneously. In another area of Rome, Augustus inaugurated his own Forum that took decades to complete, testing even his patience (cf. Box 5.10). It was built at a 90-degree angle to the Forum of Caesar (which, in turn, was connected with the Forum Romanum [Map 2]); while proceeding in a very different way from his adoptive father, *divi filius* never disassociated himself from him. Similarly, Augustus inscribed his presence on the Roman Forum by extensive restoration, the renaming of former structures, and additions. "Enhanced familiarity" was the counterpart of Constitution Plus.

Third, and connected with the other aspects, Rome now presented itself as the architecturally worthy city of an empire. The new Campus Martius conveyed world domination, and so did the Augustan Forum. It was there that foreign embassies were received and military commanders were sent out to war, while users of the Forum would walk over colored marble imported from all parts of the empire. Other buildings illustrated the same claim, such as the Porticus *ad Nationes* with its exhibit of statues personifying all nations, and the Porticus Vipsania where a map of the world was displayed. Above all, the Augustan architecture of Rome was cosmopolitan and drew on many different inspirations.

Polyvalence and Invitation to Response: Three Examples

At the beginning of this chapter I highlighted, in general terms, a central quality that cultural and political Augustan phenomena share: they invariably have multiple dimensions. That is not just a result of how they were perceived, including in later times. Rather, it is a matter of intentional design. The term "polyvalence" is apt: it expresses that there are many meanings and appeals; its own etymology, in fact, is a combination of Greek and Latin. In the same way, the creative synthesis of Greek and Roman aspects, which characterized Roman literature, art, and architecture almost from the very start, reached new heights in the age of Augustus. This chapter concludes, therefore, with a brief look at three specific examples.

1. *The Mausoleum*

Dominating the northern end of the Campus Martius (see Map 2), Augustus' tomb was his first building in Rome and would remain the tallest (Fig. 21). A few scholars posit the beginning of its construction in 32 BC, but most date it to 28 and it seems to have been largely completed by 23. Structurally, it combined concentric masonry drums with a mound, a tumulus. With this, the intentional multiplicity of traditions and associations begins. They are both architectural and cultural.

Tumulus tombs existed in the plain of Troy, home of Rome's and Augustus' ancestors, and are mentioned in Homer's *Iliad*. There was also a native Italian tradition of tumuli, going back to Etruria. The drum and podium type was also prevalent in later Greece, culminating with the tomb edifice in Halicarnassus for Caria's ruler Mausolus, which was built around the middle of the fourth century. Two massive extant tomb

Figure 21. Model of the Mausoleum of Augustus. Recent work suggests that the lower cylindrical walls may have been double the height. The obelisks may not date to the time of Augustus. Photograph courtesy Archäologisches Institut, Univ. of Cologne.

structures in today's Algeria also suggest an Egyptian tradition, hence the great likelihood that this was also the configuration of Alexander's tomb monument, the Sema, in Alexandria. Octavian made it a point to visit it (see p. 58). Alexander was a model – witness Octavian/Augustus' stylized Alexander hair lock – and the Augustan empire aimed to be the superior successor to his. And whereas Antony wished to be buried in Alexandria, the Mausoleum declared Octavian's staying power in Rome and, through its architecture, brought Alexandria to Rome. To make that message yet stronger, the two obelisks in front, which were probably added decades later, linked the Mausoleum to the central obelisk of the Meridian Plaza. The Mausoleum signified victory, too; as Penelope Davies has shown, later victory monuments throughout the Augustan empire were inspired by it. Other typological parallels include the tombs of Roman nobles on the Via Appia, which are smaller by comparison. Once thought to have been earlier monuments, they now mostly tend to be re-dated to Augustan times.

There were further messages and meanings. Pompey had been the first to monumentalize himself in the Campus Martius by building Rome's first permanent theater (see Map 2). Augustus now surpassed him and all others: this was not a building for a *civilis princeps*, but a towering structure fit for a monarch and a dynasty. The massive statue of Augustus that crowned it put him closer to the gods than anyone else. Divinity was in the air, enhanced by his statue in the anteroom of the Pantheon that was on axis to the south.

How much of this web of meanings, architectural traditions, and cultural memories would onlookers comprehend? And what aspect would predominate? That clearly would depend on the background and knowledge of each. Despite its size, the building was not simply there to overwhelm them but to engage them and to elicit their own responses and associations. The same is true of our next two examples.

2. *The Ara Pacis Goddess*

The designers of the Altar of Augustan Peace could have made it easy for themselves: they could have centered it on a direct representation of the goddess Pax; the type existed. Instead, and in typically Augustan fashion, they chose the road less travelled: the totality of the sculptural decoration, especially on the marble enclosure's outside, expresses the idea of the *pax Augusta*. Deities, the ancestors Aeneas and Romulus, the sacrificing Augustus, the relaxed demeanor of his family that includes women and children, and the senators, attendants, and priests constitute an ensemble that suggestively conveys the spirit of the Augustan peace. Since, as we have seen, "peace was born of victories" (*Res Gestae* 13), Mars, the father of the twins Romulus and Remus, was also represented – the location, after all, was the Field of Mars where his altar had formerly stood – as was the Goddess Roma, proudly sitting on a pile of arms (see Fig. 11).

Her pendant is a female deity that is polyvalent (see Fig. 10). She has been variously identified as Italia, Venus, the Earth goddess Tellus (cf. the cuirass of the Prima Porta Augustus; Box 3.4), Ceres, and even Pax. She is clearly a composite type with reminiscences and presences of the artistic traditions of all these deities. The relation of her image to the others of the sculptural program extends the web of associations. The two children she holds are paralleled by the twins Romulus and Remus as well as Gaius and Lucius; her face is not unlike Livia's (on whose birthday the Altar was dedicated; cf. Fig. 20); the vegetation surrounding her relates to fruitfulness (Ceres, Tellus) and to the extensive vegetal frieze of the lower tier; Venus was the mother of Aeneas and ancestress of the Julian family; the blessings of peace came about through war; and so on. The image is deliberately evocative, asking the viewers to make their own associations, to participate, and to reflect rather than genuflect. "Imperial" art, let alone the art of dictatorial regimes, speaks a different language. It is not surprising, therefore, that a staple of such art, grandiose battle scenes, is absent from Augustan art in Rome.

3. Vergil's Dido

In Vergil's multilayered epic, Dido is one of the most multilayered characters. She is an eastern queen in north Africa, a Roman ancestor falls in love with her, and she is trying to keep him with her – right away, there are shades of Cleopatra, who was a multifaceted personality in her own right. Dido, of course, is far more than a proto-Cleopatra. Nor is she merely The Other. In fact, she is very Roman: she is devout and a strong, principled leader. Her parting words read like the epitaph of a Roman noble, and she personifies the ideal (which she struggles against) of a Roman *univira*, a woman who would not remarry after her husband's death; even if Augustus broke with tradition by requiring remarriage, this ideal was still highly prized. Other contemporary allusions that do not fit a simple pattern include Aeneas' helping her build Carthage. It is the only city – not Lavinium, not Rome – we see him build in Rome's "national" epic, an action that poetically reflects the Caesarian and Augustan resettlement of Carthage.

Affinities between previous literary characters and Dido abound. They reach as far back as Homer and comprise Nausicaa, Circe, and Calypso. These are all prominent women in the *Odyssey*. The way in which these characters are integrated into Dido's portrait, however, accentuates a basic difference between the two epics: the *Aeneid*, appropriate for Augustan times, is a story of departure for new horizons rather than of homecoming; for good reason, the *Aeneid* lacks a Penelope figure. Just as important, Dido shares varying similarities with these characters but also is quite different in other respects. Vergil uses such literary resonances for the purpose of both similarity and contrast, asking the reader to work it all out. Besides Homer, Greek tragedy was a rich source. In contrast to pantomimic fluff, soul-searing tragedy was not the staple of the Augustan stage and Vergil reintegrated it successfully into epic. The most prominent, though by no means only model for Dido, was the oriental princess Medea, who helped Jason, only to be abandoned by him. That story had been further elaborated by Apollonius of Rhodes in his four-book epic *Argonautica* in the third century, and Vergil adapted features from it, too. And as a lover, Dido shares some behavioral traits with the lovers in contemporary Augustan love poetry. All this and more creates a rich web of associations that constantly invites the readers to participate in the creative process, make new discoveries, sort things out, and make their own connections. It is the basic reason that Dido's next life, her reception in literature, art, and music, vigorously surpassed that of any other character of the *Aeneid*, including its hero.

Great architects, artists, and writers do not simply reflect their times, they help shape them. The Augustan age was theirs as much as it was Augustus'; for good reason, Horace calls himself *princeps* in his domain (*Odes* 3.30.13). But there is no doubt that Augustus made this dynamic relationship possible. His achievement was more than political.

7

THE AUGUSTAN EMPIRE
Unity and Diversity

General Perspectives

When we look at Augustus' Roman empire, the same perspectives apply as on most Augustan phenomena: there had been substantive prior developments that Augustus continued and, at the same time, fundamentally changed. Symptomatic of this process is the Romans' use of *imperium*: before Augustus, it did not connote territorial empire but simply the power exercised by the Roman people, analogous to the *imperium* of Roman magistrates. In his *Res Gestae*, *imperium populi Romani* appears for the first time as a territorial entity: "When throughout the whole *imperium* of the Roman people *pax* had been achieved on land and sea by victories" (13). It is again typical of the Augustan blend of tradition and innovation that in the other seven mentions of *imperium* in the *Res Gestae*, the word, as before, means "power" (Richardson 2008, 118–19).

The shift reflects Augustus' view of the empire as a unified entity rather than a mere agglomeration of territories under Roman control as had been the case in republican times. Establishing that sense of cohesiveness and community, or at least a noticeable degree of it, was indeed a hallmark of his reign. Again, we are dealing with a process rather than a fixed outcome – one of the problems with the convenient term "Romanization" is that it expresses both – and, just as typical, it was not a process aiming at homogeneity. And, again characteristic of Augustus, it was not a policy announced by official proclamation. Neither was he the sole agent; effecting change was a matter of mutual contributions and depended on the provincials and Italians more than on him. The exact degree of this interaction was variable and eludes attempts to pin it down precisely. Its dynamic, however, shaped the Roman empire of Augustus, and of successors like Trajan and Hadrian, and was basic to its vitality.

The ultimate issue is *e pluribus unum*. It was not an issue of administrative fiat, which would go only so far anyway in bringing together an array of many different ethnicities, cultures, and religions. Instead, it was a matter of providing a productive setting for the interplay of local identities and a larger shared imperial and cosmopolitan identity. There were plenty of nuances in this process of reinvention. They are fascinating to trace in the evidence pertaining to social and intellectual provincial elites of the time. That, however, as we have seen throughout this book, is only one part of the picture. A central aspect of the reign of Augustus, and its efforts at building community, was precisely the involvement of much larger segments of the population in civic affairs. Civic affairs comprised a much broader area than merely Roman citizenship and electoral enfranchisement – the Roman empire was, of course, never a federal democracy. In his standard work *The Roman Revolution* (1939), in which he cast Augustus and his upstart followers as usurpers of the rightful power of the senatorial elite, Sir Ronald Syme briefly adverted to the phenomenon: "Influences more secret and sinister were quietly at work all the time – women and freedmen" (p. 384). Today, both our perspective and our knowledge are more informed, and we cannot lose sight of the majority of the empire's inhabitants and their living conditions, even if the pertinent documentation is less ample and accessible than that for the upper classes.

E PLURIBUS UNUS

Obviously, the fact that there was now one continuous ruler was of decisive importance for the reconfiguration of Rome's empire. On the strategic level, long-term policies could now be implemented for expansion, consolidation, and defense and were based on a continuing assessment of needs and resources. We saw earlier that *pax Augusta* did not mean the end of conquests, but these were guided mostly by the rationale of consolidation. Thus the northwest of the Iberian peninsula was subdued (although its mineral riches played a role in its desirability, too); the land bridge to the north of Italy was secured; and the Mediterranean became *mare nostrum*, "our sea." The result was, as Tacitus noted with his usual conciseness, that "all things were interconnected" – *cuncta inter se conexa* (*Ann.* 1.9). In pursuing this aim, Augustus did not succumb to imperial overstretch, the usual exception being the failed forays beyond the Rhine; the troop strength of the Augustan army was only 60 percent of that of the late republic.

The same characteristic of consistent policies and long-term planning applies to civil administration, and we will look at some major aspects shortly. The essential point is that there now was stability and, as time went on, an increasingly strong assurance that it would last. These developments were not an abstraction but gained a personal face – Augustus. Superseding the ever-changing cast of Roman administrators, he became the embodiment of *imperium Romanum*, and his person provided a living focus on whom people could project their hopes, their fears, their gratitude, their concerns, and much else. The emperor served as a unifying figure that had not existed before and as a representative of the empire's cohesion. Typical of the free play that prevailed, such representation could take on various forms, one of them being the imperial cult (see below). Before we turn to some particulars, however, we need to keep a central point in our sights: the Augustan dispensation worked precisely because of such aspects of soft power that accompanied its military strength. It was not system that tried to achieve unity by enforced standardization, for instance, of law (cf. p. 85) and currency. The coinage of the empire, in fact, provides a good example of the individual forces that were at work.

Besides the limited number of imperial mints, there were over 200 cities in the Augustan empire that issued local bronze coinage. They were autonomous and under no pressure from Rome. Yet they increasingly chose to put an image of Augustus on their coins. Andrew Wallace-Hadrill (1986) has studied this phenomenon in detail and points out that coins literally have two sides to them. One is legalistic, official, and economic – in this case, the choice of the imperial head was economically advantageous because it literally gave a local coinage wider currency. The other is an appeal to values shared by the user; it is more emotive and the notion of "charisma" comes into play. However we label it – and the present vogue of that label may be occasioned by a wistful reaction to current politicians and world leaders, most of whom seem charismatically challenged – this quality or aura of Augustus played as much of a role in the orderly functioning of the empire as did its nuts and bolts administration, especially as the bureaucratic and administrative apparatus was minimal.

Relief and gratefulness, which were felt in many quarters after the end of the civil wars and steadily grew as recovery and prosperity took hold, could therefore be directed at one individual. This is not to say that every last denizen of the Roman empire joined in the chorus or that prosperity was universal, but the plentiful outpourings were genuine and continued through all of Augustus' life. Shortly before his death, for instance, a ship from Alexandria sailed alongside his in the Bay of Naples. Its crew and passengers "had put on wreaths and white robes, burned incense, wished him the greatest of good fortune, and praised him to the sky. For, they said, it was through him that they lived, through him that they fared the seas, and through him that they enjoyed freedom and prosperity" (Suet., *Aug.* 98). The language of hundreds of inscriptions, especially from the Greek east, is similar; a particularly remarkable example is the decree of the Assembly of the Province of Asia, dating to c. 9 BC and proposing the introduction of a new calendar, beginning with Augustus' birthday (see Box 7.1).

Box 7.1. Honors for Augustus the Savior

"It was decreed by the Greeks in Asia…:

"Whereas Providence, which has arranged all things of our life, has eagerly and most zealously mustered the most perfect good for our lives by giving us Augustus, whom she filled with virtue for the benefit of mankind, sending him as a savior, both for us and those after us, that he might end war and set all things in order; and

"Whereas Caesar [i.e., Augustus], when he appeared, surpassed the hopes of all those who anticipated good tidings, not only surpassing all benefactors before him but not even leaving those to come any hope of surpassing him; and

"Whereas the birthday of the god [i.e., Augustus] was the beginning for the world of the good news that came by reason of him…

"Therefore, with good fortune and for our deliverance, it was decreed by the Greeks in Asia, that the New Year for all cities should begin on 23 September, which is the birthday of Augustus."

Orientis Graeci Inscriptiones Selectae
(Leipzig, 1905) 458, lines 31–41, 50–1

As early as 26/25 BC, the assembly of the province of Asia (basically today's Turkey; see Map 1) had offered a crown to anyone who would suggest the most original honor for Augustus. Augustus' own motto of making haste slowly was followed, and the prize was not awarded until c. 9 BC when a suitable proposal was made. The inscription with this resolution was disseminated even to less populated areas. Convergences have been recognized between some of its key terms and those used in the New Testament (like the beginning of the Gospel of Mark). Among them, there is the emphasis on "good tidings," or "news" (*euangelion*, hence our word "evangelical") and a divinely ordained savior, who was called a god, or "son of god," who is said to have "appeared" (*epiphaneis*, hence "epiphany"), that is, he was god

---

present among them. Some early Christians undoubtedly reacted to the imperial cult, including appropriation of its terminology, for their nascent religion, although the extent of the phenomenon has been exaggerated; see below. As for other echoes, the verb used here for Providence's arranging things is the same as that used by Augustus when he famously said that Alexander knew how to conquer, but it was more important to know how to govern (literally, "arrange" or "order") what had been conquered.

ADMINISTRATION AND ECONOMY

In contrast to many other empires and their rulers, Augustus did not impose or rely on a large, let alone massive, bureaucracy to hold his empire together. In this regard, as in others, he continued the republican tradition. The administrative staffs of provincial governors were small – scholars have suggested a figure of no more than 300 assistants – and served mostly as a liaison between the cities of the province and the imperial government. For it was the cities and towns that were the key players in the infrastructure of the empire and its economy, society, and culture. So far from getting into micromanagement, the imperial system relied on the organizational services that were in place in the various locales. This also involved, as we have seen, latitude of jurisdiction and the issuing of coinage. Coherence was a goal; uniformity was not.

An essential service for which Rome had traditionally utilized these local services was tax collection. That function continued under Augustus but with a significant change which again reflected and enhanced his authority as a sole ruler. In republican times, the amount of taxes that could be collected in a province had been let out for bids to private corporations and contractors, who could also assist the cities with collection. There were, unsurprisingly, considerable abuses, especially as tax rates could be set at an exploitative level – this all the more so as Rome and Italy were free from taxes. Augustus took steps to remedy some of the defects, even though financial operators are likely to have objected to regulations then as strenuously as they do now. In so doing, he exercised *cura et tutela*, the care and safeguarding of those entrusted to him. It confirmed his image, for all to see in actuality and not just on coins, as the protector and patron of all. It helped, too, that because he had at his disposal the wealth of Egypt, which always remained his private province, he did not have to be beholden to special interests or rely on excessive taxation.

His personal imprint – and that is the main focus of this chapter – clearly was discernible, but, quite typically, was not the result of a constant series of executive orders. Such steps were rare. An example is edicts which addressed a number of concerns that had been directed to his attention by non-Romans in Cyrene: he decreed that Roman citizens should be subject to local laws and that in trials involving Greeks, half the jury should be Greek. Similarly, he interfered little in the affairs of the towns in Italy, which numbered around 400. Road building was a priority to tie the empire together just on the material level, and imperial officials were put in charge of the task. But, as we know from what happened in Italy, they had to work through local authorities and contractors. The emperor from Velitrae would not have it otherwise, and balanced approaches like these characterize his style of governing.

In short, Augustus was an involved ruler. There was constant communication and consultation rather than intervention. He tapped into existing networks and structures but provided a sense of direction.

As for the economy of the empire, his role is far less distinct. By modern standards, the Roman economy was underdeveloped. "This means essentially," as Garnsey and Saller explain (1987, 43), "that the mass of the population lived at or near subsistence level." Even though terms like "subsistence" can be less than precise – some economic historians prefer "destitution" for further differentiation – the notion expressed here is, at least, a salutary antidote to seeing the Augustan era (and most others from Greco-Roman antiquity) in the limited light of the preserved material remains, which are mostly urban. As we have just observed, cities and towns were important, but some 80 percent of the population was rural and their living conditions were quite variable. Many workers, for instance, depended on intermittent jobs. Just as importantly, the tax burden fell most severely on the provincial poor. As with my caveats about the Augustan "Golden Age," therefore, we need to realize that beneath the attractive architectural appearance of the Augustan cities, to which I will turn shortly, lay realities, in both city and country, like the inability to "develop an extensive framework of institutions and laws capable of protecting the ordinary citizen consumer from hunger and starvation" (Garnsey and Saller 1987, 85).

For all we can tell, such effects were mitigated in the time of Augustus by his relatively more lenient tax collection policies and greater sensitivity to the needs of the provincials. During the Pannonian revolt, for instance (see p. 89), taxes were not raised in the provinces – one of the reasons for the uprising may have been harsh tax collection in that province – but a new estate tax was introduced for Roman citizens. An equally important

. BECOMING ROMAN IN SPAIN

etanians, however, and particularly those that live around
Baetis, have changed over completely to the Roman way
they do not even remember their own language anymore.
em have become Latins (i.e., having Latin rights), and they
ved Roman colonists so they are not far off from being all
he present jointly settled cities, Pax Augusta in the Celtic
sta Emerita in that of the Turdulians, Caesar Augusta in
of the Celtiberians, as well as some other settlements, show
change to the (Roman) modes of civic life I have mentioned.
all those Iberians who belong to this kind are called 'toga-
mong them are the Celtiberians, who once were regarded
t brutish of all."

Strabo, *Geography* 3.2.15

count may not be first-hand, but the archaeological evi-
Baetica (see Map 1) provides general support. It was the
ized of the three Spanish provinces, and no Roman legion
be stationed there. "Latin" rights were a stepping-stone
citizenship. They entailed commercial privileges and the
these communities automatically became Roman citizens.
nerita literally means "Augustan City of Military Retirees";
e "emeritus." It is today's Merida, and the name moved
o the capital of the Yucatan peninsula.

work created by Augustus was designed to drive the pro-
oth practical and sophisticated. He created a new category of
s" (*ius Italicum*) that were more inclusive than Latin rights
of full citizenship. At the other end of the spectrum, natives
of these rights (*peregrini*) were encouraged to found new
l. These, too, were recipients of imperial benefactions and
nbers of *imperium Romanum* rather than as conquered sub-
incentive was that any city or town, whether already exist-
ould hope for promotion to the next higher status, a matter
rely up to Augustus but encouraged the inhabitants to get
e mainstream.
y of reasons, that was a less complicated task in the west than
ast. Unlike the inhabitants of Baetica, no one would expect

mitigating factor was, of course, the return of stability and with it, prosperity. It was not that the rising tide lifted all boats, but it lifted plenty
of them. Here, typically – and to return to another aspect of the "underdeveloped economy" – Augustus did not embark on making substantive
changes. There may have been a political revolution and there was a cultural revolution, but there was no economic revolution. We are centuries
away from institutions such as a central bank or specific national policies
for managing the economy.

Instead, the economy of the empire consisted mostly of regional and
local networks. They benefited from the wider imperial framework of
greater stability, unobstructed trade routes on land and sea, and faster
connections via newly built roads, but while Rome remained a major consumer, it was not the central focus of every economic activity in the empire.
The conditions created by *pax Augusta* also led to increased economic
opportunities – whether in trade, investment, or production – and to an
increasingly large number of people who shared in the resulting profits.
In trying to unify the empire and give it reciprocal stability, Augustus'
aim was to involve far larger numbers of its inhabitants as shareholders
rather than mere subjects. The economy was an important area, and his
"policies" there worked although – paradoxically, perhaps, from a modern
perspective – they did not amount to any detailed policies.

There were side effects, however. As the population once again began
to grow and the available work force rose, wages fell, as they often do in
that setting (economic historians are fond of pointing out that one effect of
the Black Death was an increase in wages). Also, the cost of the Pannonian
wars necessitated acute financial counter measures; in AD 6, for instance,
Augustus appointed an advisory task force of three senators to scrutinize
the empire's budget for savings (Dio 55.25.6). When it came to fiscal policy, he was ready to intervene.

ADAPTING AND ADOPTING ROMAN WAYS

Imagine you were traveling through the Augustan empire in the early years
of the Current Era. What would strike you most, just as a tourist, would
be the continuing visual rhythm of buildings and structures that looked
Roman: temples, theaters, food markets, forums, aqueducts, fountains,
and so on. The degree of their Romanness varied; many were hybrids
of native styles and Roman conventions, but their totality conveyed a
supraregional aspect and commonality. As we all know, architecture plays
an important part in shaping identities as public buildings, then as now,
frame much of our daily life. To what extent can we take the Augustan

phenomenon – and there was a building boom – as indicating an increasing sense of community?

One answer is to look at the sponsors. They were a community of local elites, the emperor's family, and supralocal potentates like Herod of Judaea, and they often acted in concert with one another. For the first and largest of these constituencies, self-representation was a major motive. Sponsoring a building was one thing; building it in a Roman way gave it a larger dimension that reflected the sponsor's wider outlook and connections. "Demonstration of loyalty" is too narrow a motive here although it certainly was in play. Rather, it signified access to a larger world of power, status, and opportunity. One was not "provincial" anymore, but a participant and shareholder in the larger world of *imperium Romanum* and its culture and, just as importantly, in their future development. Certainly, the adoption of Roman architectural forms could range from purely imitative to highly creative; in this regard, too, there was no uniformity. It was an International Style that contrasted with its twentieth-century namesake precisely because it incorporated regional variations; less was not more (and, therefore, a bore). At the same time, the choice by locals of Roman models illustrates an underlying aspect of these adaptations, or people's adapting themselves to the new global context, in various areas of cultural activity: "Becoming Roman did not mean in whole or in part a single readymade Roman culture, but rather gaining the cultural competence necessary to take part in the process of deciding what Roman culture really was" (Kulikowski 1999, 2). Having been taken on by the provinces, Roman civilization no longer belonged exclusively to Rome and Italy (cf. Woolf 2005, 127). The provincials became co-owners and not just in the area of economy.

This bears directly on Augustus' role. Staying with building activity as an example, we can see that he did not impose (*potestas*). There were exceptions: in Athens, he placed a temple (relocated stone for stone from a site in nearby Attica) and a music theater (Odeion), financed by Agrippa, smack into the center of the Agora where they disrupted the flow of civic activities of a populace that had been rather uppity. Far more commonly, however, he encouraged initiatives (*auctoritas*) while providing many of his own and acting as an enabler rather than enforcer. The number of the projects he donated runs into the hundreds. They included not only new structures but also assistance in rebuilding old ones after natural disasters such as earthquakes. The really new phenomenon was the extent of it all: in republican times, there had been only sporadic building activity of this kind in Italy and the provinces. Augustus now reached out to them all, and

massively so. Here was a tangible, ubiquito
for all his subjects. The building activitie
and an enduring one at that, for him to e
with them, as well. He was not only *pater*
father of the world, as Ovid fittingly call
provinces (*Fasti* 2.130). The *princeps'* be
members like Livia and Agrippa, were th
players contributed, such as Herod and Eu
was the second biggest builder in the easte

We may compare both the procedure an
ing of Rome (Chapter 6): within the exis
figured buildings established a system of
and often idiosyncratic expanse together
seldom obtrusively. The empire began to
geographic contiguities; new roads and t
publicus), which served to transport gove
mail and supplies, improved communicatio
to the Internet in those times. The adoption
and materials, such as special, waterproof c
ash (*pozzolana*) for harbor construction c
survey methods and land division (which a
rate assessment of taxes) further helped to

Just as Roman culture itself was not m
progress, so its adoption in the provinces
fit all nor was there one size to begin with.
Gaul and parts of Spain, with effects on
continue into our days. Strabo singled ou
(see Box 7.2), and his account also highl
colonies of veterans could play in the pr
chance. The foundations of new cities and
matter of imperial approval as was the gr
"Latin" rights and Roman citizenship. In
deliberate policy of integration. Internatio
in the process, as most of the veterans di
and would spread Roman culture by thei
is much too simplistic. Instead, soldiers v
ince might settle as veterans in another a
cofounded with natives; the cities mentio
good example. The "Romans" in these c
multicultural group working together.

Box 7.

"The Tur
the River
of life, an
Most of t
have rece
Romans.
area, Aug
the regio
clearly th
Moreove
wearers.'
as the mo

Strabo's
dence fro
most urb
needed t
to Roma
leaders o
Augusta
cf. our t
westward

The fra
cess. It wa
"Italian rig
but still sho
without an
towns as v
treated as n
jects. Anoth
ing or new,
that was e
further into
For a var
in the Gree

the Greeks to forget their own language. In fact, Augustus' cosmopolitan empire was largely bilingual (in addition to having local languages). Latin was essential for official transactions, but the *lingua franca* that was used widely for communication was everyday Greek, the *koinē* Greek in which the New Testament was going to be written. Augustus himself wrote in Greek on many occasions and, most prominently, the *Res Gestae* was written in both Latin and Greek (and the Greek version was not just a mere translation of the Latin but was tailored to the mindset of a Greek audience). So far from forgetting, Greeks both in Greece and the Hellenized east used a variety of strategies to keep their cultural memories alive. How was their identity, cultural and other, going to be affected by the overlay of a Roman empire? Certainly, Roman culture had evolved as a fusion of Greek and Italian elements, but here was a new framework. What was the best way to adapt to it?

THE CULT OF THE ROMAN EMPEROR

The emergence of the imperial cult owes much to this context. The cult of the emperor was, like so many others in the ancient world, part of the civil religion. It was a civic cult that had nothing to do with a moral code, eternal salvation, or an exquisite theology. Neither, as scholars have emphasized, was there such a thing as *the* imperial cult. Instead, and in accord with the diversity of Roman and imperial civilization, it was the result of local and regional initiatives and therefore was multifarious. Starting in the east, which had a previous tradition of ruler worship, it was adapted in the other areas of the empire, too. It met the need for a unifying figure and was another way of highlighting Augustus as the representative and symbol of the empire's unity.

What direct influence did he have on it? Once more, we are looking at a familiar pattern: he mostly enabled the initiatives of others. As Octavian, and in response to requests from the provincial assemblies of Asia and Pontus/Bithynia (see Map 1), he allowed, for Roman citizens, a cult and temple of the Divine Julius Caesar and the Goddess Roma in Nicaea and Ephesus. The non-Roman "Hellenes" were granted the same for Roma and himself in Pergamum and Nicomedia; the documentation makes it clear that he was not to be called a god (*theos*). From then on, there were no further such establishments at the level of a province, but there was plenty of local activity that did not require direct, if any, permission from Rome. These cults proliferated and so did the appellations used for the emperor: "equal to a god," "son of god," "savior," "the god," and so on. Now, it is important not to view this anachronistically in terms of monotheistic practices. "God" was not a uniform notion in Greek and Roman polytheism. The writings of Greek intellectuals, among others, make it clear that the emperor was not simply "one of the gods." In the physical setting of his cult, he often shared a temple with another deity. In such cases, great care was taken, whether by the architectural configuration, the statuary of cult images, or the animals chosen for sacrifice, not to present him as the traditional gods' equal. Flexibility and variety prevailed; it is nonsense to speak of an "imperial theology" or the "Gospel of Caesar."

Instead, in Simon Price's astute formulation, "the imperial cult, along with politics and diplomacy, constructed the reality of the Roman empire" (1986, 248). After decades of war and the arrival of new order, the imperial cult expressed stability and was a way to negotiate a changed, and changing, political environment. And it gave especially the Greek communities the opportunity to shape these expressions in their own way and on their own terms. It did not manifest the heavy hand of the empire squelching their local or larger identity. Rather, and illustrating the reciprocal dynamic of the engagement that took place, "the existence of Roman rule intensified this dominance of Greek culture" (Price 1986, 100).

In the east, then, sponsorship of the cult reconfirmed the role of the local elites on which so much of the stability of the Augustan empire rested. The festivals organized by them, including showy processions and other spectacles, were of course grand occasions for the entire populace. In Italy and the west, the cult developed its own face, including the social and economic class of the people in charge. They were overwhelmingly freedmen and they formed associations (*collegia*) for the sponsorship of the cult. These *Augustales*, as they were called (Box 7.4), and their *collegia* were a socio-economic phenomenon, Rotarians rather than worshipers of the emperor in a narrowly religious sense. Much more was involved than religious pieties and ceremony. Instead, it was a matter of attaining an official status between the municipal aristocracies and the plebs. The freedmen were an energetic class and many of them were wealthy entrepreneurs. It was important to give them an outlet for substantive civic recognition and activities. Besides the imperial cult, these involved contributions to the ongoing needs of the towns, such as buildings and sponsorship of festivals and entertainments. The civic religion was a perfect avenue for broadening participation in public life for an important constituency. As we have seen, the counterpart in Rome, where Augustus did not permit a cult of the emperor, was the similar involvement of freedmen as functionaries of the neighborhood cult of the Lares and the *genius* of Augustus.

Box 7.3. Bilingual Inscription from the Theater of Leptis Magna

Figure 22. Bilingual inscription, c. AD 1. Photograph from
Wikipedia Commons.

"Imp(eratore) Caesare Divi f(ilio) Aug(usto) pont(ifice) max(imo)
tr(ibunicia) pot(estate) XXIV co(n)s(ule) XIII patre patr(iae) I Annobal
Rufus ornator patriae amator concordiae I flamen sufes praef(ectus)
sacr(orum) Himilchonis Tapapi f(ilius) d(e) s(ua) p(ecunia) fac(iendum)
coer(avit) I idemq(ue) dedicavit [followed by the Punic inscription].

"When Imperator Caesar Augustus, son of the divine, pontifex
maximus was in the 24th year of his tribunician power and held the
consulate for the 13th time and was father of his country, Annobal
Rufus, beautifier of his country and lover of concord, priest, council
member, and head of sacred rites, son of Himilcho Tapapus commis-
sioned this to be built from his own monies and dedicated the same."

Date: between July 1, AD 1 and June 30, AD 2

(continued)

This is an example of many from across the empire. There were numerous variations; in Gaul, for instance, some inscriptions were written in a Celtic language but in Latin script. Annobal Tapapius Rufus (we know his full name from another inscription) was, typically, a leading member of his community and sponsored major buildings, such as a theater with predominantly Roman features. It included a small temple, probably for the imperial cult. The combination of temple and theater had been established in Rome by the Theater of Pompey (see Map 2) and had precedents in Italy (cf. MacMullen 2000, 35–42).

The text of the inscription is taken from *The Inscriptions
of Roman Tripolitania*, ed. J. Reynolds and
J. B. Ward Perkins (1952), p. 98, no. 321

Box 7.4. *AUGUSTALES*

"Imp Caesari divi f Augusto pontif maxim cos xi tribunic potestat xi Magistri Augustal prim Philippus Augusti libert M. Aebutius Secundus M. Gallius Anchia[l]us P. Fidustius Antigonus"

"To Imperator Caesar son of the divine Augustus Pontifex Maximus in the 11th year of his consulship in the 11th year of his tribunician power, the Head Officials of the Augustales Philippus freedman of Augustus Marcus Aebutius Secundus Marcus Gallius Anchialus Publius Fidustius Antigonus (dedicated this)."

CIL 11.3200

This is one of the earliest inscriptions (c. 12 BC) from an association of *Augustales*. It was found in Nepet, a small town in Etruria. The names indicate foreign origin, which is demonstrably Greek for the last two. It is not atypical of the state of our evidence that the *Augustales* are mentioned only once in literature (in Petronius' *Satyricon* from the time of Nero) but attested in some 2,500 inscriptions.

See S. Ostrow, "The *Augustales* in the Augustan Scheme,"
in Raaflaub and Toher (1990) 364–79

So we come back to the role of Augustus again – was this deliberate social engineering on his part? In the case of the Lares cult in Rome, his role was direct: he reconfigured it in connection with his reorganization of the districts and neighborhoods of Rome (see p. 102). For the *Augustales* and their cult, there is little evidence of any direct intervention on his part. Instead we see a multitude of local initiatives, motivations, and purposes, as well as intercity imitation and competition. Clearly, however, the whole development was one to which Augustus would give his blessing and support. The rapport he established with this important segment of society is also reflected by the presence of emblems of the battle of Actium – scenes of clashing ships, ships' prows, and crocodiles – in the art of the freedmen "because his victory had indeed been theirs" (Kellum 2011, 201). In sum, we see Augustus once more in his favorite role as an *auctor*, permitting and encouraging the initiatives of others but staying in the background. The imperial cult and its management, whether in the east or west, were not administered from the center. That was another, major reason for their success and vitality.

Final Perspectives: Religious and Cultural Pluralism, Toleration, and Some Realities

Like so many other Augustan topics, the imperial cult should be viewed not in isolation but as part of a wider spectrum. Just in terms of its material presence, it was embedded in a larger religious landscape of temples and shrines to a great number of gods. The religious pluralism they comprehended can be considered an even stronger factor in the empire's cohesion and stability – much more so than a unitary religion might have been. Many principal deities, of course, had a recurring presence throughout the empire, often with a local and regional flavor. In addition, that flavor was well represented by native deities; cosmopolitan Romans would view many of them as local variations of their own gods and interpret them accordingly (*interpretatio Romana*), which was yet another way of accommodating religious variety. Most important, everywhere one went there was religious freedom; religious wars were to be the product of later ages and seemingly more advanced civilizations. Such an atmosphere and practice of toleration has, in fact, been a major characteristic of other large empires at their height, as Amy Chua has illustrated in her stimulating analysis of such powers (2007). Toleration was the concept that bound the many components together instead of letting them become centrifugal forces. Precisely because of the absence of competing supremacy claims, toleration did not have to be an active, programmatically articulated policy. Rather, it was more of a matter of *laissez faire* and another tradition that carried over from republican times.

The supermarket of religions was only one aspect the larger cultural pluralism. Roman culture became a world culture because it let others in and allowed for contributions from many quarters; the parallels with the global character of American culture – "Americanization," parallel to "Romanization" – are suggestive (see Box 7.5). Again, this tradition reaches back to the republic but became even more pronounced as the Augustan empire (and its successors) developed. In terms of administrative and military directives, the flow came from Rome and the ruler. As for culture, the relation was far more reciprocal. Rome became the true head of the world, *caput mundi*, in that regard too, as it attracted an increasing number of residents from the provinces who brought their cults and culture with them. The cosmopolitan character of the city came to reflect that of the empire at large. The total number of Rome's population under Augustus is estimated at around one million.

Box 7.5. Global Cultures

"America's culture has not turned the world into a replica of the United States. Instead, its reliance on foreign cultures has made America a replica of the world."

Pells (2011, 405)

"What I want to emphasize, therefore, is how *reciprocal* America's connections with other countries really are. The United States has been a recipient as much as an exporter of global culture."

"But the power of American capitalism and the worldwide familiarity with English do not by themselves account for America's cultural ascendancy. American entertainment has always been more cosmopolitan than 'imperialistic.' It is this cosmopolitanism that helped make America's mass culture a global phenomenon."

"The heterogeneity of America's population – its regional, ethnic, religious, and racial diversity – forced the media, from the early years of the 20th century, to experiment with messages, images, and story lines that had broad multicultural appeal."

Pells (2002)

> *Mutatis mutandis* (as we say so elegantly in Latin), these are apt characterizations of Roman imperial culture, too – simply change "America"/ "United States," "American" to "Rome" and "Roman," and "English" to "Latin."
>
> Pells, R., *Modernist America: Art, Movies, and the Globalization of American Culture* (New Haven 2011). An earlier summary article appeared in *The Chronicle of Higher Education* (April 12, 2002), pp. B7–B9.

That said, it would be misleading to conjure up the notion of Augustus' empire as an enlightened paradise. As we have seen, some 80 percent, if not more, of the empire's population was rural, and "Romanization" in many of those areas was only skin deep, if at all existent. These country folk were the later "pagans" (*pagani*), so named after the nonurban districts (*pagi*) where they lived. Living conditions varied, but for most dwellers of the empire, as we have seen, they hovered around the subsistence level and even the cities were no bulwark against famines and ill health. Further, as David Mattingly has usefully reminded us, "the Roman empire was not run on altruistic lines; it developed mechanisms for the exploitation of land and people" (2011, 164). At the same time, Augustus, the richest man in the Roman empire, was also its greatest benefactor. Striking the right balance here was another work in progress, as was the empire itself and its culture.

8

THE FINAL DAYS AND AN ASSESSMENT

DEATH OF AN EMPEROR

"So Augustus fell sick and died," writes Dio (56.30). Of course, no respectable biographer, ancient or modern, would be content with such a shocking display of brevity, and Dio was not either. The death of a legend, and especially a legend in his own time, called for more detail and drama. It was supplied in ample doses; most writers, for instance, reach into the usual grab bag of omens similar to those that, retrospectively, presaged his birth, and the procedure makes for nice bookends of his life. Besides, hooting owls and thunderbolts, for example, handily negotiate the space between the grossly incredible and the merely humdrum.

When we sift through the accounts especially of Suetonius, Dio, Tacitus, and Velleius, we can arrive at a reasonably accurate reconstruction that stays clear of biases such as Tacitus' usual demonization of Livia. In August of AD 14, Augustus sent Tiberius to Illyricum, the territory of the provinces of Dalmatia and Pannonia (see Map 1), to "strengthen the peace" there. He planned to accompany him as far south as Beneventum and also wanted to take in some athletic contests in Naples. On the way, he fell sick – precisely because diarrhea is so banal, it sounds authentic – and took a break of a few days on Capri. According to Suetonius (*Aug.* 98), it became the occasion for tangibly promoting the mix, endemic to Roman culture, of Greek and Roman: "He distributed togas to the Greeks and Greek cloaks (*pallia*) to the Romans; insisting that the Romans should speak Greek and dress like Greeks, and that the Greeks should do the opposite." Ever the jovial host that we know from the Palatine, he presided over a lively dinner party where the young guests had a great time and Augustus gleefully took part in the general merriment (p. 139). He also joked about some events on the island and teased Tiberius' astrologer. No gloomy premonitions here.

On he went to Beneventum to bid Tiberius goodbye. Soon after the start of the return trip, his illness got worse, and he had to turn in at Nola, in fact, at the same house where his father Octavius had died. The accounts diverge here; Tacitus, for one, has Livia assert her evil control, which Dio spins into her feeding Augustus poisoned apples; both authors also elaborate on the murder of Agrippa Postumus. Another part of the melodrama is Tiberius' being recalled – did he get back in time to speak with Augustus or not? Velleius asserts that he did, and even if his version provides the touchy-feely counterbalance to the others (Augustus' "mind was now at ease, with the arms of his beloved Tiberius about him," 2.123.2), it is unlikely that, subjected as he was to the scrutiny of contemporary witnesses, he would simply have invented the final meeting of the two.

Last words are always a big part of the production, and here, too, Augustus would set a trend. This applies not so much to his parting words to Livia, cited earlier (p. 111), which in all their simplicity attest the lifelong bond between the two, as it does to the preceding scene: he asked for a mirror, had his hair combed and sagging cheeks propped up, and then called in a group of friends. We may pause here for moment: if we had to put some final words in his mouth, what would we suggest? A ringing message to the world about the *pax Augusta*? An uplifting citation from Vergil's *Aeneid*? Or maybe a thoughtful maxim from Horace? This is not what happened. Instead (Suet., *Aug.* 99), he asked them: "Have I played my role in the mime-play of life suitably?" And he added, in Greek, no less, the usual appeal for applause at the end of a play:

> If I have pleased you, kindly signify,
> Appreciation with a warm goodbye. (trans. R. Graves)

With that the official part was over, and only members of the family were present. He inquired about the health of one of his granddaughters, addressed Livia, and then, as his mind was failing, cried out, "Forty young men are carrying me off!" As Suetonius points out, that was exactly the number of praetorians that were to form the honor guard as he lay in state.

What are we to make of Augustus' departing this world in the role of a play actor? There is no need to overinterpret, but his choice certainly was meaningful. After all, all the world's a stage. Play is not divorced from reality but allows us to view it from a distance. The mime was not heavy drama but a lighthearted farce. While being the patron of a culture that was second to none in sophistication – whether in art, poetry, or architecture – Augustus, as we have seen, never presented himself as highbrow but truly enjoyed popular entertainments, such as the mime and pantomime. And he was good at staging shows and being a showman; this meant anything but lack of substance. The staged final vignette, then, is classic Augustus: the seriousness of end of life mitigated by light-heartedness, prodding the onlookers to reflections: what a life indeed, what an achievement, and how many roles did Augustus truly play – and have to play – to pull it all off. Later emperors would imitate the model, though not its many dimensions: Vespasian kept the humor by exclaiming, "My god, I'm becoming a god," whereas Nero remained true to his delusions: "What an artist the world is losing!" The exact date of Augustus' death was August 19, AD 14; on this very day, fifty-seven years earlier, he had become consul for the first time.

The body was transferred to Rome where senators tried to outdo each other in proposing honors for the deceased; naming the period of his reign "the Augustan century" was one of them. The senate also gathered for the reading of his will. It was quite detailed; besides the actual will specifying inheritances, there were four appendices, including instructions for his funeral and a record of his deeds that is basically the *Res Gestae*. Unsurprisingly, Tiberius (two-thirds) and Livia (one-third) were named his personal heirs; the senate granted her an exemption from the statutory limit of the amount a woman could inherit. The list of recipients of additional largess was extensive and included some foreign kings; as we have seen, such players and networks were an essential factor in the stability of the Mediterranean *pax Augusta*. As for beneficiaries in the city, we again have an element of closure: just as the young heir of Caesar had paid out his adoptive father's legacies, so Augustus now left 40 million sesterces to the "Roman people," meaning the plebeian heads of household in the city who were on the grain dole. Further bonuses were given to the soldiers. True to his life, different sides of Augustus' character inscribed some of these provisions. On the one hand, solicitude for children of fathers who had left him a bequest in their wills: Augustus simply kept the monies in trust and returned them to the children when they were grown. On the other, no forgiveness for Julia: she inherited nothing, and he explicitly abrogated her right to be buried in the Mausoleum.

Then came his truly final show, the funeral that had been scripted by him. Fittingly, it incorporated many elements of a triumph and triumphal procession. Harking back, perhaps, to the only triumph he granted himself, the triple triumph of August 29 BC, there were three images of him, including one of wax in his triumphal garb and another, made of gold, on a triumphal chariot. As we have seen throughout, Augustus both followed tradition and broke with it, and this was no different: his images were at the head of the procession rather than the end. He led, rather than followed; the parade itself was made up of Roman and family ancestors going back to Aeneas and Romulus, including even Pompey, and of nations that had been conquered. Some of the former would be images kept in the family homes; others would be actors wearing masks. The procession made its way to the Roman Forum, where Tiberius and the younger Drusus delivered funeral orations. Following them, all the senators, equestrians, their wives "and practically all others who were in city at the time" (Dio 56.42.1) joined the cortège to the Campus Martius, where the body was placed on a pyre at the Ustrinum (see Map 2) and burned. An eagle was released to soar heavenwards, but this symbol was not enough: as in the aftermath of Romulus' death (see p. 67), a respectable witness (senator, former praetor) materialized who swore that he had seen Augustus ascending to heaven. On September 17, then, Augustus ceased being only *divi filius* and the senate decreed him to be *divus* Augustus. He had achieved the goal he set himself in one of his first speeches at Rome: "To aspire to the honors of his father." Caesar's image could not be shown in the funeral procession because he already was *divus*, but once more that absence translated into a stronger presence. That presence was made palpable by Tiberius' delivering his eulogy from the platform of the Temple of Divus Julius.

Did the death of Rome's ruler cause any unrest? Augustus was concerned about it, and on his deathbed repeatedly asked for Tiberius. The concern was about areas such as Pannonia and Germany, where some uprisings indeed broke out. Tacitus, the ceaseless advocate of republican *libertas*, twists and spins the issue into a lurid description of a Rome crawling with armed soldiers to intimidate the populace from rioting during the funeral. Once more, however, reality trumps jaundiced projections. The only occasion on which the Roman masses saw fit to riot at the time was the holdout of popular pantomime actor. Like athletes today, he wanted a higher fee than that stipulated in his contract, and the folks backed him up. The matter was taken to the senate, which apparently caved in. It is with this episode that Dio's account of Augustus ends (56.47.2), just as Augustus ended the story of his life with a mime scene.

ASSESSMENT

Augustus' impact on his world, and on world history in general, was monumental. He was indeed a key figure of classical antiquity. He ranks next to Alexander, whose forelock, controlled in a characteristically Roman way, became his signature emblem. It is his overall achievement that we need to keep in our sights amid the usual controversies and debates about individual aspects of his life and work that any outstanding historical personality will inevitably engender. Emphasis on, and inspection of, one or the other part of the multifaceted record of a multifaceted individual – the emperor Julian (AD 361–3) famously compared Augustus to a chameleon – is completely appropriate but, almost by definition, ends up being partial. Instead, we have to look at the total picture, which is not the equivalent of a bland synthesis. Leaders are not leaders unless they provoke disagreement.

Augustus certainly did, and Tacitus schematized it (see Box 8.1a). Like America's current favorite news channel, he claimed his presentation was "fair and balanced" (his equivalent wording is "without ire and partiality"), but as always, that very assertion and its follow-up ("I am far removed from any reasons for such sentiments") alert the reader that such is not the case: the cons, stated last and with greater length, clearly have it (see Box 8.1b). What is typical, however, of his and similar denunciations is that their bulk concerns Octavian's ascent to power and, especially, his actions during the triumvirate. It was, as we have seen, the most brutal period the Romans had yet experienced. Octavian was aware of it, and of his deep involvement, then; hence his efforts to destroy its memory by the systematic burning of official documents. He realized, as memory scholars do today – and, as always, I leave academic moralizing to others – that forgetting and oblivion are complementary counterparts of remembering. At the end of that period, there needed to be some closure; a formal, legal precedent in Athens was the so-called amnesty decree of 404/3 BC in Athens that forbade "remembering past injuries" – in this case, the atrocities committed by the terror regime of the Thirty Tyrants. Cicero had invoked that precedent in a speech two days after the murder of Julius Caesar, helping to persuade the senate to decree amnesty for his assassins. A more recent application, which takes nothing away from the *gravitas* of such issues in the political and historical realm, is the stated necessity of deletion and forgetting in the digital age.

Box 8.1a. Augustus: Pros

"Some said he had been driven to civil war out of duty to his father and because of the necessities of the *res publica* in which at that time there was no place for laws, a course of action which no one could prepare for or carry out in any good way. And when he was seeking to take revenge on the murderers of his father, he had made many concessions to Antony, and many to Lepidus. Once the latter had become senile through indolence and the former had been ruined by his vices, there was no other remedy for this country, torn by discord as it was, than to be ruled by one man. Yet he had put the *res publica* together not as a king or dictator but under the name of *princeps*; the empire's boundaries were now the ocean and faraway rivers; legions, provinces, fleets, all things were now connected with one another; there was law for the citizens, and the allies were treated with decency. The city itself had been magnificently adorned; only in a few instances had there been a use of force in order to secure tranquility for the rest."

Tacitus, *Annals* 1.9.3–5

Box 8.1b. Augustus: Cons

"The counterargument was: duty to his father and the crisis of the *res publica* masked his real intentions. It really was from a lust for despotic power that he had incited the veterans by bribing them, raised a rogue army as a private citizen, and corrupted the consul's legions.... Then, after he had usurped, by means of a senate decree, the status and functions of a praetor, he took possession of the armies of Hirtius and Pansa after their deaths; those deaths may have been due to enemy action or, in the case of Pansa, poison administered to his wounds or, as for Hirtius, mutiny by his soldiers and the young Caesar's treacherous machinations. He then extorted the consulship from an unwilling senate and turned against the republic the very forces with which he had been entrusted against Antony. Citizens were proscribed and lands were confiscated, often without so much as the approval of those who were behind these deeds. Even granting that the deaths of Brutus and Cassius settled a score that he owed to his father (though it is perfectly lawful to let go of private feuds for the sake of the public welfare), he deceived [Sextus] Pompey with a phony peace agreement and Lepidus with the pretense of friendship. Next, Antony was led on by the treaties of Tarentum and Brundisium and by the marriage to his [Octavian's] sister and paid with his life for a spurious kinship. No doubt, there was peace after all that, but a bloody peace it was: there were the disastrous defeats of Lollius and Varus and the murders in Rome of men such as Varro, Egnatius, and Jullus [Antonius].

(continued)

"His domestic life was not spared either. Nero's [Tiberius Claudius Nero, Livia's first husband] wife had been abducted from him, and there was the farce of consulting the priests whether she could legally marry before the birth of her child with whom she was pregnant.... Finally there was Livia, a noxious mother to the state and a noxious stepmother to the house of the Caesars.... As for Tiberius, he had chosen him as his successor not out of high regard for him but because he full well knew his arrogance and cruelty; by this most wretched contrast he aimed to increase his own glory."

Tacitus, *Annals* 1.10.1–7

The key point is that Augustus moved beyond the triumviral period, and his behavior then, in all ways. It was time to move on, for all. This is the major juncture, and it was not simply to be expected. His assertion that he "had power over all things" was not an overstatement; all options were open to him. For most people around the Mediterranean, the end of ruinous wars and a return to normal life, domestic tranquility, and some material security would have been enough. If it took a monarch to guarantee these basic blessings, so be it. At least he was "the monarch of everybody" (Momigliano 1940, 80) instead of being interested only in the welfare of a small clique; of course, that monarch should not be a paranoid dictator or bloodthirsty tyrant, either. A return to "laws and rights" (see Fig. 7) would have sufficed, but other frameworks were available besides the republican constitution, which had not been up the task. The converse parameter for Octavian was that, no, he was not about to give up his power but would try to exercise it in a way that was acceptable to most. And there were several advantages, as we have seen, of doing so within a modified republican system, Constitution Plus, as I called it in Chapter 3.

For many scholars and partisans (see Box 8.2), the resulting dynamic has become the central issue. Augustus then appears as the Great Pretender, bamboozling the Romans with a display of the hollow trappings of "the Republican constitution" that he was craftily subverting in order to cling to power. I have deliberately refrained from rehearsing and rehashing those endless arguments. The reason is simple: there is more to Augustus and his impact. Fixation on this issue is fine but should not be projected back on him as his exclusive concern. Quite simply again, power for him became the means to an end and not an end in itself. This aligns well with modern studies of leadership, which have moved away from preoccupation with power and instead emphasize the more important task of a leader to inculcate purpose.

Box 8.2. Augustus in "Augustan" England: Not Just Praise

"The most important objection to Augustus was not that he was a butcher, or a torturer, or a pathic, or a lecher, or incestuous, or a legacy-hunter, or a censor, or even a book-burner. Nobody is perfect, as the nation successively ruled by Oliver Cromwell and Charles Stuart no doubt remembered. The dominant objections were to his destruction of the balanced constitution of the Roman Republic, the fatal precedent he set for other rulers, and the establishment of the empire whose slavery and fall were inherent in its creation. Moreover, as either rhetoric, or genuine belief, or both had it, Augustus was consciously and maliciously guilty of murdering the republic. As Tacitus and Dio Cassius had taught the eighteenth century, Augustus selected Tiberius knowing that he was evil, knowing that he would further ravage the empire, and hoping that his own memory would be further enhanced as a result of the contrast. Augustus' rule, then, served British theoreticians, historians, and politicians as a practical guide: it showed them what not to do in their own nation, and they saw what happened in Britain and France when Augustus' ways were followed."

H. Weinbrot, *Augustus Caesar in "Augustan" England*
(Princeton 1978) 86

Given the range of his activities and his significance as Rome's first emperor, Augustus has been invoked as a model and exemplar continuously from ancient to modern times. That exemplarity could be viewed in all kinds of ways and has covered the whole spectrum – from utter damnation to effusive hagiography. In the arts, the term "Augustan age" was appropriated for high points of literary and artistic achievement. Examples are eighteenth-century England, seventeenth-century France, and Saxony especially under Frederick Augustus I, also known as August the Strong (1670–1733), who made

(continued)

Dresden a cultural metropolis. As the above quotation illustrates, such efforts could provoke a backlash; after Mussolini, for instance, effectively usurped the Augustan era for Fascism, the association stuck for decades, and scholars were reluctant to say anything positive about Augustus so as not to appear as sympathizers.

That purpose had multiple aspects, as we have seen throughout this book. Significantly, it did not exhaust itself in the material and physical reconstruction of Rome and Italy. That effort was certainly needed after the ravages of decades of civil war and represented transactional leadership, to use the definitions of Burns (1978) and others in a broad sense. Augustus' achievement went beyond these aspects: he was a transforming leader who aimed higher – witness the marriage legislation, the shaping of the empire into a community, and the civic enfranchisement of the freedmen class. In the process, he transformed Rome and its culture; as the ancients already recognized, his dictum that he found Rome as a city of bricks but made it into a city of marble is both reality and metaphor.

We need to remind ourselves again at this point that not everything that happened under Augustus happened because of Augustus. He was not simply the super ruler or demiurge who created everything anew. Much of his leadership consisted precisely in recognizing the significant changes that were already under way, whether the shift in the Roman system of knowledge or burgeoning social change in the Mediterranean world, and in channeling them and directing them with both flexibility and steadiness. His guiding policy, if we wish to call it that, was to reshape as well as remake. Hence, too, the constant blending of innovation and tradition that is one of hallmarks of his reign. Another, related ingredient was the combination of vision and pragmatism. Certainly, from today's world that is poisoned by ideologies and afflicted by religious strife, it is refreshing to look back at a time that was free of them and prospered.

When we look at personal qualities of Augustus that factored in his achievement, two stand out in particular. One was his tenacity, combined with perseverance. It was evident, as we have seen, from the very beginning. Physical strength and robust health were not among his natural endowments, and he had work for everything he got. What made up for it and more was his surpassing mental stamina. To have withstood the unrelenting barrage of physical exertions, often almost to the point of death, and emotional and psychological wounding was itself an extraordinary achievement in the years from Caesar's death to the conquest of Alexandria. The challenges and pressures after that were different but just as stressful. Of course, one's greatest strength can also be one's greatest liability, as evidenced by his tenacious, and often disastrous, management of family members.

The other quality that allowed Augustus to achieve all he did was his capacity to grow. Conquest and warring down an enemy was one thing; effectively governing the resulting reign was another – here is where Augustus saw the biggest difference between himself and his model Alexander. Given the generally static view of character in Greco-Roman antiquity (to which I adverted at the very beginning of Chapter 1), his development after 30 BC was not to be expected, and some understandable mistrust kept lingering. This change should not be rendered simplistically with phrases like "a kinder, gentler Augustus" and similarly reductive characterizations. He still was the same man with the same steely determination. But he saw that the task he was facing now, and the way he chose to engage it, required qualities beyond those that had been in evidence. He addressed the problems that had been neglected, and he planned for the long term and not just for his own gain. The way he and his advisers went about this with hard work, patience (we may recall his motto "make haste slowly"), fairness, and vision resonated. This was a ruler and leader one could respect (cf. Box 8.3).

Box 8.3. Augustus Today: A View from Outside Academe

"If Augustus could be restored to life from the pages of history, his leadership skills would be highly valued and very much in demand. Today, when many large companies … are in severe disarray, his ability to instill confidence and provide direction would make him as close to being the perfect CEO as anyone could be" (p. 252).

"One reason for Augustus' success as a leader was that, unlike so many contemporary politicians and CEOs, he had a practical sense of limits. Doing his own version of cost-benefit analysis for Rome's frontiers, he calculated that it was time to stop expanding. He knew instinctively that to push the boundaries of the empire farther simply for his own glory, as Alexander did, would be immensely costly and ultimately self-destructive. In today's world, Augustus would never have binged in sub-prime mortgages, gagged on derivatives, or over-leveraged his balance sheet.

(continued)

"Like other leaders we have examined, Augustus had a vision and knew how to inspire. He possessed enormous energy, which he proved capable of focusing for the good of Rome in a disciplined way. But he never lost his appetite for managing detail or let himself fall victim to hubris. He was that managerial rarity – both a first-rate strategist and politician – who never let success warp his judgment or control his behavior" (p. 279).

From Steve Forbes and John Prevas, *Power, Ambition, Glory: The Stunning Parallels between Great Leaders of the Ancient World and Today ... and the Lessons You Can Learn.* Foreword by Mayor Rudy Giuliani (New York 2009).

The overall result, often heralded as his greatest achievement, was the stability he gave the Roman rule in the form of the principate for almost 200 years. It was a stability that frustrated and survived madmen such as Caligula, who wished that the Roman system had only one neck so he could sever it. Important and long-lasting as this concrete and tangible achievement was, it was exceeded and complemented by an expansion of horizons. The outlook became universal. It is reflected in the world histories (there had been only one before, that of Polybius, the Greek Alexis de Tocqueville, in the second century BC) of three contemporary historians who, tellingly, came from different parts of the empire: Diodorus (Sicily), Nicolaus of Damascus (Syria), and Pompeius Trogus (Gaul). The universal and cosmopolitan perspective also informs Strabo's *Geography* and master works such as Vergil's *Aeneid* and Ovid's *Metamorphoses*. They were only the beginning – the dialogue would continue for centuries. In sum, "the Roman world was opened up both physically and mentally" (Treggiari 1996, 902), and that was one of Augustus' greatest legacies.

SELECT BIBLIOGRAPHY
AND REFERENCES
FOR FURTHER READING

General

Bleicken, J., *Augustus: eine Biographie* (Berlin 1998).
Bringmann, K., *Augustus* (Darmstadt 2007).
Champlin, E. and others, eds., *The Cambridge Ancient History*, vol. 10, 2nd ed. (Cambridge 1996).
Cooley, A. E., *Res Gestae Divi Augusti: Text, Translation, and Commentary* (Cambridge 2009).
Galinsky, K., *Augustan Culture: An Interpretive Introduction* (Princeton 1996).
  ed., *The Cambridge Companion to the Age of Augustus* (Cambridge 2005).
Kienast, D., *Augustus: Prinzeps und Monarch*, 4th ed. (Darmstadt 2009).
Raaflaub, K., and Toher, M., eds., *Between Republic to Empire: Interpretations of Augustus and His Principate* (Berkeley and Los Angeles 1990).
Scheid, J., *Res Gestae Divi Augusti* (Paris 2007).
Syme, R., *The Roman Revolution* (Oxford 1939).
Zanker, P., *The Power of Images in the Age of Augustus* (Ann Arbor 1988).

Sourcebooks

Cooley, M. G. L., ed., *The Age of Augustus*. LACTOR 17 (London Association of Classical Teachers 2008).
Sherk, R., *Rome and the Greek East to the Death of Augustus*. Translated Documents of Greece and Rome 4 (Cambridge 1984).

CHAPTER 1

Goldsworthy, A., *Caesar: Life of a Colossus* (New Haven 2008).
Malitz, J., *Nikolaos von Damaskus: Leben des Kaisers Augustus* (Darmstadt 2003).

Smith, C., and Powell, A., eds., *The Lost Memoirs of Augustus and the Development of Roman Autobiography* (Swansea 2009).

CHAPTER 2

Goldsworthy, A., *Antony and Cleopatra* (New Haven 2010).
Kleiner, D., *Cleopatra and Rome* (Cambridge, MA 2005).
Mackay, C., *The Breakdown of the Roman Republic* (Cambridge 2009).
Osgood, J., *Caesar's Legacy: Civil War and the Emergence of the Roman Empire* (Cambridge 2006).
Schiff, S., *Cleopatra: A Life* (New York 2010).

CHAPTER 3

Feeney, D., *Caesar's Calendar* (Berkeley and Los Angeles 2007).
Flower, H., *Roman Republics* (Princeton 2010).
Gowing, A., *Empire and Memory: The Representation of the Roman Republic in Imperial Culture* (Cambridge 2005).
Purcell, N., "Romans in the Roman World," in Galinsky (2005) 85–105.
Wallace-Hadrill, A., "*Mutatas Formas*: The Augustan Transformation of Roman Knowledge," in Galinsky (2005) 55–84.
   Rome's Cultural Revolution (Cambridge 2008).

CHAPTER 4

Gruen, E., "Augustus and the Making of the Principate," in Galinsky (2005) 33–51.
Lintott, A., *The Romans in the Age of Augustus* (Oxford 2010).
Lott, J. B., *The Neighborhoods of Ancient Rome* (Cambridge 2004).
Mattern, S., *Rome and the Enemy: Imperial Strategy in the Principate* (Berkeley and Los Angeles 1999).
Rich, J. W., "Augustus, War and Peace," in J. Edmondson, ed., *Augustus* (Edinburgh 2009) 137–64.
Scheid, J., "Augustus and Roman Religion: Continuity, Conservatism, and Innovation," in Galinsky (2005) 175–93.

CHAPTER 5

Balsdon, J. P. V. D., *Roman Women: Their History and Habits* (London 1962).
Barrett, A., *Livia: First Lady of Imperial Rome* (New Haven 2002).
Bartman, E., *Portraits of Livia: Imagining the Imperial Woman in Augustan Rome* (Cambridge 1999).

Dennison, M., *Empress of Rome: The Life of Livia* (London 2010).
Fantham, E., *Julia Augusti: The Emperor's Daughter* (New York 2006).
Kleiner, D., "Semblance and Storytelling in Augustan Rome," in Galinsky (2005) 197–233.
Levick, B., "Tiberius' Retirement to Rhodes in 6 BC," *Latomus* 31 (1972) 779–813.
Purcell, N., "Livia and the Womanhood of Rome," in J. Edmondson, ed., *Augustus* (Edinburgh 2009) 165–94.
Raaflaub, K., and Samons, L., "Opposition to Augustus," in Raaflaub and Toher (1990) 417–54.
Roddaz, J.-M., *Marcus Agrippa* (Rome 1986).
Treggiari, S., "Jobs in the Household of Livia," *Papers of the British School at Rome* 43 (1975) 48–77.
Wiseman, T. P., "The House of Augustus and the Lupercal," *Journal of Roman Archaeology* 22 (2009) 527–45.

CHAPTER 6

Davies, P., *Death and the Emperor: Roman Imperial Funerary Monuments from Augustus to Marcus Aurelius* (Cambridge 2000).
Favro, D., *The Urban Image of Augustan Rome* (Cambridge 1996).
Hardie, P., ed., *Paradox and the Marvellous in Augustan Literature and Culture* (Oxford 2009).
Haselberger, *Urbem adornare: Rome's Urban Metamorphosis under Augustus* (Portsmouth, RI 2007).
Stern, R., *Modern Classicism* (New York 1988).
Strong, D., and Ward Perkins, J., "The Temple of Castor in the Roman Forum," *Papers of the British School at Rome* 30 (1962) 1–32.
White, P., *Promised Verse: Poets in the Society of Augustan Rome* (Cambridge, MA 1993).

CHAPTER 7

Ando, C., *Imperial Ideology and Provincial Loyalty in the Roman Empire* (Berkeley and Los Angeles 2000).
Chua, A., *Day of Empire: How Hyperpowers Rise to Global Dominance – and Why They Fall* (New York 2007).
Galinsky, K., "The Cult of the Roman Emperor: Uniter or Divider?" in J. Brodd and J. Reed, eds., *Rome and Religion: A Cross-Disciplinary Dialogue on the Imperial Cult* (Atlanta 2011) 1–21, 215–25.
Garnsey, P., and Saller, R., *The Roman Empire: Economy, Society and Culture* (London 1987).
Harris, W., *Rome's Imperial Economy* (Oxford 2011).

Kellum, B., "Representations and Re-Presentations of the Battle of Actium," in B. Breed et al., eds., *Citizens of Discord* (Oxford 2011) 187–207.

Kulikowski, M., Review of G. Woolf, *Becoming Roman: The Origins of Provincial Civilization in Gaul* [1998], *Bryn Mawr Classical Review* (1999) 02.09.

MacMullen, R., *Romanization in the Time of Augustus* (New Haven 2000).

Mattingly, D., *Imperialism, Power, and Identity: Experiencing the Roman Empire* (Princeton 2011).

Price, S. R. F., *Rituals and Power: The Roman Imperial Cult in Asia Minor* (Cambridge 1986).

Revell, L., *Roman Imperialism and Local Identities* (Cambridge 2009).

Richardson, J., *The Language of Empire: Rome and the Idea of Empire from the Third Century BC to the Second Century* (Cambridge 2008).

Wallace-Hadrill, A., "Image and Authority in the Coinage of Augustus," *Journal of Roman Studies* 76 (1986) 66–87.

Whitmarsh, T., ed., *Local Knowledge and Microidentities in the Imperial Greek World* (Cambridge 2010).

Woolf, G. "Provincial Perspectives," in Galinsky (2005) 106–29.

CHAPTER 8

Burns, J. M., *Leadership* (New York 1978).

Galinsky, K., "Vergil's *Aeneid* and Ovid's *Metamorphoses* as World Literature," in Galinsky (2005) 340–58.

Levick, B., *Augustus: Image and Substance* (London 2010).

Max-Planck Award Project "Memoria Romana" on memory in Rome, available at: http://www.utexas.edu/research/memoria.

Mayer-Schönberger, V., *Delete: The Virtue of Forgetting in the Digital Age* (Princeton 2010).

Momigliano, A., Review of R. Syme, *The Roman Revolution* (1939), *Journal of Roman Studies* 30 (1940) 75–80.

Treggiari, S., "Social Status and Social Legislation," *Cambridge Ancient History* 2 10 (1996) 873–904.

INDEX

INDEX OF PASSAGES
AND INSCRIPTIONS